COMPARATIVE
STATE
FEMINISM

COMPARATIVE STATE FEMINISM

DOROTHY McBRIDE STETSON
AMY MAZUR

EDITORS

SAGE Publications
International Educational and Professional Publisher
Thousand Oaks London New Delhi

For information address:

SAGE Publications, Inc.
2455 Teller Road
Thousand Oaks, California 91320
E-mail: order@sagepub.com

SAGE Publications Ltd.
6 Bonhill Street
London EC2A 4PU
United Kingdom

SAGE Publications India Pvt. Ltd.
M-32 Market
Greater Kailash I
New Delhi 110 048 India

Printed in the United States of America

Library of Congress Cataloging-in-Publication Data

Main entry under title:

Comparative state feminism / edited by Dorothy McBride Stetson, Amy G. Mazur.
    p. cm.
    Includes bibliographical references (p.   ) and index.
    ISBN 0-8039-5829-3 (cloth: acid-free paper).—ISBN
0-8039-5830-7 (pbk. : acid-free paper)
    1. Women—Government policy—Cross-cultural studies. 2. Feminism—Cross-cultural studies. I. Stetson, Dorothy M. II. Mazur, Amy G.
HQ1236.C62 1995
305.42—dc20   95-12280

This book is printed on acid-free paper.

95 96 97 98 99 10 9 8 7 6 5 4 3 2 1

Sage Production Editor: Diana E. Axelsen

Contents

Abbreviations

These abbreviations apply to all of the chapters. Those that are not country-specific are found in the first category.

General

CEDAW	Convention for the Elimination of Discrimination Against Women
CSW	UN Commission on the Status of Women
DAW	UN Division for the Advancement of Women
EC	European Community (before 1994)
EEP	Equal Employment Policy for Women
EU	European Union (after 1994)
FLS	Nairobi Forward Looking Strategies
ILO	International Labor Organization
IWY	International Women's Year
MP	Member of Parliament
NGO	Nongovernment organization
OECD	Organization of Economic Cooperation and Development
UN	United Nations

Australia

ERC	Expenditure Review Committee
OSW	Office of the Status of Women
OWA	Office of Women's Affairs
PM&C	Prime Minister and Cabinet
WBP	Women's Budget Program
WEL	Women's Electoral Lobby

Canada

CACSW	Canadian Advisory Council on the Status of Women
CEWC	Committee for the Equality of Women in Canada
CIDA	Canadian International Development Agency
IDC	Interdepartmental Committee
NAC	National Action Committee
SWC	Status of Women Canada

Denmark

DESC	Danish Equal Status Council
DWS	Danish Women's Society
WC	Women's Commission

France

CETF	Comité d'Etudes et de Liaison des Problèmes du Travail Féminin
CIDF	Centre d'Information de Droits des Femmes
CSEP	Conseil Supérieur de l'Egalité Professionnelle
CTF	Comité du Travail Féminin
DNCF	Délégation Nationale à la Condition Féminine
LDF	Ligue du Droit des Femmes
MDCFF	Ministère Déléguèe auprès du Premier Ministre à la Condition Féminine et à la Famille
MDDF	Ministère Déléguèe auprès du Premier Ministre chargé des Droites de la Femme

mdf	Mouvement Démocratique et Féminin
MDF	Ministère des Droits de la Femme
MEP	Mission pour l'Egalité Professionnelle
mlf	Mouvement de la Libération des Femmes
PS	Parti Socialiste
SDF	Service des Droits des Femmes
SECF	Secrétariat d'Etat à la Condition Féminine
SEDF	Secrétaire d'Etat aux Droits des Femmes
SEDFVQ	Secrétariat d'Etat aux Droits des Femmes et à la Vie Quotidienne
SEEF	Secrétariat d'Etat à l'Emploi Féminin

Germany

CDU	Christian Democratic Union
CSU	Christian Social Union
FB	Frauenbeauftragte (Women's Affairs Offices)
FDP	Free Democratic Party
FRG	Federal Republic of Germany
GDR	German Democratic Republic
SPD	Social Democratic Party
UFV	Unabhängiger Frauenverband (Independent Women's Association)

Great Britain

CBI	Confederation of British Industry
EOC	Equal Opportunities Commission
EPA	Equal Pay Act
NIEOC	Northern Ireland Equal Opportunities Commission
QUANGO	Quasi Nongovernment Organization
SDA	Sex Discrimination Act
TUC	Trade Union Congress
WNC	Women's National Commission

Ireland

JOCWR   Joint Oireachtas Committee on Women's Rights
MELR   Ministry of Equality and Law Reform
MSWA   Ministry of State for Women's Affairs
TD   Teachta Dala (member of parliament)

Italy

ESC   Equal Status Committee
ESONC   Equal Status and Equal Opportunity National Commission
PDS   Democratic Party of the Left
PCI   Italian Communist Party
UDI   Unione Donne Italiane

Netherlands

CCWP   Cabinet Committee for Women's Policy
DCE   Directie Coordinatie Emancipatiebeleid
            (Department for the Coordination of Equality Policy)
EK   Emancipatiekommissie (Emancipation Commission)
MVM   Man-Vrouw-Maatschappij
STEO   Stimuleringsgroep Emancipatieonderzoek
            (Steering Committee for Women's Research)

Norway

ESC   Equal Status Council

Poland

LK   Liga Kobiet
PNOW   Polish National Organization of Women
PUWP   Polish United Workers Party
USWF   Undersecretary of State for Women and Family

Spain

CCPP	Comisión consultiva para el seguimiento del Primer Plan para la Igualdad
CR	Consejo Rector
IM	Instituto de la Mujer
PSOE	Partido Socialista Obrero Español

Sweden

EOA	Equal Opportunities Act
JÄMO	Jämställdhetsombudsmannen (Equality Ombudsman)
SEOC	Swedish Equal Opportunities Commission

United States

AAUW	American Association of University Women
ACLU	American Civil Liberties Union
cacsw	Citizens Advisory Council on the Status of Women
CLUW	Coalition of Labor Union Women
ERA	Equal Rights Amendment
NOW	National Organization for Women
OFCC	Office of Federal Contract Compliance
PCSW	President's Commission on the Status of Women
PDA	Pregnancy Discrimination Act
WB	Women's Bureau
WUW	Washington Union Women

Preface

This book presents the results of a research project, the first stage in a multinational study of institutionalized feminism. The introduction describes the project design, the country case studies compose the data, and the conclusion presents the findings. Our goal—to direct and produce a work of comparative political analysis—has been realized only through the collaboration of a remarkably talented and knowledgeable group of scholars. Their individual achievements are demonstrated in each of the country case studies that make up *Comparative State Feminism.*

While the plan and results of the research project are found in the introduction and the conclusion, the case studies provide the essential empirical component for the comparative project. Each chapter offers information on the complex interaction between feminism and the state in a unique political culture, and we urge readers to study them in detail. The findings outlined in the conclusion about the extent to which the state can act to achieve feminist political goals have depended on the expertise of the contributing authors. We remain, however, responsible for the decisions about classification of the cases in the typology and comparisons discussed in the conclusion.

Our goal is to contribute to the development of a comparative theory on the subject of feminism and the state. In launching this effort, we have benefited from commentary, advice, and encouragement from many scholars of comparative politics and state feminism whose work is not a formal part of the comparative study. They include Hester Eisenstein, Sylvia Bashevkin, Phil Cerny, Susan MacManus, Martha Cottam, Barbara Nelson, David Collier, Anna Birte Ravn, Birte Siim, Elizabeth Meehan, Eva Kolinsky, and Sophie Watson. We look forward to working with them and others as we move to the next stage of this project.

Collaboration, these days, is enhanced by the tools that information-age technology has produced. Although we are grateful for these aids, they make us even more aware of our dependence on the assistance of our universities' computer and office staffs. Thus we wish to acknowledge the library, computer, and department staffs at Florida Atlantic University and Washington State University. For compiling a coherent manuscript and bibliography from 14 international case studies we are especially grateful to John Tennert of Washington State. We would also like to thank our editor at Sage, Carrie Mullen, and the attentive editorial staff for encouragement and care in transforming the raw materials into the finished volume.

—DOROTHY MCBRIDE STETSON
—AMY G. MAZUR

1

Introduction

Dorothy McBride Stetson
Amy G. Mazur

Social movements provoke official action, especially by democratic governments. Whereas movement activists seek real change and permanent access to arenas of power, government actions may be symbolic or even cosmetic, a way of damping the fires of reform. Second-wave women's movements in advanced industrial societies have generated an assortment of responses from their governments.[1] The most striking consequence of over 25 years of women's movement activism has been the array of institutional arrangements inside democratic states devoted to women's policy questions. Such a widespread change in institutions has the potential of turning the state into an activist on behalf of feminist goals,[2] embedding gender issues in national policy agendas and giving advocates for the advancement of women permanent access to arenas of power. The purpose of this book is to study systematically this cross-national trend of establishing state structures to improve the status of women.

The concept *state feminism* in this work refers to activities of government structures that are formally charged with furthering women's status and rights. At issue is the extent to which these agencies are effective in helping women as a group and undermining patterns of gender-based inequities in society. To many women's movement activists, the idea that the state could further such a feminist agenda is problematic if not impossible. Their skepticism triggers the central questions of this comparative study. First, does state feminism exist? That is, do state structures assigned by political leaders to address women's inferior position in society contribute to policies that reduce gender-based inequities and provide an opportunity for women's movement activists to influence feminist policy formation? Second, if state feminism exists, are there variations in the abilities of these state structures to promote feminist political agendas in the context of the different political, social, and cultural traditions of various countries? *Comparative State Feminism*, therefore, has three major objectives:

1. To describe the range and diversity of state structures formally responsible for promoting women's position and rights in advanced industrial societies
2. To analyze the extent to which these state offices achieve feminist goals within the social, political, and historical context of each nation-state and the variations in achieving goals across different countries
3. To propose, based on this cross-national comparison, the combination of political and social factors that appears to produce state structures prone to pursuing effective state feminist action

Women's Policy Machinery

No single inventor claims to have developed the idea that the state could, through its institutions, become an actor in promoting equality between men and women. One of the first countries to have a permanent agency for women was the United States, where Congress established the Women's Bureau of the Department of Labor in 1920. Over the years, especially during World War II, women's agencies and offices appeared in other countries. More recently, successive governments have added offices, commissions, agencies, ministries, committees, secretaries, and advisers to deal with women's issues. A source of encouragement and advice to them has been the United Nations.

The United Nations has its own institutions devoted to women's agendas: the Commission on the Status of Women (CSW) and its administrative arm, the Division for the Advancement of Women (DAW). Through these structures, the United Nations has recommended, since the 1960s, that governments around the world establish similar structures. The CSW coined the term *national policy machinery for the advancement of women* to refer to agencies devoted to women's policy issues. Following this UN definition, this book will use the term *women's policy machinery*[3] to describe any structure established by government with its main purpose being the betterment of women's social status. Often set up in name only, formal women's policy structures may not actually achieve state feminist goals.

Both domestic and international influences have led states in advanced industrial societies to create women's policy machinery. Domestically, the second wave of the women's movement emerged in the context of social and economic changes after World War II. Stimulated by the rise of other movements, especially on the Left, activists used various strategies to protest against pervasive male dominance. The women's rights strategy focused on using conventional pressure-group tactics for seeking changes in policy and practice to promote antidiscrimination and equality. Other activists worked on leftist parties to include women's demands in socialist and social democratic agendas. Adding energy to the women's movement were the radicals of the women's liberation wing, inventing a variety of unconventional means to change gender relations at the personal level.

Whatever form the second wave took, political leaders were faced with a challenge to take action. Demands came from sectors they were used to working with, such as unions and parties. But they also came from formerly nonpolitical women's organizations and newly formed groups skillful at attracting media attention. In crafting a response or, in come cases, a diversion, most leaders found it useful to create some sort of office to be responsible for dealing with the movement's concerns. At the time, many politicians believed that, at the very least, adding women's policy machinery would show the growing number of women voters that the state was responding with attention to some version of a women's policy agenda.

The CSW has viewed policy machinery as a means of implementing its resolutions on equality and opportunity for women at the national and local levels. As the UN activities on behalf of women have become more ambitious, especially with the International Women's Decade (1975-1985), its attention to policy machinery has intensified. Beginning in 1975, the Decade for Women: Equality, Development, and Peace conferences (Mexico City, 1975; Copenhagen, 1980; Nairobi, 1985) focused on setting a worldwide agenda for women as elaborated in *Nairobi Forward-Looking Strategies for the Advancement of Women* (United Nations, 1985/1993b). Central to the implementation of this agenda has been the establishment of a national policy machinery by each member state.

Since the Nairobi Conference in 1985, and leading up to the Fourth Women's Conference in Beijing in 1995, DAW has gathered information on machinery in many countries and studied the range, diversity, and effectiveness of various efforts. Leaders of UN member states are frequently called upon to report to DAW on the types of machinery they have established. Furthermore, since 1979, over 120 countries have ratified the UN's Convention for the Elimination of Discrimination Against Women (CEDAW). Signatories must file periodic reports with the oversight committee on the "legislative, judicial, administrative, or other measures which they have adopted to give effect to the provisions" of the convention (Article 18). Pressure from domestic movements, together with monitoring by international agencies, has encouraged political leaders in many countries to establish and retain some sort of institution to treat women's issues.[4]

Reports to the United Nations about national machinery indicate a wide variety of forms: permanent national commissions on the status of women, ad hoc and regional commissions, advisory committees, permanent bureaus within departments and ministries, and, in Communist countries, administrative committees within ruling parties (United Nations, 1987). These structures vary by their level of organization, authority, and power and by their links to governmental and nongovernmental agencies. Women's issues are complex, affecting a cross section of conventional governmental activities from social and labor to economic and legal. As a consequence, machinery is also complex and adapts to fit the needs and political context of each country. UN studies show that the national machineries do not lend themselves to easy categorization.

It is important to contrast this focus on policy machinery with other ways of looking at women's role in government. Policy machinery refers to structures in government—those agencies that are established by statute, administrative directive, or political resolution. Thus, studies of machinery are different from studies of women in government and political office. Participation of women in elective office is defined according to the rates of representation in legislatures, cabinets, and executive positions (e.g., Darcy, Welch, & Clark, 1994; Lovenduski & Norris, 1993; Randall, 1987). Studies of state feminist offices are also different from studies that look at the role of women in public administration or feminist scholarship on organizations (e.g., Ferguson, 1984; Guy, 1992; Staudt, 1990). The establishment of women's policy machinery does allow some women to work full-time inside government, designing and implementing projects devoted to the improvement of women's status rather than being restricted to a part-time role outside as supplicants. Unlike much research in this area, this study calls women who staff women's policy agencies *femocrats* to distinguish them from other women in government.[5] In this book, therefore, the term *women's policy machinery* refers to state structures established to advance the status of women; state feminist women's policy machineries are those agencies that concretely achieve their formal charge in some way.

State, Women, Feminism

When scholars have turned to assess the record of the state in promoting the status of women in advanced industrial societies, many, especially those from Western Europe, have done so to counter results from mainstream research. Their work represents an effective critique of the assumption that state implementation of a social democratic ideology produces widespread gender equality. Other feminist scholars, mostly from the United States, turn their attention to the claim that constitutions based on liberal democratic ideology can attack gender hierarchies. These critiques of the welfare state and the liberal state fuel the skepticism among feminists that the state has the capacity to achieve equality or the means to bring women into the policymaking arenas that affect their lives.

As this chapter will show, this study of comparative state feminism has benefited from the lively debate that has arisen in comparative social science over the "return to the state" (Almond, 1988; Caporaso, 1989; Mitchell, 1991; Rockman, 1990). Many writers have advocated taking a look at the question of the capacity of the state and its effects on political representation (Evans, Rueschemeyer, & Skocpol, 1985). Feminist scholars are also taking another look at the state, especially at the record of women's policy machinery, for evidence of possible state feminism. In this section, we will summarize feminist critiques of the welfare state and the liberal state and contrast them with the recent literature on state feminism, which sees a less monolithic state as a potential ally to women's diverse interests.

FEMINIST CRITIQUES
OF THE WELFARE STATE

European feminist scholars have focused on the institutional frameworks that states created when they adopted welfare policies and the effect of these creations on women. Scandinavian feminist scholars, for example, look at the social democratic welfare state as a relationship that has arisen between the state, the market, and families to regulate economic production and human reproduction (Borchorst & Siim, 1987; Hernes, 1987). British Marxist feminists see the state as the instrument of capitalist production (McIntosh, 1978; Wilson, 1977). Through specific social policies, the capitalist state creates the welfare state, an instrument that particularly oppresses women. American analysts, on the other hand, have employed frameworks that separate state institutions from government policies and programs (Diamond, 1983; Gordon, 1990). Welfare policies in all systems appear to be well-intentioned efforts to provide social benefits to workers and their families. Hernes, Borchorst, and Siim admit that the often-envied array of birth-to-earth programs in Scandinavian countries has produced, or at least coincided with, a high standard of living and quality of life for women. Borchorst (1994b) points out that the emphasis on mother-workers has increased options and economic independence of women. Nevertheless, the effect of the welfare state policies has been to institutionalize women's roles as mothers and workers—a double role and hence a double burden—without significantly altering the roles of men (Lewis & Astrom, 1992, p. 61). Although policies encourage waged work for all women, the workplace remains segregated and hierarchical. Despite generous assistance to families for help in child rearing, women do not have equal status with men in society. The welfare state has weakened male dominance in the family while strengthening those aspects of the public realm where men continue to dominate.

When assessing the British welfare state, McIntosh (1978) and Wilson (1977) also recognize some benefits to recipients of health care, social services, and pensions. From their perspective, however, motives remain the important thing. Because the architects of these welfare state policies represent the interests of capitalists, the critics ask how such policies benefit capitalist production. The answer is that the British welfare state tends to emphasize the role of women as economically dependent mothers. This dynamic works to the advantage of capitalists by ensuring the reproduction of a workforce healthy enough to sustain economic relations. Female dependency on husbands has been replaced by female dependency on the capitalist state.

Critics of U.S. welfare state policies, although avoiding a Marxist analysis, agree with their European counterparts that insofar as women may have benefited from some social policies, the primary effect has been that government has supplanted the family as the means of sustaining the dependency of women. A "two-tier" system separated work-related programs serving a male clientele from social compensation programs for a female, economically dependent, clientele. There was no effort to help women gain a foothold in well-paid jobs. Instead, protective labor laws for women reinforced the gendered division of labor.

Feminist critics also diverge in their interest in and conclusions about the effect of the welfare state on the political participation of women. Statistics show that Scandinavian parties and legislatures have the highest proportions of female members of all the democratic countries. But Hernes (1987) argues that this situation is "not synonymous with power nor with the ability to shape and influence their own status" (p. 73). This is due to the fact that the welfare state has institutionalized a pattern of corporatist decision making involving peak interest groups and bureaucratic agencies, rather than political parties and legislatures, in which women are active. The interest groups that are part of this system tend to be trade unions and businesses whose leaders are men; women's many organizations are not considered politically relevant at the national level. Hernes's conclusion is that "women have become clients without having gained the status of citizen" (p. 86) Borchorst and Siim (1987) agree that although women have achieved freedom from traditional patriarchal family structures, the welfare state has strengthened their subordination in the public sphere, where sex segregation in the workforce has limited women's influence in corporatist channels. It's not that women aren't participating. It's that the welfare state has empowered the very areas of participation—neocorporatist interest group/state relations—where men dominate.

While critics confront European welfare states that are the product of class politics, feminist critics of U.S. welfare policies must contend with a historical record that shows these policies are the product of political action by feminists. From the 1880s to the 1930s, women were influential in the development of protective legislation, widows' pensions, and mothers' aid through the progressive and social feminist organizations (Sarvasy, 1992; Skocpol, 1992, pp. 311-524). At the very least, the development of the U.S. welfare state coincided with increased political participation of women. Did this mean that the United States, unlike its European counterparts, brought women into the political process on a permanent basis?

Mink (1990) admits that some women did have influence in the development of social policy as "direct participants in politics and government—as members of commissions, school superintendents, health officers, social workers, and even as chiefs of the federal Children's and Women's Bureaus" (p. 101). Nevertheless, she points out, class and race affected such participation. Only a few middle-class White women played even a minor role in politics. Most women, due to economic status and/or race, remained outside the political process. The institutionalization of the motherhood role in welfare state social policy undercut whatever influence might have come to poor and minority women when they gained formal political rights.

FEMINIST CRITIQUES
OF THE LIBERAL STATE

Feminist critiques of the liberal state are really critiques of liberal feminism, aimed at women's movement activists who pursue their agenda through changes in laws and integration of women into the public sphere. The critics' intent is to show that no matter how many laws are passed or how many women hold public office, the state reflects, promotes, sustains, and responds to a hierarchy of male prerogative and female subordination (Elshtain, 1983, 1990; Ferguson, 1984; MacKinnon, 1989). The liberal belief, derived from contract theory, that the state (defined as government) is a neutral arbiter capable of responding to any group that develops political resources is a myth, a myth perpetuated by liberal feminists. It is a cruel myth because it serves the interests of the powerful.[6]

According to the critics, bureaucratic-legal states perpetuate women's subordination, no matter how many gender-neutral or equal rights policies they pursue. Public policies aimed at equality tend to bring women from private into public roles and politicize the private relations between men and women. If women are successful, they must conform to the norms and discourse of the bureaucracy, which is fundamentally grounded in hierarchy and inequality. As Elshtain (1983) states,

> [The] individuals located in highly centralized and hierarchical bureaucracies operate in conformity to certain impersonal, abstract, and rational standards today; this is the "price of entry" into the *predominant* public identity available to anyone, male or female. (p. 303)

Bureaucracies are the very essence of inequality; therefore, the policies of bureaucracies cannot produce equitable results (Ferguson, 1984, p. 23). Bureaucratic discourse itself produces clients, not participants. Thus, women end up subordinate to the state. Similarly, the law and the courts enforce rules that in turn reinforce societal gender relations. The result is that no matter how many cases liberal feminists win, most women remain poor and dependent, as breeders and marginal workers (MacKinnon, 1989).

According to Elshtain and Ferguson, women who join the bureaucratic state do so at the expense of their own potential female power derived from private realms. Elshtain (1983) reminds readers of the power of "maternal thinking" based on human dignity and community values that reject "amoral state craft" (p. 310). Ferguson (1984) warns that playing the bureaucratic game means the loss of an alternative feminist discourse based on "characteristic experiences of women as caretakers, nurturers, and providers for the needs of others" (p. 158). Such a discourse has revolutionary possibilities: "A specifically feminist discourse can suggest a reformulation of some of the most central terms of political life: reason, power, community, freedom" (p. 155). For MacKinnon (1989), who writes in the area of law, such a change would create a legal system based on women's experience and concrete reality, a form of substantive rather than procedural equality. The male-defined power structure would be replaced with mechanisms for really changing the conditions of women's lives in all respects including, through a new feminist jurisprudence, women's relation to the law.

STATE FEMINISM

While feminist theorists have been writing about the welfare state and the liberal state, 30 years of women's movement activism has coincided with changes in actual nation-state structures. Many advanced industrial democratic states have established agencies ranging from equal opportunity commissions and councils to departments and ministries for women. Governments have given these institutions the responsibility to achieve what Hernes (1987, p. 11) calls "feminism from above," or state feminism. The meaning of the term *state feminism* has evolved in its brief public life. Originally, the Scandinavian literature refers to state feminists as "both feminists employed as administrators and bureaucrats in positions of power and to women politicians advocating gender equality policies" (Siim, 1991, p. 189). Then Australian writers coined the term *femocrat* (Sawer, 1990) to describe the individuals referred to by Siim. The creation of the notion of a femocrat allowed scholars like Eisenstein (1990) and Outshoorn (1992) to focus on the institutionalization of feminism in public agencies promoting a women's policy agenda and to analyze the women staffing them.[7] It is a logical step, then, to use state feminism to refer to this institutionalization of feminist interests. It is important to avoid, at this point, any assumptions about a universal definition of feminism. As we will see, the definitions of both *state* and *feminism* are questions for cross-national research.

The scholars who have begun to turn their attention to women's agencies offer a fresh look at the state and its capacity to achieve feminist goals. These writings on state feminism differ from previous feminist research in that they question the notion held by many critics that the state is a single entity acting in society in defense of its own interests. Whether influenced by postmodernism's obliteration of grand design or sobered by their encounters with the world around them (both explanations are offered), writers of state feminist literature avoid such global definitions of the state (Pringle & Watson, 1992). A more useful approach is to conceive of the state as the site or location of a variety of internally differentiated structures and processes (Franzway, Court, & Connell, 1989). Furthermore, for purposes of comparative research, these analysts recognize that whatever the state means is relative; conceptions vary from political culture to political culture, and these differences affect the way the state agencies may intervene in women's lives (Pringle & Watson, 1992; Sawer, 1993).

Deconstructing the monolithic state has reconstructed the question of its impact on women. Until now, empirical research on state feminism has been limited to a few case studies (e.g., Sawer, 1990, 1993; Stetson, 1987; Walker, 1990). Research in state feminism in Australia, for example, shows that through the intervention of femocrats and state offices, organizations have been successful in securing funds for many projects based on feminist collective ideologies. Sawer (1993) argues that the operation of these agencies cemented a bond between the state and women's groups that strengthened the nongovernmental bodies' influence over policy. Work on these structures in Canada, on the contrary, suggests that subsidies from women's agencies to feminist groups were limited and were seen by political leaders as too radical (Walker, 1990). Still, as Stetson (1987) has shown in the case of France, the Ministry of Woman's Rights under the first Socialist presidency of Mitterrand (1981-1986) took over the agenda-setting role that had previously resided in nongovernmental feminist groups.

These initial forays to explore the records of action by specialized agencies have led many to agree with Drude Dahlerup (1987) that in order to develop a feminist theory of the state, we need less abstraction and more studies of "the scope and context of government action and its consequences for the position of women" (p. 108). Theories about the state and feminism must be examined cross-nationally, given the cultural differences in the ways both these terms are understood. Eisenstein (1990) agrees that the question of whether the state has helped or hurt women requires comparative research to assess the impact in a variety of contexts. In this book, we offer the first systematic cross-national examination and analysis of states' records and potential to further feminist goals.

Method of Comparison

We have selected the *comparative method* to conduct this study. The comparative method—as contrasted with the case study and experimental or statistical methods—uses a small number of cases, subjected to close systematic analysis (Lijphart, 1971). The cases are selected to represent a larger population of political systems. Data are collected from these cases according to a framework that sets forth a common set of research questions for each case. Then the cases are classified according to similarities and differences found in the central variables of the study. The final step is to suggest explanations of the similarities and differences found. The analysis of this book, therefore, will use the comparative method to yield hypotheses about cross-national variations in state feminism.[8]

There are a number of important decisions that must be made in designing a study using the comparative method. First, the cases must be selected according to clear criteria. This involves a decision about whether to opt for the "most similar" approach, in which cases are selected in order to maximize their similarities, or the "most different" approach, which would focus on contrasting cases. There are good arguments for both approaches (Lijphart, 1975; Przeworski & Teune, 1970). Second, authors must be recruited to prepare the case studies, and they must have a framework that will help them gather similar kinds of data about each case. The framework must be carefully constructed to avoid "conceptual stretching," that is, the use of concepts whose meanings do not apply to all cases (Collier & Mahon, 1993; Sawer, 1993).

Third, the framework must be based on a set of research questions that delineate all relevant variables for the generation of hypotheses, that is, both dependent and independent variables. These must also be anchored in a carefully constructed theoretical foundation. We turn now to the research plan for this book, describing the selection of the country cases and authors and the analytical framework's dependent and independent variables, including a discussion of how we treated the problem of conceptual stretching.

SELECTING THE CASES

The population from which the cases were drawn is composed of advanced industrial societies.[9] In selecting the cases, we used primarily the most similar approach, choosing countries that had many characteristics in common. Thus, we reduced our population to those advanced industrial societies with stable democratic political systems. Because we are studying a phenomenon that arose from the second wave of feminism beginning in the 1960s, we confine our cases to those countries that have had democratic governments continuously since the 1950s.[10] From this population, we have selected 12 cases: Australia, Canada, Denmark, France, Germany, Great Britain, Ireland, Italy, the Netherlands, Norway, Sweden, and the United States.

Our study also includes two contrasting cases, representing political change among the advanced industrial societies: Spain and Poland. Spain, a member of the European Union and classified among the advanced industrial societies by the World Bank, has had continuous democratic rule only since 1975, when the authoritarian Franco regime was replaced. Poland, a member of the Communist bloc until 1989, represents the more recent trend of democratization in Europe: the transition of Eastern European countries from communism to market economies and democratic regimes. This set of 14 cases, therefore, simultaneously provides a solid foundation to develop propositions about cross-national variations in state feminism in democratic states and suggests explanations for the existence of women's policy machineries in systems that are not as prone to democratic stability. As Collier (1991, p. 17) notes, these strategies of most similar and most different case analysis can be combined in the same study to set better future research agendas.

We sought authors for these cases who were either native scholars or had extensive experience living and doing research in the country.

We also searched for authors who had published research on women and politics in the country and, preferably, on some aspect of the national women's policy machinery. We have been extremely fortunate to assemble distinguished contributors, each of whom meets all criteria. We are also gratified that they were willing to structure their individual projects according to the common framework we set forth.

DEPENDENT VARIABLES: CRITERIA FOR STATE FEMINISM

Central to this study is the following question: Is women's policy machinery feminist? To answer this question requires setting forth categories of agency activities to study and criteria for determining whether they are feminist or not. To develop the categories of agency activities, we drew upon literature from comparative social science on the state, particularly the work of Skocpol (1985). She suggests two important categories for studying state action: the *capacity* of the state, through policy, to have an impact on society and the impact of the state on political relationships or *state-society relations*. Adapting these two analytical angles to the study of women's policy machinery yields two areas of inquiry:

1. State capacity: To what extent does women's policy machinery influence feminist policy?
2. State-society relations: To what extent does women's policy machinery develop opportunities for society-based actors—feminist and women's advocacy organizations—to have access to the policy process?

When these questions are examined in a variety of different country case studies, problems of "conceptual stretching" may arise.[11] Most social science concepts are subject to various interpretations in different cultures and languages. And we have used two concepts—state and feminist—that are subject to intense debates both cross-nationally and within countries. The contemporary scholarly debates on the use of the state in political research have revealed one area of agreement: Conceptions of the state in society are grounded in history and political culture (Rockman, 1990). Such conceptions range from societies where the idea of the state has little political meaning, the so-called stateless societies, such as the United States, to nations where several ideas of state as actor in society coexist, such as Germany (Caporaso, 1989; Dyson, 1980; Joppke, 1992; Nettl, 1968). We seek to solve this problem by incorporating a country's conception of the state into the framework as a possible explanatory variable (see below).

The problem of defining *feminist* or *feminism* is especially important and thus especially difficult to resolve because these terms are central to the phenomenon we are trying to document and compare, namely whether the state can further feminist goals. There is much controversy among women's movement activists, self-defined feminists, and women's studies scholars about what is meant by these terms and whether a particular action is feminist. In the area of gender studies and especially feminist theories of law and policy, feminist concepts tend to be grounded almost exclusively in the writings of Anglo-American scholars and activists (Fineman & Thomadsen, 1991; MacKinnon, 1989; Smart, 1990).

It is conventional in this literature to set forth a list of feminist ideologies limited to varieties of modified feminism: liberal feminism, Marxist feminism, socialist feminism, and radical feminism. Recent studies of gender and international relations have added ecofeminism and postmodern feminism to the list (Peterson & Runyan, 1993). The problem with this approach is that it tends to restrict the vision of researchers to a predetermined set of categories and cause them to overlook gender-based ideologies that are politically important but do not fit on the list. It thus denies the right of women in various countries to set forth their own versions of feminist agendas. Many a Western feminist scholar has been criticized for claiming to have determined whether a pattern of gender politics in another country is feminist or not (see, for example, Nesiah, 1993).

Furthermore, rather than developing an analytical concept of feminism, many scholars who work with the term tend to reify the concept by placing the notion of feminism on a pedestal. The notion of feminism becomes, for many, the endpoint of analysis rather than the means to an analytical end.

Sensitive to the potential misuse of the central concept of this study, we separated its use into two categories permitting two definitions: (a) the definition to be used by authors of the case studies and (b) the definition to be used for the overall comparison of case studies. The authors were asked to include information on ideologies and politics of self-defined feminists pertinent to the politics of the countries they studied. They were also asked to include information on organizations that had the objective of improving the status of women, however defined, and whether or not these organizations proclaimed themselves feminist. For the purposes of the comparison of the case studies we used the following working definition:

> An ideology, policy, organization, or activity is feminist to the extent that it has the purpose of improving the status of women as a group and undermining patterns of gender hierarchy.

INDEPENDENT VARIABLES: EXPLAINING STATE FEMINISM

In identifying factors that explain cross-national variations in state feminism, it was important in the design of this study to choose independent variables that would affect the two dimensions of state feminist offices: their policy influence and their ability to provide access to women's groups. Early in our research we noted that despite the common environment of the second-wave women's movements and the international impetus from the United Nations, the politics that led to the establishment of agencies seemed to vary. In some countries, political leaders, hoping to win over women voters, created an agency or appointed an adviser for women in the absence of any demand from outside the government. In other countries, the issue became part of party platforms pushed by women within party organizations. In still others, leaders sought to respond to increased activism from women's movement organizations. These observations suggest that a major area of explanation for the nature and degree of state feminism in a given country will be the circumstances of office creation. In other words:

- ◆ Does the pattern of politics surrounding the establishment of women's policy machinery affect the degree to which it is able to achieve feminist political goals?

The form of women's policy offices also appears to have an important influence on cross-national differences in the effectiveness of their activities. UN studies have shown a broad array of types of agencies and locations, from ministries of the national cabinet to ad hoc committees and regional advisers. There are equal opportunity agencies, bureaus, and autonomous commissions. As a consequence, the second area of explanation for divergences in state feminism will be the specific type of agency. The analytical question for this second independent variable is the following:

- ◆ Do certain organizational forms increase the likelihood that policy machinery will further feminist goals?

Looking at the organizational forms alone might omit the effect of expectations of and cultural attitudes about state action in the political culture. Here is where the cross-national diversity of conceptions of the state can be included in the analysis. The capacity of the state to resolve social problems may be greater if the agencies operate in the context of cultural beliefs that define these agencies as the main vehicles for social action. Women's policy machinery would draw resources from this view to further feminist policy. At the same time, cultural traditions of a strong state, especially those embraced by state elites, may hinder efforts to strengthen nongovernmental women's advocacy organizations, by opening access to the policy process without making these society-based organizations dependent on the state or coopting them. On the other hand, groups may not look to the state as an arena for social change in the so-called stateless societies such as the United States, where the government operates within a cultural context that does not recognize a coherent entity—the state—acting for social goals. In such societies, policy machinery would be seen as just another social agency with limited potential for changing anything. The importance of cultural notions of the state leads to this question:

- ◆ To what extent does the conception of the state affect the likelihood that women's policy machinery will further feminist political goals?

Finally, we must include variations in the politics of the women's movement as a possible explanation of patterns of state feminist action. Specifically, we focus on activists' views of the state, whether they see it as a possible vehicle to improve the status of women or as an instrument of male power that is not to be trusted. Also of interest is the pattern of organization that developed in the second-wave women's movement, whether it was a coherent national network sponsoring a professional women's lobby, a diverse set of small loose-knit women's liberation groups, or a combination of the two. This fourth independent variable will be looked at in terms of this last question:

- Is a particular form of the women's movement more compatible with the development of active state feminist offices?

ANALYTICAL FRAMEWORK
FOR CASE STUDIES

This description of the research design sets the stage for the common framework we presented to the authors of the case studies and the outline for each country-specific chapter that follows. First, we set forth criteria for defining policy machinery, specifically, for locating the major structures. Any agency that met these criteria was to be included in the case study:

It was in operation for some portion of the period since 1960.
It had the primary responsibility to develop and/or implement policy to promote the status of women.
It was established by statute or executive order.

Authors were able to locate institutions that met these criteria in all countries.

Then the authors were asked to provide a detailed description of the process that led to the establishment of the agency. In this section, they discuss the conception in the political culture about the proper role of the state and the role of feminist and women's advocacy organizations interacting with the political and administrative leaders. This information about the process of establishment is followed by a description of the organization and activities of the agency, including forms of administration, powers, budget and other resources, and typical activities.

The next section for each case includes an analysis of the role of the agency in policy formulation and implementation. Authors were encouraged to focus on specific policy areas, such as equal employment or reproductive rights. Finally, the authors were asked to include an analysis of the relation of the machinery to nongovernmental organizations, especially focusing on the record of the agency in strengthening the organizational network and facilitating its access to policymaking arenas.

An Invitation to Compare

The concluding chapter of the book presents our analysis of the case studies according to the analytical framework described here. That is, the conclusion will discuss to what extent women's policy machineries in each country were state feminist and to what degree they actually influenced feminist policies and provided access to women's groups that also sought to affect feminist policy formulation and implementation. Cross-national variations in levels of state feminism will then be discussed in terms of the values of the four independent variables mentioned above for each of the 14 countries. In this way, this study will propose a set of conditions associated with high levels of state feminist activity.

Although these findings suggest one way of thinking about state feminism and women's policy machineries, they do not in any way exhaust the potential for comparative analysis of these 14 case studies. Indeed, the excellent scholarship of these chapters provides a wealth of comparative data that can be analytically cut up in quite different ways than this book has chosen, for entirely different theoretical purposes. For example, one could use these chapters to examine the extent to which women's policy machineries created regional and territorial bureaus. Thus, we invite readers to use these chapters to explore new analytical questions that arise from reading the stories of feminists and their governments in these varied political systems and cultures.

Notes

1. Students of women's movements agree that there have been two major waves of feminist political activity in most Western democracies, with the first wave occurring around the turn of the century. The second wave began in advanced industrialized countries in the late 1960s and early 1970s, thus coinciding with the creation of new women's policy machineries. Historians note that in some countries, including the United States, the contemporary movement is, in fact, the third wave.

2. It is important to note that feminism is a highly contested concept that has different meanings in different political, social, and national contexts. The controversies over this notion and the way in which this study deals with the problems of defining the term will be discussed at further length in this chapter.

3. The use of the term *women's policy* raises questions about the existence of *women's interests*. Clearly there is no way to verify that a particular demand is in the interest of all women (see, e.g., Molyneux, 1985). However, the United Nations charges women's policy machinery with improving the status of women by identifying the needs of women in various situations. Similarly, the term women's policy is used here to include actions to promote women in various situations in advanced industrial societies. Such actions promote equality and respond to women's concerns about maternity leave and child care. This contrasts with the use of the term by Hernes (1987, Chapter 1), who separates equality policy from women's policy.

4. For the most recent official list of women's policy machineries worldwide see United Nations, 1993a.

5. Franzway et al. (1989, Chapter 7), for instance, state that the word femocrat is "sometimes spoken pejoratively, it refers to those women appointed to work in 'women's affairs' and women's units in the state apparatus, the bureaucracies" (p. 133). An invention of Australian feminists, the term is also used to refer to any feminist in a government bureaucratic job (Eisenstein, 1991; Watson, 1990).

6. These criticisms do not focus much on the state itself, but on the limits of the liberal ideology of rights in eliminating the subordination of women. The idea of rights, as Pateman (1988) and others point out, is based on dichotomies that separate public arenas from private ones; the state may not interfere unduly in the private ones. Although this approach may safeguard the lives and liberty of male citizens, it does not further the rights of women, whose lives are often enclosed by private boundaries under male dominance.

7. Hatem, in a study of Egypt published in 1992, departs from the pattern of usage by Outshoorn, Eisenstein, and this book's authors by using state feminism to mean the same thing as welfare state policies and programs.

8. The methodological approach of this study uses one of three types of comparative method outlined by Skocpol and Somers (1980), the use of cases for the "generation and testing of hypotheses." The other two types are using cases to demonstrate theory and using cases to highlight difference. See Collier (1991) for a summary of the comparative method.

9. This does not mean that these are the only countries with active women's policy machineries; many less industrialized societies in the southern hemisphere have national policy machinery as well.

10. These include the following 20 countries: Austria, Belgium, Denmark, Finland, France, Germany, Iceland, Ireland, Italy, Luxembourg, the Netherlands, Norway, Sweden, Switzerland, the United Kingdom, Australia, New Zealand, Canada, the United States, and Japan.

11. For a discussion of the problem of conceptual stretching in comparative research and proposed solutions, see Collier and Mahon (1993).

2

"Femocrats in Glass Towers?"

*The Office of the Status
of Women in Australia*

Marian Sawer

The Australian government has had a network of agencies that focus on women's policy issues for over 20 years. The record of this machinery suggests that feminist interventions in the state can result in positive gains for women. It will be argued in this chapter that the combination of femocrat advocacy from within government with grassroots pressure from outside has resulted in better policy outcomes for women, including a wide range of government-funded and feminist-inspired services. This is particularly so in the context of the erosion of social liberal traditions in Australia in the 1980s and an increased reliance on market forces in many areas of government policy.

Femocrat is a term invented in Australia in the 1970s to describe feminists who took up women's policy positions that were being created in government at the time. Later, it was also used for feminists who moved on to mainstream positions in the bureaucracy. Originally a term of abuse or ironic self-deprecation, the term femocrat is now perhaps an icon of the Australian experiment with feminist interventions in the state. Today, the term femocrat appears in feminist discourse,[1] as well as in wider political discourse in Australia, for example, in newspaper headlines about appointments to women's policy positions. It is sometimes used in a hostile fashion by critics, such as the right-wing trade union official Joe de Bruyn. In objecting to the influence of the prime minister's femocrat advisers in obtaining large new child-care commitments rather than incentives for women to stay home, he concluded: "Radical femocrats ensconced in glass towers in Canberra have no idea what ordinary working women want" (*The Age,* 15 April 1993).

This chapter will be concerned with the evolution of the Office of the Status of Women (OSW) in the federal Department of Prime Minister and Cabinet (PM&C). One should keep in mind that this agency, as well as the network of women's units of which it forms the hub, is a structure or strategy that has been replicated in all the Australian states and territories. The analysis draws on extensive interviews (Eisenstein, 1995; Sawer & Groves, 1994). We will begin by sketching some of the background to the adoption of this strategy and the political tradition and circumstances that made it possible, then turn to the development of its organization, role in policymaking, and relations with women's organizations.

Establishment

In late 1969, the polite lobbying of generations of Australian women for equal rights was overtaken by the arrival from the United States of a more assertive form of feminism—women's liberation. Like the United States, Australia was home to increasing numbers of women with higher education who had been politicized by the antiwar movement and were ready to rebel against the constriction of their roles. Women started collectively naming the sources of their oppression, using new words such as *sexism* and *male chauvinism* and urging social transformation. By 1972 many women wanted change, and some were looking to the government.

It is part of the Australian political tradition to look to the state for a response to social issues. Australia's nation building took place during a period when social liberalism was on the ascent in the United Kingdom. The concept of the state as a vehicle for social justice and for the civilizing of capitalism has been embodied in the state experiments of Australia and New Zealand since the 1890s (Encel, 1994; Sawer, 1994). Distinctive Australasian institutions were created at this time, such as centralized conciliation and arbitration systems, which removed the setting of wages from the higgling (or haggling) of the marketplace (Macintyre, 1989). Both progressive liberals and the new labor parties shared in this pro-state orientation, which was an important element in the parliamentary alliances of the first years after federation (1901-1910).

At the beginning of the 1970s at least one wing of the women's movement drew on this tradition of pragmatic orientation toward the state. "People thought, the government can do useful things. And our generation were thinking '. . . well, why can't it do our things then?' " (Eisenstein, 1995). "Our things" included child care, equal pay and equal opportunity, and reproductive freedom. The emergence of the nonparty Women's Electoral Lobby (WEL) in 1972 and its highly successful election strategy of that year (Preddy, 1985) were largely responsible for bringing the demands of the women's movement to the attention of politicians.

With the election of the Labor Government in December 1972, after 23 years of conservative rule, women were able to see immediate returns for their efforts. The new prime minister, Gough Whitlam, moved swiftly on women's issues. He decided to appoint a women's adviser to his staff, the first step in the evolution of the current OSW. The decision arose from a suggestion by the convener of WEL-ACT to her husband, Peter Wilenski, then the prime minister's principal private secretary.

The appointment of the adviser immediately became a focus for media interest—the selection process was sensationalized as the "hunt for the PM's 'supergirl'" or the "supergirl contest." The successful candidate was Elizabeth Reid, then a senior tutor in philosophy at the Australian National University and later to become a senior UN bureaucrat. Reid, who was active in women's liberation and was teaching one of the first women's studies courses, was selected on the grounds of both her demonstrated commitment to women and her outstanding intellectual abilities.

Reid set about systematically raising women's expectations that government would listen to them. One of the slogans of the feminists entering government in the 1970s was the need to "take every woman seriously" and to get as much information about government services out to women in the community as possible. This soon led to the creation of woman-friendly information services. In the meantime, Reid's position was identified as women's access point in government and, as a result, she was overwhelmed with work: "I was receiving more letters than anyone else in government other than the Prime Minister," Reid (1987, p. 15) said.

The creation of a women's adviser position was controversial among feminists. The position of such a post inside the male bastion of government was seen by some as an attempt to buy off the revolution: "No woman chosen by men to advise upon us will be acceptable to us. We believe that it is not your right to choose for us our spokeswoman, any more than it is any woman's right to act as the single spokeswoman for the rest of us" (personal communication, Editorial Collective, *Mejane* newspaper, March 26, 1973).

Other activists, however, soon followed Reid into government. For instance, a number of the other 17 women short-listed for the women's adviser position entered the bureaucracy and became the first femocrats (Ryan, 1990). So many WEL members took up these positions that the phenomenon became known collectively as "WEL entering government."[2] WEL was also instrumental in getting women's adviser positions and women's policy machinery established in state and territory governments.

The expansionist social policy agenda of the Whitlam Government, particularly before the economic problems engendered by the oil price hike in 1974, presented political opportunities that were readily taken. There was also a happy coincidence of a peak of feminist activism and the election of reform-minded governments, both in Canberra and in some states. This is not to say that the transition from the women's movement into the hierarchical world of the federal bureaucracy was an entirely easy one, even under reform administrations. Femocrats appointed because of their expertise in gender issues and their advocacy skills developed in the women's movement often knew little about the bureaucracy and "learned more from the stenographer than anyone else" (Sawer, 1990, p. 23).

At first there was some optimism that the structures could be changed: "The women's movement in Australia has now entered into the decision making world, not merely in order to be equal with men, or to learn to play tired old games, but in order to change that world" (Australian National Advisory Committee, International Women's Year, 1976, p. 27). Along the way, however, compromises were inevitably going to be involved.

Organization and Activities

THINKING THROUGH THE STRUCTURES

Although femocrats working at the center of government were able to provide vital support for feminist forms of service delivery elsewhere, they themselves had to operate within very hierarchical structures. Early rebellions against hierarchical norms only fueled the suspicions with which more traditional bureaucrats viewed femocrats. In the late 1980s, senior bureaucrats still regularly referred to one important federal women's unit as "the feminist collective."

Basically, in thinking through the kind of structures necessary for women to be effective in the bureaucracy, WEL members, with their new experience of government, were determined that women's structures in government should not be just a "wastepaper basket for women's problems"; rather, they should have the more strategic role of conducting a "gender audit" of all policy and program administration. Reid announced this orientation on the day of her appointment in 1973 when she called for "impact on women" statements to be attached to all cabinet submissions.

Structurally her new position was anomalous. She was a member of the prime minister's personal staff and worked from his office. In principle, her role was to provide private advice to the prime minister, like any other staff member. In fact, she took on a very public, quasi-ministerial role. In 1975, when the Government was already under siege from conservative forces, the hostile media treatment of International Women's Year (IWY) events and fears of further revelations damaging to the Government led to a decision to move her into the PM&C, as head of an expanded Women's Affairs Branch. Emotionally and physically exhausted, she decided instead to resign over what she described as an attempt to silence her.

```
┌─────────────────────────────────────────────────────┐
│                   Evolution of OSW                    │
│             Women's Affairs Section 1974              │
│             Women's Affairs Branch 1975               │
│            Office of Women's Affairs 1977             │
│          Office of the Status of Women 1982           │
└─────────────────────────────────────────────────────┘
```

Figure 2.1. Evolution of the Office of the Status of Women in Australia

Reid's achievements had been remarkable: initiation of federal government funding for women's refuges and a range of other women's services, such as women's health and rape crisis services; the funding of a national child-care program; and the substantial government funding for IWY. Under Reid, the birth of what was to become the OSW took place. She was insistent that the Women's Affairs Section should be focused on policy and coordination functions and not become absorbed in program administration. Thus, the logical location for Women's Affairs would be the PM&C, central to the whole decision-making process of government. Figure 2.1 shows the evolution of the OSW, beginning with the creation of the Women's Affairs Section in 1974.

1975 was a very stormy year in Australian politics, culminating with the governor general sacking the Labor prime minister on November 11 and the subsequent election of the conservative Government of Malcolm Fraser. During the campaign, Fraser had promised to retain the Women's Affairs Branch in his department if he was elected. Early in 1976, he also agreed that it should become the nucleus of a network of women's policy units to be established in various functional departments. Later in the same year he increased the recognition given to the Branch by appointing a minister assisting the prime minister on women's affairs, the first time such a portfolio had been created in Australia. There has been a women's portfolio ever since. Today all states and territories, as well as the Commonwealth, have ministers responsible for the status of women, and there is a regular ministerial conference that includes the relevant New Zealand minister.

WEL was influential in shaping the form of policy machinery with its 1974 submission to the Royal Commission on Australian Government Administration. With some reservations, the Royal Commission accepted the logic expressed in WEL's proposal of the network model rather than a separate bureau or commission. It recommended that a number of departments should "be encouraged to develop women's policy units on an experimental basis" (Royal Commission on Australian Government Administration, 1976, p. 345). This proposal is often expressed in the image of a wheel, with the Women's Affairs Branch as the hub and the units in functional departments as the spokes.

At the 1975 Women and Politics Conference, Sara Dowse, who headed the Women's Affairs Branch after Reid's resignation, suggested that the adoption of the center-periphery model of women's policy machinery, rather than vertical integration, was structurally appropriate to feminist philosophy. The wheel of women's affairs, in which functional experts, backed up by a strong coordinating body with access to all cabinet submissions, examine policy at its point of origin for its impact on women, has been a characteristically Australian contribution.

POLITICAL FORTUNES AND MISFORTUNES

The Fraser Government in the 1970s established 12 women's policy units and formed an Interdepartmental Working Group on Women's Affairs chaired by the head of the Women's Affairs Branch. After this promising start, the wheel of women's affairs started coming unstuck. A new head of the PM&C resented the access enjoyed by Women's Affairs to the cabinet process. After the December 1977 election, it was announced that the newly upgraded Office of Women's Affairs (OWA) was to be moved to the newly created Department of Home Affairs, which then ranked 26th out of the 27 ministries. Relocation from a central coordinating department to a peripheral one meant increased difficulty in gaining access to cabinet submissions. Nor was the Office able to play an effective role as the hub of the women's affairs wheel. The Interdepartmental Working Group became moribund, as did a number of the women's units. The workload of the Office increased commensurately, as proposals came through to the cabinet with little prior analysis of their impact on women.

While the interdepartmental network sagged, however, a new intergovernmental network came into being. As we shall see below, regular meetings of Commonwealth and state women's advisers beginning in 1978 helped maintain momentum in women's policy across the Australian federal system. At the same time, through its years of exile, the Office was able to build up its staff resources as it took on the secretariat duties for the new National Women's Advisory Council and then the national consultations leading up to the UN Mid-Decade Conference in Copenhagen (1980). The Office played an important role in the preparatory work for all four UN world conferences for women, internationally as well as domestically. Through these activities, close relations were developed with a range of women's organizations, including relatively conservative ones that provided vital political support for the Office (still staffed by Labor appointees) during these years. In return, the Office helped where possible to aid these organizations in their advocacy work.

When a federal Labor Government was eventually reelected in 1983, it was committed to the return of the Office to the PM&C, to upgrade it to divisional status, and to restore women's units within "relevant government authorities." The return of the Office had great symbolic importance as a statement of the Government's commitment to women. It also strengthened the role of the Office in monitoring cabinet submissions and advising on budget proposals and enabled it to function once more as the hub of a network of women's units. The relocation of the Office facilitated the briefing of the prime minister, the minister assisting the prime minister for the status of women, cabinet ministers, and other staff and made it easier to make submissions to the Expenditure Review Committee (ERC). Some quick decisions were achieved: For example, all cabinet submissions were to carry an impact on women statement. And, as one senior staff member said, being in the PM&C gave the Office "the advantage of location, location, location" (Patricia Kelly, quoted in Sawer & Groves, 1994, p. 29).

The advantages of location were compounded by the appointment of a new head, journalist Anne Summers, who had high political credibility and ready access to the prime minister, as well as a background in women's liberation. She led in the introduction of a major new coordinating exercise for the Office: the Women's Budget Program (WBP; called the Women's Budget Statement after 1987). Women's advisers had long been discussing the need for a mechanism that would look at the Government's budget as a whole and try to shift main-

stream funding in ways that would benefit women, rather than min-
uscule targeted programs.

The WBP was introduced on a trial basis in 1984 and was implemented
for all federal departments and agencies in 1985. For the first time,
departments were required to account for their impact on women in a
document published on budget night. The WBP was soon adopted by
the states and territories as well, some of which succeeded in maintaining
a greater analytic edge than the federal prototype. The Office presented
a case study of the program to an "Expert Group" meeting held by the
UN Branch for the Advancement of Women in 1987.

The kind of audit involved in the Women's Budget Statement was
supplemented by the introduction, in 1988, of "gender equality indicators" to measure from year to year how women's status relative to
men was faring on a range of dimensions including income, dependence on income support, and representation in decision making. The
indicators were developed in conjunction with the Australian Bureau
of Statistics and published in the Women's Budget Statement and in
National Agenda Implementation Reports.

Another way in which the OSW is involved with policy coordination is through regular meetings of Commonwealth, state, and territory women's advisers (now known as the Standing Committee of
Women's Advisers). These meetings were initiated in 1978 and were,
particularly for the next decade, a frank and off-the-record way in
which femocrats working for different governments could pool ideas
and provide mutual support. Another important player in the area of
women's policy under recent Labor Governments has been the Parliamentary Labor party's Committee on the Status of Women. The
Committee meets every Tuesday during the parliamentary session, is
open to all Labor women MPs, and works to focus the minds of
ministerial colleagues on the impact of their policy proposals on
women. The Committee now includes a number of former ministers
responsible for the status of women and reinforces at the political level
the work of the Office at the bureaucratic level. In addition to its
primary policy advisory and policy coordination functions, the OSW
has also had responsibility for consultation and information functions, providing secretariat services for national women's advisory or
consultative councils and other consultative bodies. The National
Women's Advisory Council of the Fraser years played an important
role in building up pressure for Commonwealth antidiscrimination

legislation as well as serving as a parachute that provided political support for the Office. The National Women's Consultative Council of the Hawke years also provided a public voice for the Office on a number of issues, from taxes to the ratification of the ILO Convention on Equal Opportunity for Workers with Family Responsibilities. The 1989 Women's Tax Convention, cohosted by the Council and WEL, forcibly put the case for the Government to give priority to low-income earners in forthcoming tax cuts: Almost 75% of women earned less than $20,000 a year, the level at which some unions had wanted tax cuts to start. This helped the Office to an unaccustomed win on a mainstream economic decision.

Another aspect of the OSW's consultation role has been through operational and project grants to women's organizations. OSW grants were of importance both in enabling new sections of women to become organized and in assisting more established groups to fulfill their representational and advocacy roles in more professional ways. Demands for submissions were increasing exponentially, and some femocrats were highly critical of the quality of the submissions coming forward from underresourced women's organizations. The level of operational grants was increased significantly in the context of the 1993 federal election, in which the Labor Government was trying to close a wide gender gap. Apart from the consultation and grants programs, the Office has also had a role from time to time in the direct provision of information services to women in the community, disseminated through women's shopfronts and through newsletters sent to community organizations, neighborhood houses, women's refuges, and other women's services.

A NEW DIRECTION

During the late 1980s there was a proliferation of councils and other bodies being serviced by the Office, in addition to the National Women's Consultative Council: the Commonwealth/State Domestic Violence Coordinating Task Force (replaced by the Commonwealth/State National Committee on Violence against Women in 1990), the National Working Party on the Portrayal of Women in the Media, and the Commonwealth/State Council on Non-English Speaking Background Women's Issues. The fact that these secretariat and support functions were absorbing some 25% of staff time in the Office was becoming a cause for alarm by 1993. There was a perception among politicians and bureaucrats that the Office had lost influence and focus. The newly appointed minister undertook a review for the prime minister of future directions for the Office. The review suggested that the Office should maximize the benefit of its location through greater integration within PM&C, backed up by strong support from the departmental executive and the prime minister's office.

The number of bodies being served by the Office was reduced as they completed their terms. The National Women's Consultative Council was replaced by a smaller specific-purpose council responsible for coordinating preparation for the 1995 UN Women's Conference in Beijing. A twice-yearly roundtable between the minister and national women's organizations was instituted as a forum where other concerns could be raised. Decreased confidence in the representative character of women's organizations (particularly their failure to attract young women) was reflected in increased emphasis on market research to test attitudes about specific policy issues. With the ending of the advisory and consultative bodies, the publications program of the Office was significantly reduced and the newsletter, OSWomen, was also discontinued.

Although nongovernment organizations endorsed the new strategic policy focus of the Office, they were concerned about how abandoning community outreach would affect the relationship between the Office and women in the community. Some believed that an effective relationship between the Office and community organizations also required the latter to become more strategic in their policy focus and to improve political communication within the nongovernment sector. Progress is being made in this direction through the creation of the information-sharing CAPOW! network,[3] which encompasses most national women's organizations (linked by fortnightly fax), and through work (at the insistence of the new minister) on the feasibility of a peak body representing women.

Policy Formulation and Implementation

The women's budget process introduced in 1984 had the potential to enhance the OSW's role in coordinating the gender audit of policy.

It had an important educational effect, requiring departments to think about policy decisions in gender terms and consider, for example, how decisions about tariffs, industrial relations, taxation, and industry policy might have different effects on women, due to their different location in the workforce and the family. As former Cabinet Minister Susan Ryan has said, "It was a powerful tool for drawing the attention of ministers and the public to the impact of government programs on women" (quoted in Sawer & Groves, 1994, p. 32).

The Women's Budget Statement has caused considerable annoyance to some departments whose staff believed their work was in the interest of the economy as a whole and could not be disaggregated in terms of sex-specific outcomes. With the support of the Permanent Heads Task Force on the Status of Women, OSW insisted that the supposed gender neutrality of policy and programs be demonstrated rather than asserted and that gender-specific data be provided. In general, feminist surveillance of policy raised some hackles: "We made ourselves very unpopular as we poked around in other people's policies and made comments on their Cabinet submissions" (Summers, quoted in Sawer & Groves, 1994, p. 30). But the greatest resistance came from those involved with economic policy development. As one current staffer commented to us: "When we push against the barriers, get involved in 'their' issues, then there's resistance. . . . The attitude of the men in, say, the Economic Policy Division is 'It's an economic issue, what's it got to do with you?' " (staffer quoted in Sawer & Groves, 1994, p. 11).

The struggle for mainstream policy legitimacy is a continuing theme in the history of the Office. The problem under Fraser was dealing with a Government that in practice was economically interventionist in a traditional Australian way but that was held back on women's issues by its conservative rural coalition partner, which believed women's place was in the home. The problem under the Hawke Labor Government was its domination from the mid-1980s by anti-Keynesian economic rationalists. Feminist economists employed by the Office produced important papers for the Economic Summit of 1983 and for the Tax Summit in 1985. Their contributions, however, were far from welcome. They showed that women would benefit from enhanced progressiveness in income tax and more expenditure on services, contrary to the new economic wisdom, which proposed a shift from direct to indirect taxation and reduction in the size of the public sector. The economic rationalists, inspired by public choice theory, believed that women were a special-interest group with no right to stake claims in arenas where the objective determination of policy was to take place.

The Office was pushed toward "women as victim" issues, on which it could at least make some headway, even if only for the wrong reasons. One former head of the Office said: "I think it was easier to get progress on areas where male politicians felt chivalrous. Domestic violence, child sexual assault, rape" (Helen L'Orange, quoted in Eisenstein, 1995). Nonetheless, the same femocrat played a key role in ensuring that feminist analysis remained central to government strategy on violence against women (i.e., that the root cause was gender inequalities in power). She was also one of the experts appointed by the UN Secretary General to draft the UN Declaration on the Elimination of Violence against Women, which was adopted by the General Assembly in 1993.

Relationship With the Women's Movement

Communication with bureaucrats and ministers is one issue. Relations with the women's movement is another. The constraints under which femocrats work have often been poorly understood by feminists outside. For instance, one feminist critic lamented, "The leaflets put out by the Office are frustratingly bland about their activities. You would think they never had any disagreements, never got into any fights, never ran into any hostile opposition" (Pringle, 1979, p. 59).

For good political and bureaucratic reasons, femocrats often have to encourage others to take credit for policy changes that they achieve. Hence femocrats may be blamed for government policies they have been powerless to change and miss out on credit for policies that are changed. They may be attacked for decisions that are in fact the least-worst outcomes. Dr. Meredith Edwards, a WEL activist before becoming a femocrat, has commented on her distress in this situation. "The options you have fought against never become public knowledge" (Sawer, 1990, p. 25), she said. A central dilemma for femocrats is that they need to forge alliances within the bureaucracy and with the women's movement to be effective, but the compromises and secrecy/trustworthiness required to maintain the former may sour relationships with the latter (Levi & Edwards, 1990). As one recent recruit to the office said,

> In the early '70s I had no real understanding of what was going on inside the bureaucracy. I was working with radical women's organizations, Rape Crisis, and women's health centres and so on, and I didn't see the inside. Now I see that it is important to have people inside government, doing the behind-the-scenes stuff as well as outside. (staffer quoted in Sawer & Groves, 1994, p. 90)

Tensions between femocrats and their sisters in the broader women's movement were particularly evident in the early years. Some of those outside felt that the femocrats had sold out and joined the patriarchy rather than challenging its structures. As advisor Reid (1985) states,

> Every time a move was made in a public arena by people like myself, women in the women's movement reflected upon its impact, whether it was counterproductive. We were constantly assessed for our level of compromise, co-operation, and corruption by the structures we were in. (p. 13)

Those inside often felt aggrieved by the lack of understanding and support from those outside, particularly as they themselves were constantly under suspicion from the rest of the bureaucracy because of their assumed closeness to the women's movement. Femocrats were simultaneously being denounced for being missionaries and mandarins. While traditional bureaucrats suspected them as missionaries, pushing a woman's agenda, women in the community often believed that they had sold out to become mandarins (Summers, 1986).

Such suspicions were fueled by the prevalence of what was called "power dressing" in the 1980s and the ubiquitous shoulder pads. Sisters in suits became a familiar sight (Lynch, 1984). Besides adopting institutional dress codes, femocrats had to become bilingual, speaking in the economic rationalist terms that gave them credibility with senior decision makers while trying to remember the value language they shared with women outside. Deborah McCulloch (1988), who worked as the first women's adviser to the premier of South Australia, pleaded with feminists in community agencies to understand the dilemmas femocrats were placed in as gatekeepers: "Make friends with your femocrat. The position of femocrats is as unenviable as your own. Pushed by the pollies, bullied by the bureaucrats, denounced as wimps by the women, they are squeezed from all sides" (p. 19).

As the 1980s wore on, the women's movement was learning to become more tolerant of diversity; bureaucratic feminism could become one among a multitude of feminisms.[4] Greater knowledge also cooled the passion of debates over femocracy at women's conferences. For example, by 1984 almost all members of the editorial collective of *Refractory Girl*, a radical feminist journal founded in 1972, were public sector employees, which strongly suggests where the feminist activists of the 1970s were employed. The increased presence of women as political commentators in the mainstream media has also improved the level of debate over the Office and its effectiveness on different issues.

Also from the alleged glass tower of women's policy offices, many had a clear view of the complementary relationship between femocrats and the women's movement outside: "The radical demands of the women's movement prepare the ground for the less threatening, but nevertheless important changes to policy and legislation that are pushed through by feminists in the public service" (Anon, 1987). Moreover femocrats were sometimes able to alert those outside to the need to exert pressure on an issue, without betraying bureaucratic confidentiality.

Some femocrats felt that contact with the women's movement was important to reaffirm the values that had taken them into the bureaucracy in the first place: "It's like going to church" (Meredith Edwards, quoted in Eisenstein, 1995). Another femocrat commented,

> It's very hard working here at times not to believe your own rhetoric. And it's easy to get really angry with people who criticize you . . . you need some mechanism whereby you can keep clearly in your mind why you're there. Too often you're so busy you don't. (Frances Davies, quoted in Eisenstein, 1991, p. 39)

During the 1980s the Office was affected not so much by accusations of compromise or co-optation as by the subsiding political energies of the women's movement. As the women's movement opened up more avenues for women's careers, it disappeared into institutions, leaving less energy for engaging in community activism or bringing pressure to bear on governments from outside. Moreover, the hostility of large parts of the women's movement to conventional norms of organization inhibited its development as a well-organized political lobby group to which government would be forced to respond. For this reason, budget cuts at the expense of women were sometimes viewed as not particularly sensitive. Fortunately the situation was repaired by the reopening of the gender gap in support of the Labor Party in the late 1980s; hence the increased sensitivity of government to this constituency, well-exploited by femocrats. For example, in the run up to the 1993 federal election, Anne Summers was able to win some notable victories for this reason, including, at last, the cashing out of the demeaning "dependent spouse" tax rebate and its payment instead as a "home child care allowance."

There still remained the accusation that femocrats did not represent the interests of "ordinary women." As Anna Yeatman (1990) has pointed out, on one hand femocrats enjoyed an economic independence deriving from their primary labor-market jobs that was unknown to most Australian women. On the other, their function was to analyze the impact of policy on women who were predominantly in situations of economic vulnerability resulting from caring responsibilities. This experience indeed radicalized some women who ended up in femocrat positions without a background in the women's movement, such as the economist who headed the OSW from 1986 to 1988. As younger women have been recruited to the Office, they often lack the movement background of earlier recruits. Still, some come from women's studies and see work in the Office as an applied version of what they have learned at university.

Some right-wing media commentators express the view that femocrats are"radical, hairy-legged lesbians" and could not therefore represent real women. There have been particular objections to increases in expenditures on child care from groups representing "the family" or full-time homemakers; they have portrayed such expenditures as discriminating against women who look after their own children. Pro-family groups have advocated and femocrats have opposed family unit taxation for reasons of the disincentives it creates to women's participation in the workforce.

Conclusion:
Outcomes for Women

Two decades after the creation of the Office of the Status of Women, we asked a number of people what they thought its major achievements had been. During the years of conservative government much of the work of the Office was defensive, for example, fending off moves toward family unit taxation. But research commissioned in the course of this campaign was to prepare the way for the further shift in family support toward primary careers. The Office also provided strategic advocacy that helped in the steady growth of government-funded women's services over 20 years, despite periodic crises. Femocrats did much to protect these nontraditional forms of service delivery from bureaucratic interference or attempts to impose more hierarchical management structures (Hopkins & McGregor, 1991, p. 142).

In the area of social policy, femocrats inside and outside the Office played vital roles in the gradual expansion and diversification of the national child care program and services such as respite and domiciliary care services to support those who care for the aged and people with disabilities. For many, the most obvious victories of the Office were in the area of national sex discrimination and affirmative action legislation, because here the Office had primary responsibility up to the point at which legislation was handed over to other agencies to implement, rather than simply being in a coordinating role. Another victory was ratification of the ILO Convention on Workers with Family Responsibilities and action around this agreement. For an Aboriginal respondent, one of the most significant achievements was Women's Business—the first nationwide consultation with Aboriginal women.

We might also conclude that a major achievement was simply being there as an institutionalized feminist presence to remind policymakers that good policy must serve women as well as men; that women, regardless of their marital status, have equal rights to, for example, labor market and job creation programs but at the same time have special needs arising from caring responsibilities. Ideally, the OSW would no longer need to ring up policymakers to say "what about women?" In the meantime, it has an important role in teaching governments about the gender effects of supposedly neutral policies and in working for women from inside the state.

Notes

1. The term *femocrat* has been included in the titles of academic books, such as Anna Yeatman's (1990) *Bureaucrats, Technocrats, Femocrats,* as well as being incorporated into feminist culture more generally.

2. By the time WEL celebrated its 20th anniversary, many of its founding members had also become members of parliament and cabinet ministers. For example, five of the six women who have held federal portfolios for the status of women have been WEL members, with the sixth only holding the position briefly.

3. CAPOW! stands for Coalition of Participating Organisations of Women, but the long form is rarely used.

4. A recent review of what might constitute distinctively Australian feminism has identified two main elements: first, the theory and practice of "official feminism" (that is, state-oriented feminism) discussed in this chapter; second, an eclectic "clearing house" approach to international feminisms, exemplified in current French-influenced work on "theorizing the body" (Sullivan, 1994).

3

An Array of Agencies

Feminism and State
Institutions in Canada

Linda Geller-Schwartz

In the turbulent world of feminist politics, it is little wonder that the few existing analyses of women's policy structures in Canada are colored by the political agendas of the actors. Socialist feminists have characterized them as the product of a conscious attempt by the liberal state to organize and confine feminist demands into manageable proportions (Findlay, 1987, p. 33). Conservative women's groups have viewed the same structures as cadres of radical feminists trying to hijack the legitimate, democratic, policymaking process of government. But when one looks closely at the complex—or even chaotic—array of agencies concerned with women's issues in this federal system, it is more tempting to attribute its shape to "muddling through" rather than to any single controlling purpose.

Although a single, visible, defining goal may have been missing during the past few decades, it is clear that there has been an ongoing conscious effort by numerous governments and coalitions of women's groups to find the appropriate structures to represent women's interests within the state. And just as interpretations of women's place in society have changed over time, so have the state agencies for women. The prevailing ideology of the state in Canada, the country's fundamental political structure, and the importance of its international image have also profoundly influenced the shape of these institutions.

This chapter attempts to accomplish three tasks. First, it describes the establishment and organization of women's policy agencies at the national level and suggests why they have assumed a particular configuration. Second, it explores ways in which the staffs in these agencies have attempted to influence the policymaking process, and it assesses their success in doing so. Finally, the chapter attempts to shed some light on the complex relationship between women's advocacy groups and the federal government.

Establishment and Organization of Women's Policy Institutions

Canada readily responded to national and international demands to advance the status of women by creating permanent government institutions charged with women's policy concerns. This section describes each successive action by the government of the day (i.e., prime minister and cabinet) beginning in the 1950s and ending with a flurry of innovations in the early 1970s. Although the focus here is on activities at the national level, it should also be noted that all 10 provinces have established a variety of agencies and programs to address women's concerns. As a result, Canada has an array of women's agencies that no government, regardless of its desires to cut back on government spending, has thus far felt strong enough to dismantle.

THE WOMEN'S BUREAU, 1954

In 1954, the Minister of Labour announced to the House of Commons during a routine debate on departmental budgets that a Women's Bureau would be established with a mandate to address, through research, study, and the dissemination of information, the "special problems facing women workers." He acknowledged that this move was in response to the urging of "women's organizations, speaking for large numbers of women" and, in particular, their concern "that some women in employment are handicapped by some common prejudices of employers which are not founded on fact" (*Debates, House of Commons*, 1952-1953, p. 5420).

The minister appeared to respond to claims women made that, after their massive war effort, they were being denied adequate opportunities to participate in the postwar workforce. A coalition of groups, including such organizations as the YWCA, the Canadian Federation of University Women, and the Canadian Federation of Business and Professional Women's Clubs, lobbied the government to address these problems (Vickers, Rankin, & Appelle, 1993, p. 47). The United States provided a model: The Women's Bureau in the U.S. Department of Labor had been in existence since 1920.

The Canadian Bureau was to be headed by Marion Royce, a well-respected activist on women's issues. But what the minister did not tell the House of Commons was that Royce and an assistant were to be the only full-time employees of the Bureau. Thus the first state agency in Canada to be concerned with the status of women was born. For a decade and a half the Women's Bureau remained the only women's policy agency at the federal level.

It was clear from the beginning that the Bureau was a pale replica of its American antecedent. Despite its limited resources, the Bureau managed to carve out a niche for itself. As one commentator has remarked, "the Bureau, however small, at least anchored a pragmatic feminist viewpoint in the business of the state" (Bégin, 1992, p. 27). This "feminist viewpoint" was bolstered by its collection and analysis of some of the first survey data on working women and the publication of innumerable studies on issues important to women.

During the 1950s, the Bureau began its efforts to cultivate relationships with women's groups. The director was actively involved in women's service groups on the outside, such as the Committee on Homemakers' Services and the Vocational Training Council. The Bureau started publishing a Directory of National Women's Organizations. The director worked with women in the unions and established a committee of representatives of federal and provincial labor departments to discuss issues relevant to working women. An especially important operational activity was in the international arena, where the director served on the United Nations Commission on Status of Women.

MINISTER RESPONSIBLE
FOR THE STATUS OF WOMEN, 1971

The growing political importance of women's issues eventually led the government to appoint a minister responsible for the status of women in 1971. However, it took an influential report of a royal commission to persuade the government to do so.

By the mid-1960s it was evident that the discrimination facing Canadian women would not be corrected by the activities of a tiny bureau buried in the Department of Labour. Armed with the 1963 report of President Kennedy's Commission on the Status of Women in the United States, a coalition of 32 women's organizations, calling themselves the Committee for the Equality of Women in Canada (CEWC), aggressively lobbied the Canadian government for a similar commission. Their efforts were largely responsible for the appointment of a Royal Commission on the Status of Women.

The Royal Commission reported in 1970, with 167 recommendations covering a wide and diverse range of issues. The Commission's recommendations would provide years of grist for the policymaking mills. Its specific recommendations on mechanisms for building women's concerns into the day-to-day business of the state created, in effect, a blueprint for future women's policy machinery. The Commission (1970) concluded that the Women's Bureau was insufficiently autonomous from political and administrative control and that its mandate was too narrowly focused on employment (p. 391). It recommended the appointment of a permanent Status of Women Council that would report directly to Parliament on the overall progress being made by women. The Council would have the resources to undertake research, establish programs, and propose legislation.

The Liberal Government of Pierre Trudeau, in the face of a very cogent and popular report, knew it had to act, but it was not entirely happy with the proposals. Instead of creating a full-fledged Status of Women Council, it appointed a coordinator for the status of women in the Privy Council Office, the department serving the prime minister. The primary task of this officer was to head an Interdepartmental

Committee (IDC) composed of representatives from all government departments to oversee the analysis and implementation of the report. By this action, the cabinet appeared to recognize the importance of the Commission by giving its recommendations high priority (Gelber, 1971, p. 21). In years to come, however, commentators would view this response as a cynical way to bury the report's initiatives in a cumbersome bureaucracy (Findlay, 1987, p. 36).

In 1971, the Government, anxious to show its commitment to women's concerns, appointed a minister responsible for the status of women. Usually a minister is the political head of a department, with responsibility for a panoply of programs and policies. However, in this case there was no department of women's affairs. Although such a department was considered, there were fears that concentrating all responsibility for women's issues in one department would ghettoize women and their needs. An interdepartmental committee, the Government concluded, could "raise the consciousness" of the whole state (Bégin, 1992, p. 34). That goal aside, the minister responsible for status of women was, and continues to be, a junior minister in the cabinet, a position of limited influence.[1]

ADVISORY COUNCIL FOR
THE STATUS OF WOMEN, 1973

Despite the appointment of a coordinator and a minister for women at the cabinet level, women's groups became concerned that the Government was not acting quickly enough on the Royal Commission's many policy-related recommendations. In 1971, a coalition of 30 women's groups joined together to form the National Action Committee (NAC). Its purpose was to lobby the Government to implement the report and, in particular, to establish more effective policy machinery in the form of the Council for the Status of Women (Vickers et al., 1993, p. 26).

In 1973, the Government complied by announcing the creation of the Canadian Advisory Council on the Status of Women (CACSW). The Council is composed of 27 part-time and 3 full-time members to be appointed by the Government of the day. The mandate of the CACSW was to "bring before the government and the public matters of interest and concern to women." The CACSW was to be an "independent organization, funded by the government, but situated outside of the government structure" (Status of Women Canada, 1993, p. 5). But, to be "outside" the government structure, the Council would have to report to Parliament, as the Royal Commission had proposed, not the executive. However, CACSW was to report to the Minister Responsible for the Status of Women, a member of the executive. The NAC saw the establishment of the CACSW as its first lobbying victory (Vickers et al., 1993, p. 78). Although they were pleased that the Government had acted, it soon became evident, from the partisan nature of its appointments and the fact that it reported to the minister, that the CACSW was not independent, except in the eyes of the Government. The unfortunate result was to undermine the potential role of the CACSW on behalf of women: Its formal independence made it untrustworthy from the Government's point of view, whereas its substantive links to the Government made it suspect from the perspective of women's groups. Although members of NAC at first participated directly in the activities of the CACSW, it was later shunned by many women's groups.

In the 20 years of its existence, the CACSW has done some excellent research and stimulated public debate on many important issues. Yet, as its former directors have acknowledged, the Council has seldom been able to be an effective critic of government policies or have a significant impact on the policymaking process (Anderson, 1991, p. 213).

WOMEN'S PROGRAM, 1973

While setting up the CACSW, the Government acted on another Royal Commission (1970, p. 49) recommendation—to provide support to nongovernmental organizations working for women's equality. Since 1973, the Women's Program, a branch of the Department of the Secretary of State, has provided such support.[2] Over the years, hundreds of voluntary women's groups have received funding from the Women's Program.

According to one of its former directors, the staff of the Women's Program considered themselves accountable to the agenda of the women's movement rather than to government priorities. It was the one place in the state where genuine, grass-roots feminists were in control. This was possible, she claimed, because of the "relative invisibility of its activities," buried, as they were, deep within the bureaucracy of a government department (Findlay, 1987, p. 40).

However, this low profile was short-lived. In 1974, the Women's Program clashed with the central agencies of government over what kind of programs and organizations should receive funds in connection with International Women's Year. The Privy Council wanted to use the allocated money to promote the Liberal Government's priorities on women's issues—primarily a moderate equal rights approach. The Women's Program staff wanted the money to be used to help women's groups across the country achieve their own self-defined purposes. With the help of the CACSW and by bringing the conflict to the attention of the public through leaks to the press, the Women's Program managed to prevail in the allocation of the available money. As a result, some of that money was used by women's groups to criticize government's inactivity on many issues (Findlay, 1987, p. 41).

As soon as International Women's Year was over, the central agencies resolved to bring the "wild-eyed feminists" under control. This was done by imposing, in the name of efficiency and accountability, a bureaucratic procedure for allocating grants so burdensome that the staff in the Women's Program felt they no longer had time to work with the women's movement. The feminist perspective in the bureaucracy thus lost its material base (Findlay, 1987, p. 43).

Despite being "tamed" in this way, the Women's Program continues to exist. It has weathered an assault from conservative women's groups and survived eventual budgetary cutbacks by a Conservative Government (Anderson, 1991, p. 212). In the late 1980s, the Program had an annual budget of some $13 million, which it distributed to several hundred women's groups (Vickers et al., 1993, p. 146).

STATUS OF WOMEN CANADA, 1976

In the fall of 1974, as a prelude to International Women's Year, the United Nations sponsored an international seminar in Ottawa to discuss national machinery for the advancement of women. At that seminar, the Privy Council's Coordinator of the Status of Women (PCCSW) declared that Canada was committed to the "full integration of women in all aspects of society, and an end to discrimination," adding optimistically that "when this is achieved, the national machinery . . . will become obsolete" (Canadian Department of Labour, 1975, p. 11). *Integration* appeared to be the watchword of the seminar. To effect change, women and their policy concerns had to be fully integrated throughout the policymaking process.

The 1975 UN International Women's Year World Plan of Action also spurred the Canadian Government into further action on behalf of women. In 1976, the Government elevated the coordinator's office (established in 1971) into a separate department, Status of Women Canada (SWC), reporting to the Minister Responsible for the Status of Women. SWC was given a mandate that went beyond the traditional research, education, and coordinating roles of such state institutions to include "analyzing policies, programs, and legislation for their impact on women" and "recommending changes" as well as "initiating" policies to "advance women's equality" (SWC, 1993, p. 4).

As part of this new perspective, the Government also required each department throughout the national bureaucracy to set up an internal mechanism to act, in effect, as the institutionalized watchdog for women's concerns and "to provide direct input into policy and program development" (SWC, 1993, p. 6). The underlying ideological premise was that women's issues are not discrete items. Almost all policies and programs of government have an impact on women, and it should be the responsibility of the Government to examine differential impacts and take them into account in the development and implementation of policy.

Initially, the new process of institutionalizing women's concerns throughout the machinery of government appeared to work quite well. SWC coordinated a comprehensive process, with representatives of almost all government departments, to develop Canada's plan of action for the Decade of Women. In 1979, the Plan of Action was released. The SWC reported that by 1982, 96% of the measures in the plan had been either fully or partially implemented (SWC, 1993, p. 9). However, there remains some question about whether the success of the new process of "integration," as manifested by the plan, was not more apparent than real. The plan was tailored for immediate success, not fundamental change. In the first place, women's groups had very little input in the process (Findlay, 1987, p. 46). Second, the bureau-

cratic process weeded out policies and refined issues and recommendations until the only ones left in the plan were those that the departments could live with.

With respect to the mechanisms that were to be established in the
various departments, very few responded in a meaningful way. Despite these limits, SWC did, at times, play an effective role during the
1970s, largely because of the qualities of the coordinator, who was
given deputy minister status and thus participated in high-level
meetings. In addition, since all cabinet memoranda had to include a
section on policy implications for the status of women, SWC retained
some clout in cabinet.

THE CURRENT SITUATION

Once established, women's policy agencies in Canada do not fade
away. Successive Governments may reorganize structures or change
their names and mandates, but the institutions themselves seldom
disappear.[3] The result is an eclectic array of national policy machinery:
the Women's Bureau, the Minister Responsible for Status of Women, the
CACSW, a central department on the Status of Women, senior advisers
or divisions in various departments, and a couple of permanent
interdepartmental committees. All of these are ostensibly there for the
purpose of providing material on behalf of women for the policymaking process. In addition, some women's groups receive extensive state
funding through the Woman's Program to provide this input.

The pattern of growth that characterizes women's policy machinery
in Canada is consistent with an incrementalist or "muddling through"
approach to policy problems. There are no grand schemes laid on to
resolve social issues. Nor do Canadians look to the state to harness its
resources toward a goal of resolving group demands. Rather, the
government of the day, be it Liberal or Conservative, selects from a
repertoire of bureaucratic tools—royal commissions, advisory councils, special advisers, special bureaus. In this way, each government
can point to a variety of illustrations of its responsiveness to people's
needs without investing much political or administrative capital. Still,
on the basis of the sheer volume of paper and the numbers of people
involved, one would expect that such institutions could have a sig-

nificant impact on policymaking in Canada. The next section examines this proposition.

Role and Effect in Policy
Formulation and Implementation

In the 1950s, the women in white gloves and hats who politely lobbied the government to establish the Women's Bureau assumed that education was all that was needed to correct the problem women faced, namely, discrimination in the workplace. As time passed, the analysis of the problem broadened, and the understanding of how to effect change evolved. The result was an application of the integration model: an attempt to institutionalize attention to women's concerns throughout the bureaucracy. Yet a real understanding of the bureaucracy of the liberal Canadian state would have revealed that this policy was doomed to failure.

Canada is a constitutional monarchy with a parliamentary system of government. Ministerial responsibility and cabinet solidarity are central principles in the Canadian system of government. With the exception of a few key government advisers in the central agencies, most civil servants are expected to be disinterested career public officials, prepared to serve the current government, whatever its political persuasion. Civil servants are supposed to be the anonymous, efficient, unbiased administrators of the machinery of state. The integration policy implied that civil servants could be internal lobbyists for women's interests. Even if the male-dominated bureaucracy had been prepared to recognize that certain policies (other than obvious issues such as maternity leave) could have a differential impact on women, the idea that civil servants should adopt the role of internal lobbyists for women as a definable group was an anathema.

The Canadian International Development Agency (CIDA) did briefly manage to build an analysis of the impact on women of their policies into their programs and even attempted to train their employees to understand and use this process (CIDA, 1986). But this success was short-lived and failed to survive subsequent changes in personnel.

When I took over as director general of the Women's Bureau in 1984, CIDA was held out to me as a model. We made some attempts to develop a similar integration process within the Labour Department. But the protectiveness of the bureaucrats over their small areas of authority; the antagonism toward internal lobbyists, as they saw us; and the general cynicism about women's issues meant that there was no support for such a policymaking model. When internal reviews of policies were taking place, the Bureau might be asked for comments, but this was an ad hoc discretionary practice, not a formal institutionalized process.

Although the integration model did not work, Canadian femocrats have had some success in bringing about change in substantive policy. They have done so by working effectively within the Canadian model of policymaking and implementation. Bureaucrats and politicians respond to pressure from nongovernment interest groups, while resisting internal lobbyists. Femocrats have worked directly, indirectly, or even surreptitiously, using external organizations to further their own institution's policy goals. On the one hand, they marshaled their resources within the state through research, public education, and, when possible, direct subsidy, to foster pressure from domestic lobbies, and on the other, they exerted pressure for compliance with Canada's international commitments.

Sometimes, these domestic and international pressures have worked together. The Women's Bureau effectively used international contacts and commitments to induce change through such combined public pressure on Canadian labor policy. The advanced social policies of European countries and the discussions in the United Nations and International Labor Organization (ILO) helped shape the Bureau's research and publication agenda. Women's groups used such information to develop recommendations and lobby for policy changes. At the same time, the Bureau asserted that Canada's ratification of ILO Conventions and its prominent international profile meant that such policies as paid maternity leave, equal pay for work of equal value, and antidiscrimination human rights legislation had to be implemented at home.

One account of how equal pay for work of equal value was introduced into Canada demonstrates how the major woman's organization in Canada, the NAC, reinforced the efforts of femocrats to get the legislation passed (Marsden, 1980). For many years the Women's Bureau had been researching and publicizing the pay issue. Finally, in 1972, following a recommendation by the Royal Commission on the Status of Women, Canada ratified ILO Convention 100 on Equal Remuneration. At the same time, NAC used public and private lobbying to promote direct action on the issue of equal pay. The president and key executive members of NAC had very close links to the governing Liberals and met frequently with the prime minister and various cabinet ministers. It also appears that they got unmarked brown paper envelopes from anonymous "friends" within the bureaucracy, feeding them useful inside information and warning them of pending developments. Aided in these ways, NAC's lobbying efforts were successful in getting legislation passed.

A favorite way in Canada to induce legislative change is through a more elaborate form of research and education, namely the public commission of inquiry. Governments find commissions a handy response to pressure from women's groups to do something. The Royal Commission on the Status of Women in the 1960s perhaps was the prime example of this. The sole female cabinet minister at the time had been unsuccessfully pressing the prime minister for months to appoint such a commission. But, as she indicated, it took the "remarkable organization" of the Committee for the Equality of Women in Canada for it to be finally established (Vickers et al., 1993, p. 53).

A royal commission can draw public attention to specific issues and invigorate femocrats working inside the government through the creation of new agencies, additional resources, and enhanced credibility. There has been considerable dispute about how many of the recommendations of the Royal Commission on the Status of Women were ultimately implemented, but no one questions the key role the Commission played in putting women's issues on the policy agenda (CACSW, 1979).

In the early 1980s, another royal commission was appointed to examine whether the government should adopt a U.S.-style policy of affirmative action (Royal Commission on Equality in Employment, 1984). When it reported in 1984, a new Conservative Government had just taken power, and the minister of employment was a woman with considerable political influence. In this propitious environment, the Government acted quickly to implement an employment equity policy based loosely on the recommendations in the report. Feminists criticized the policy as being toothless, and employers regarded it as a bureaucratic nightmare, yet it was a formal policy, something that could not have been achieved without the existence of a thoroughly researched and well-written public report.

However, this process of research and public education generating external pressures for change does not always work. In the mid-1980s, the Conservative Government embarked on free-trade talks with the United States. NAC and other women's groups, as well as unions, social welfare organizations, and environmental activists, feared the impact of free trade on their constituencies (Cohen, 1992). The Government was firmly committed to implementing a free-trade agreement, and any attempts within the bureaucracy even to do research on the differential impact of free trade upon particular groups were closely and firmly controlled. Free trade was an issue too central to Government priorities to be sidetracked.

This was made clear from the Government's reaction to the challenges to free trade. When external groups started to release their research, the Government hastened to produce its own pamphlets to counter any adverse conclusions. It even lined up the minister responsible for status of women and civil servants to neutralize the potential impact of the unfavorable studies and promote the Government's policy (Cohen, 1992, p. 223). Femocrats within the government who tried to raise questions about the Government's plans were quickly silenced.

When feminists in Canada are asked whether they have managed to have any significant impact on national policies, they often point to their success in producing an equal rights clause in the constitution. Ironically, the process through which this clause was won reveals the limited effectiveness of state women's agencies on policy issues that are of vital importance to the Government. In the early 1980s, the Liberal Government indicated that it was going to repatriate Canada's constitution, which at that time existed only as a British Act of Parliament, and include in it a Charter of Rights and Freedoms. The CACSW commissioned major research papers and undertook a public campaign to ensure that the charter would effectively protect women's rights. As part of this campaign, it planned a national conference on the issue. The Government was afraid that the conference would occur just as the charter was being debated in Parliament, so it exerted pressure on the CACSW to cancel the conference. Its members, all of whom were appointed by the Government, acceded to those wishes. Doris Anderson, the CACSW president, who is an effective and well-respected feminist, resigned in protest (Anderson, 1991, p. 222).[4]

Her resignation acted as a catalyst uniting women across Canada. About 1,000 women bypassed the femocrats and held their own conference in Ottawa. They aggressively lobbied the federal cabinet and provincial premiers and won the clauses protecting women's rights they wanted in the charter. These clauses have had an important impact on women's rights in Canada, including their right to serve in the military and their right to an abortion (Black, 1992, p. 105).

The Canadian case shows that the existence of a wide variety of state agencies devoted to women's policies is not in and of itself an effective way to influence policy to advance women's interests. At the same time, it demonstrates that such machinery can provide resources for a dedicated staff of femocrats to use to stimulate public pressure on behalf of specific goals. When the women's policy agenda conflicts with priorities of the government of the day, however, femocrats can find themselves ignored, silenced, or used to subvert the very goals they seek.

Relationship of Women's Policy Machinery to Women's Groups

Until the mid-1980s, the relationship between women's groups and the federal government and its women's policy agencies appeared to be symbiotic. This relationship was encouraged by the ideology, activities, and personnel of the established visible women's groups and by the Government's financial support. From the beginning, advocates for women spoke principally through the NAC. Formed in 1971, NAC grew from a coalition of 30 groups to an umbrella organization with about 600 member groups, representing about one third of the organized women's movement (Vickers et al., 1993, p. 4). From the perspective of the federal government and the media, NAC was the only politically relevant national women's movement until the early 1980s. Thus the ideology and tactics of NAC largely defined the initial relationship between women's groups and the state.

NAC was firmly anchored within the centrist, pro-state, liberal tradition of Canadian society. The kind of feminism practiced by NAC has been defined as "subdued feminism," radical liberalism, centrist, and pro-statist (Adamson, Briskin, & McPhail, 1988, p. 62; Cohen, 1992, p. 217; Vickers et al., 1993, p. 35). Its advocacy of greater state intervention to improve social services and to correct discrimination placed it slightly left of center in the Canadian political spectrum. Because NAC was a moderate political player, it rarely questioned capitalist institutions. Few radical feminist or socialist feminist voices were heard in the organized movement.[5] NAC subscribed to a liberal feminist ideology, with its focus on the value of dialogue and educa- tion and the importance of the state as the principal instrument of change. As a coalition of women's groups, it was formed with the goal of lobbying government to implement the recommendations of the Royal Commission on the Status of Women in the 1970s. After that, it continued to demonstrate a firm commitment to the ordinary policy process and to the value of trying to exercise power behind the scenes. NAC operated through annual lobbying sessions with the cabinet, briefs on a variety of issues to government, and all sorts of informal contacts with politicians and civil servants.

The zenith of NAC's clout was seen to be the 1984 federal election, when it hosted a historic national television debate among the party leaders devoted entirely to women's policy issues. As indicated above, NAC's activity did contribute to the establishment of state agencies for women and the implementation of a number of policy changes. By the late 1970s, NAC had such a high profile that one prominent member of the press referred to it as the "most powerful lobby in Canada" (Marsden, 1980, p. 246).

Beyond the core values of Canada's political culture, a number of reasons account for the moderate, liberal stance assumed by the women's movement as represented by NAC. First, in order to have any success in mobilizing women in a country as large and diverse as Canada, experience had shown that it was essential for NAC to practice "integrative feminism" (Vickers et al., 1993, p. 23). NAC was a coalition of a wide variety of separate organizations, rather than a single organization, such as the U.S. National Organization for Women (NOW). It had to adopt a political practice that would hold these groups together. Second, individual members of the executive of NAC had close ties to different major political parties. So many NAC presidents went on to become elected politicians, including cabinet ministers, that it has been claimed that NAC served as an "alternative training ground for aspiring women politicians" (Vickers et al., 1993, p. 283). These political links were seen as a strength, but they limited NAC's ability to stray beyond an ideological middle ground.

Third, the Government encouraged NAC's moderate approach through funding, beginning with the subsidy that permitted its initial organization meeting. By the mid-1980s, the majority of NAC funds came from the government—some $400,000 in annual grants (Vickers et al., 1993, p. 141). Individual member groups of NAC also received extensive funding.

In the 1980s, however, a number of factors converged to change NAC's situation and feminist politics in Canada. In 1984 a Conservative Government was elected after 20 years of Liberal party rule. The economy had taken a serious downturn during the decade, and budgetary constraint was the watchword. NAC had few political friends in the new Government, and instead the conservative women's movement had the ear of many in the cabinet (Cohen, 1992). At the same time, changes were occurring within the women's movement itself. Although there had been, since the 1960s, extensive grass-roots, feminist activity in Canada, the Government had taken little notice, finding it diffuse and incomprehensible. It was content to deal with NAC, which provided the public face of feminism.

By the mid-1980s, feminists from the Left had assumed more power within NAC. The definition of women's issues changed from the focus on equal rights and antidiscrimination to encompass all economic and social policies that might have an effect on women. Thus, the Canadian women's movement took a more radical stance. NAC joined with unions, environmental groups, and poverty organizations to develop coalitions on such issues as the social welfare agenda. They accused the Government of trying to deconstruct feminist theory into isolated issues and to exhaust the largely volunteer movement by constantly requiring them to respond to a wide range of individual issues (Anderson, 1991, p. 213). The "cozy" relationship with government had ended. Under the influence of NAC's new leadership, lobbying now involved more loud and public confrontations.

At the same time, a barely concealed rift with Quebec's women's movement further inhibited the ability of the women's movement to speak with one voice. The history of the women's movement in Quebec is different from that of the rest of Canada (Dumont, 1992). In the federal system, most of the power over social welfare is located in provincial governments; thus, women's groups have usually organized locally and provincially to seek change. In Quebec, with its cultural, religious, and linguistic differences, the focus on the provincial government was even more pronounced.

Although French-Canadian feminists in Quebec were involved in the creation of NAC, their interests gradually shifted away almost entirely from the national feminist agenda to the provincial arena. This was in large measure due to the rise of separatism in the province of Quebec and the growing disputes with the federal government. By the mid-1980s, most of the women's movement in Quebec had rejected the liberal, individualist, federalist stance of NAC and opted for a much more collectivist view. For these activists, equality and feminism became intimately linked to the independence of Quebec. The separatist struggle between Quebec and the rest of Canada thus was reflected in the ideological and organizational schism within the Canadian women's movement.

The Conservative Government responded to these changes in the Canadian women's movement by boycotting the annual lobbying day with NAC and cutting its funding in half. Barbara McDougall, the minister for status of women at the time, indicated that she thought the lobby had outgrown its "usefulness" and that NAC leaders should meet with cabinet ministers in private (Anderson, 1991, p. 213). The ministers questioned whether NAC still represented women's interests and was competent to work with the state agencies.

Relations between feminists and state agencies have changed from symbiotic in the 1970s to problematic and contentious in the 1990s. The status of femocrats has been affected by this change. Civil servants in women's policy agencies, with the exception of those briefly in the Women's Program, have seldom been drawn directly from the activists in the women's movement. Rather, they were career civil servants who happened to be women and who happened to be sufficiently committed to women's rights that they were prepared to accept the job of femocrat, a job that was almost certain to hamper their future career in the bureaucracy. Holding a job in a women's agency identified them as feminists, a role seen as incompatible with the duty of an unbiased civil servant. As such, their loyalty and discretion could be questioned, and they immediately became suspect.

Conclusion

Women's policy institutions have existed in Canada for four decades. Those of us who have served in them usually left totally discouraged about their effectiveness. A lack of political will seemed to stymie even modest changes, and we saw ourselves as the unwitting defenders of inadequate government policies. Repeated efforts to structure government to formally integrate women's interests were met by a bureaucratic wall of indifference, if not hostility.

Yet it is clear from a review of history that when conditions are right—a new government, a sympathetic minister, international pressure, and effective lobbying by women's groups—even such seemingly innocuous activities as research and public education can have an impact in the long term. But without external pressure, these structures have little hope of doing more than holding the fort or maintaining the status quo.

Notes

1. When the former director of research for the Royal Commission was elected to Parliament, she refused an appointment as minister responsible for the status of women on the ground that little, if anything, could be accomplished from a position of such limited influence (Bégin, 1992, p. 35).

2. The Department of the Secretary of State was responsible for a diverse range of social programs, including policies on official languages and programs for Canada's aboriginal peoples, citizens with disabilities, and youth, as well as the Women's Program.

3. In 1993, both the departments of the Secretary of State and of Labour were eliminated, and their programs were distributed to other departments. The Women's Bureau is now part of a new department of Human Resources, and the Women's Program is being transferred to Status of Women Canada. In March 1995, the Liberal Government indicated that many of the key functions of the Advisory

Council would be assumed by Status of Women Canada, leaving the future existence of the Council in serious doubt.

4. Anderson (1991, p. 223) subsequently headed NAC, where she felt she could make a difference. Yet, she acknowledged that the extensive research and public information campaign of the CACSW was important in getting the women's groups to focus on the issue.

5. See analysis of Lynn McDonald, the president of NAC in 1979, cited in Adamson et al., 1988, p. 62.

4

A Political Niche

Denmark's Equal Status Council

Anette Borchorst

Denmark's Equal Status Council (DESC) constitutes a landmark in the institutionalization of gender equality. The government created the DESC in the 1970s to promote equal opportunity policy. Women's rights organizations obtained representation in this permanent state agency. The Council is not the only locus of operation for feminists in the state, but it has been the dominant agency for gender equality ever since it was established. It plays a decisive role in the preparatory phases of amendments and new legislation, and it is heavily involved in the implementation of existing equal opportunities legislation.

This chapter examines the process that led to the establishment of the DESC, paying special attention to the composition of the Council.[1] Due to the influence of corporatism, representation of interests and organizations is highly structured. A second concern here is to describe the activities of the DESC and its achievements, especially with respect to the legislation of equal opportunity. Information about the notion of the state in Denmark's political culture is pertinent to the analysis of the role of the DESC in policymaking and implementation. Finally, the relation between the state equality agency and the two wings of the women's movement, the women's rights organizations and the women's liberation groups, will be discussed. The significance of ideological, economic, and international factors is also considered.

Although the Danish state's position on women's status has been discussed by several scholars, specific studies on the DESC are few in number. The core material for my analysis includes publications from the Council, especially its annual reports; it is also based on personal experience. Since November 1988, I have been a member of the Council representing women's studies. Hence I am presently, if only temporarily, a femocrat myself.

The Establishment of
the Equal Status Council

The prime minister created Denmark's Equal Status Council in 1975 by administrative order, to investigate and help coordinate government concerns with gender equality issues. This act followed a decade of controversy among groups and parties over the proper state response to women's rights issues. In 1965, the Social Democratic prime minister appointed a Commission on the Position of Women in Society, also called the Women's Commission (WC). This initiative originated with women politicians in the Social Democratic party who were also members of women's rights organizations. In the mandate of the WC, the prime minister noted the discrepancy between gender equality in almost all laws and the actual differences in women's and men's position in society (Kommissionen vedrørende, 1974).

The original concept was to appoint a small number of experts and representatives from the women's rights organizations to the WC, but the prime minister found it necessary to yield to the requests of many organizations to obtain representation. The WC ended up being a mastodon, with 55 members in all (Borchorst, 1986). Besides feminists and experts, representatives from organizations of workers and employers, politicians, and civil servants from many different ministries sat on the Commission. Questions of composition continued to plague its efforts to determine the state institutional structure for gender equality.

The majority of the WC recommended establishment of a permanent state agency. When the parliament debated the reports of the WC in 1974, only 5 of the 10 parties supported this recommendation, and the motion was rejected. The prime minister, who was from the Liberal party and headed a right-wing coalition government, sided with the opponents. He argued that bureaucratic and administrative regulations, papers, and documents would not advance more equal conditions between the sexes (Folketingstidende, 1974, p. 2427).

By the next year, a new Social Democratic Government had come to office, and the prime minister acted on the recommendation with an administrative order. The Equal Status Council was to be an independent body under the Prime Minister's Office with its own secretariat. The Council was to concern itself solely with gender equality issues; questions of race and ethnicity were not incorporated.[2] In 1978 the parliament confirmed the Council by law with support of five of the nine political parties.[3]

The forces affecting the Government's decision to create a women's policy agency were multiple and interrelated. The Danish political culture includes the long-standing belief that the state should embody equality and democracy. The idea of the democratic state emanates from the folk high school movement and the peasant and consumer cooperatives in the 19th century. Later it became a guiding principle for the social democratic labor movement (Andersen, 1983). The Danish welfare state, like the other Nordic welfare states, was founded on these ideas, and citizens have become used to addressing the state and the politicians to ask for governmental action to solve collectively experienced problems (Hernes, 1987; Siim, 1991). Initially, the idea of equality in the Danish culture pertained to class relations rather than gender relations, but eventually the egalitarian ideas were extended to women.

Women's rights organizations, such as the Danish Women's Society (DWS) and the National Council of Women, which advocate the legal expansion of women's rights, were at the forefront of the campaign for a permanent state agency for gender equality. They built on the idea of the democratic state. These organizations had a long history of demanding governmental action on gender issues and the situation of women. Conversely, the more radical women's liberation movement adopted a hostile attitude toward the state. This wing of feminism was leftist and anarchic, even more so than its sister movements in the other Nordic countries (Haavio-Mannila et al., 1985). The liberation movement's flat organizational structure and unconventional actions were not suited to the task of approaching public agencies directly.

The influence of this more radical wing of the women's movement was felt not in the politics of establishing the DESC, but in the ideological debate over women's position. It raised questions that were crucial to the fundamental shifts in perceptions of women's position in the 1960s. The intensive public debate centered around the question of whether married women should stay at home or engage in paid work and what situation was beneficial to small children. The issue divided women and generated deeply felt cleavages within the women's rights movement. As a result, the membership of the Danish Women's Society declined. Large numbers of housewives left the organization, because they found that it embraced the interests of working women more than those of housewives (Borchorst, 1989).

These contradictory arguments about women's role also were reflected in the policy debates of the 1960s. One prime minister created a Ministry for Family Affairs to support a traditional family model in which women's primary role was to take care of the children. At the same time, a number of policies facilitated the entrance of women into the workforce. Public programs to support the care of small children were substantially extended, along with those to assist people who care for the sick and the elderly. Choice in childbearing was increased when the contraceptive pill was released in 1966, and free abortion up to the 12th week of pregnancy was approved in 1973.

Along with these aspects of the culture, ideological debates, and policy, economic factors also formed a necessary prerequisite for the creation of the DESC in Denmark. The Women's Commission was appointed in 1965 during a period when improvement in the economy produced an increased demand for labor. Needed workers were acquired mainly by integrating married women into the labor force rather than by admitting immigrants or "guest workers," as many other West European countries did. By the time the DESC was established in 1975, a downturn in the economy had caused increased unemployment, but the political process leading to the institutionalization of women's policy issues was already fully under way.

The commitment of the Danish government to cooperate in international initiatives was the final, but certainly not the least important, contributing factor to establishment of the DESC. Of particular significance was the tradition of Denmark's cooperation with other Nordic countries, especially the countries with Social Democratic parties: Sweden, Norway, and Finland. Denmark has often followed their lead by adopting and modifying initiatives from these countries. Thus, Denmark established both its Women's Commission and the permanent agency for gender equality some years after similar entities in Sweden, Norway, and Finland (Haavio-Mannila et al., 1985).

During the period of establishment, international organizations were also recommending initiatives for women's rights, and these required a response from successive Danish governments. Directives of the European Community (EC) on equal pay and equal treatment in the 1970s largely determined the content of Danish policies as well. The appointment of the Women's Commission coincided with recommendations of the United Nations Commission on the Status of Women. Activities related to International Women's Year in 1975 and the Women's Decade from 1975-1985 reinforced the UN call to nations to establish women's policy machinery. Hence, the appointment of the DESC closely coincided with the UN Commission's recommendation.

Organization of the DESC

Decisions about the composition of the DESC were very controversial aspects in the establishment process. The decisions were so crucial because of the corporatist framework in which interest groups relate to the state in Denmark. The strong corporatist tradition means that groups gain access to policymaking primarily through their representation on statutory commissions and committees in the executive and the bureaucracy, rather than by lobbying members of the legislature. Thus, the failure by any interest group to gain formal representation on the DESC might permanently curtail any prospects of influencing policy. At the same time, close attention to the composition reveals important players in the policy process as it relates to women.

The WC had proposed that the agency consist of a chair and 12 members: 4 to be appointed by the social partners, that is, the main organizations of workers and employers; 2 to be named by the women's rights organizations; the remaining 6 to be selected among people who had participated extensively in the public debate on equal opportunities and societal matters (Kommissionen vedrørende, 1974). This proposal mirrored the difficulties in finding a compromise among the many different interests and viewpoints represented in the commission.

When finally established in 1975, the size and the composition of the Council did not match any of the WC's proposals. The DESC was to have eight members:

A chair, appointed by the Government

Three members appointed by the social partners (the Danish Employers' Association, the Federation of Danish Trade Unions, and the Federation of Danish Civil Servants and Salaried Employees' Organizations)

Three members appointed by the National Council of Women in Denmark, an umbrella organization for a number of women's rights organizations, established in 1899

One member representing Greenlandic women's organizations

By this action, the Government, controlled by the Social Democrats, gave organized interests precedence and completely ignored the suggestions of independent experts and the women's liberation movement.[4]

In 1988, the representative of the Greenlandic women's organizations was dropped because Greenland, which had been granted some autonomy from the Danish state, had passed laws for its own gender equality committees. Instead, a representative was appointed from another women's rights group, the Danish Women's Society, established in 1871. Also in 1988, a ninth member—a specialist in feminist research—was added to the Council in 1988; this answered the demand for a member who is independent of organized associations. The Council itself selects this ninth member.

The continued presence of the social partners (three of nine members) in the Council reflects the particular form of corporatism that characterizes the political system in Denmark. The representation of the social partners in public policymaking was strengthened in the postwar period, when the modern welfare state was established. Neocorporatism is founded on industrial arbitration, collective bargaining, and a separate court system to resolve conflicts among workers and employers. Because a large majority of both workers and employers are organized, the social partners are able to determine working conditions through collective agreements. The state has undertaken a mediating role in case of conflict, but it should also be noted that the state, nationally and locally, is an employer for a very large part of the Danish workforce. Therefore, public employers and unions organizing public employees are key players.

The importance attached to class as a basis of policy interest is accentuated by the formal representation of business and labor. Gender interests have not been considered relevant criteria for representation in the same way as class interests. Policymakers do not recognize that gender relations are hierarchical and conflictual. This is to be expected, because the social partners represent male interests; organizations of workers and employers have been extremely male dominated, and they have made assumptions from the perspective of male norms in collective bargaining.

Thus, the establishment of the DESC was significant for gender politics because it showed an acknowledgment of specific interests of women in a distinct policy area—equal opportunities. Yet, the representation of the social partners in the DESC suggests a confirmation of their continued dominance in regulating the labor market. Although they constitute a minority of the Council, they gained total control in one major area of policy: that of dealing with exemptions from the Equal Treatment Act, which allows for affirmative action provisions. Initially, the social partners shared a very restricted view of equal opportunities, and, in particular, they opposed positive actions for women. During recent years, however, union representatives often hold the same views on equal treatment issues as the women's organizations in the Council. This change is attributable to a feminization of unions from below: More than 40% of the members are women. Although most unions are still male-dominated, women have also become more visible at all levels. Another incentive for the unions to seek an alliance with the women's organizations has been that their access to the government has been reduced as a result of the right-wing government coalitions during the 1980s.

The association of private employers remains opposed to many equality initiatives, often issuing minority statements disagreeing with the rest of the Council. They are especially reluctant to join with other members in stating that employers in particular cases have violated the gender equality laws. Employers have been skeptical of equal opportunity goals from the beginning. They argued that gender equality could be reached more effectively through changes in individual attitudes rather than collective actions. In recent years, decisive rulings against employers by the EC Court of Justice on equal pay cases have, however, forced them to pay more attention to gender equality. These decisions have shifted the burden of proof in equal pay cases from employees to employers, making gender equality a policy they can no longer afford to ignore.

The chair of the Council plays an essential role, especially for the external image of the DESC. She gives statements to the press and is the link to the government. There have been four chairs to date. The first, appointed in 1975, was a Social Democratic politician who had been involved in the Women's Commission. She resigned in 1981. The second chair, also a Social Democrat, was much younger and identified herself with the women's liberation movement. She was chair until 1987, when the prime minister appointed a conservative who was a former president of Danish Women's Society. In 1993 she was forced to resign after considerable pressure from the majority of the Council, critical of her role in the illegal suspension of entitlement of refugees to family reunification. Her successor was a former politician from the extreme Left, the first DESC chair who was not a member of parliament at the time of her appointment.

Activities and Responsibilities

Unlike the agencies in the other Nordic countries, the DESC in Denmark was set up as an independent unit. Nevertheless, the Government has exerted influence on the activities of the Council. The prime minister appoints the chair and lays down the term of reference for the Council. The cabinet sets the parameters for its activities through the budget. Governments headed by Social Democrats tend to ascribe higher priority to gender equality than liberal-conservative governments. The activities and responsibilities of the Council have increased regardless of changes in the party coalition in power. These changes were effected by initiatives of chairs, the growing demand of international commitments, and, in the late 1980s, new statutory responsibilities.

The initial terms of reference of the DESC, laid down by the prime minister in 1975, charged it with the following tasks:

1. To follow the development of gender issues in society, in legislation, and in the labor market; to investigate measures preventing gender equality; and to suggest measures for change
2. To act as an organ of initiation and coordination for public authorities on questions of gender equality
3. To suggest an agenda for research and for obtaining further information on equality

In the first years, the activities of the Council covered the first two points, and efforts were mainly devoted to dealing with the inquiries and complaints of individuals. Having been established by a minority Government without parliamentary ratification probably narrowed any room for maneuvering. The first chair held views that conformed to this relatively restricted role. Finally, the financial and human resources of the Council were modest. Legal confirmation of the Council in 1978 provided a sense of security, although the terms of references and the tasks of the DESC remained unchanged. In 1981, after the appointment of a new chair, the Council became more outgoing and engaged in principal policy debates.

Denmark's growing commitment to international cooperation on gender issues has increased the Council's activities. The secretariat is fully involved with the units of gender equality within the European Union (EU), the Nordic Council, the Council of Europe, and the United Nations; their matters appear regularly on the agenda of the Council. Responding to these issues requires coordination of policy initiatives, preparation of amendments, and development of new policy initiatives.

By far the most important activity of the Council relates to its responsibility for equality policy. At first, this mainly involved making statements on complaints about infringement and compliance with major legislation—the Equal Pay Act of 1976 and the Law on Equal Treatment for Men and Women as Regards Employment and Related Matters in 1978. In 1988, parliament enacted the Act on Equal Opportunity Between Men and Women, which committed all public authorities to be active about gender equality. This Act also affected the composition of the Council and its activities by authorizing the DESC to investigate matters by its own initiative. Also, employers, employees, and public authorities became obliged to make information available at the Council's request. Amendments of the Equal Pay Act and the Equal Treatment Act in 1989, 1990, and 1992 have confirmed these principles.

ROLE OF THE DESC IN POLICYMAKING AND IMPLEMENTATION

The activities of the DESC have been primarily directed toward equality, but only regarding some of the policies that affect gender differences. Hernes (1987, Chapter 1) makes a distinction between equality policy and women's policy. Her distinction is based on the content of the legislation. Equality policy aims at giving women access to decision-making roles in different spheres, concerns the redistribution of status and social power, and is often related to elite recruitment. Women's policy aims to improve the quality of life of women and children through a system of transfers and services. This area has mainly belonged to social or welfare state policy. Hernes also indicates that the two kinds of policies imply different equality principles: equal versus differential treatment.

The Council's activities have primarily related to equality policies, as Hernes defines them. Equal pay and equal treatment are concerned with money and working conditions, but the scope of equality embedded in these laws only serves to eradicate the most obvious discrimination against women. The policy of equal opportunity and the Council, therefore, exist in a political niche. It is not a small niche and it has been enlarged, but this expansion has been limited.

The Council itself has sought to expand its activities to include other elements directed toward women's well-being. The inclusion of maternity leave and parental leave in the Equal Treatment Act integrated one element of women's policy. The DESC's equal pay project is another example of this effort to combine antidiscriminatory equality policy with actions to aid women as a group. Rather than limiting attention to narrow comparisons of men and women in similar jobs, the Council has started to focus on comparable worth and the effects of conflicts between work and family responsibilities on pay. By including reconciliation of work and family issues in the discussion of pay, they set the framework for widening the concept and scope of equality. So far this has mainly resulted in publications and information. The sphere of the Council has been expanded, however. It now has a mandate to request information from throughout the government, and it also has the ability to take up cases by its own initiative. Notwithstanding the success in incremental policymaking, it is true that women's policy by and large is outside the competence of the Council. Thereby, policies of vital significance to women are not recognized formally as gender policies by the political system.

The restricted scope and content of equal opportunity is mainly attributable to the wish to maintain the political consensus that has characterized policies of equal opportunity. As demonstrated earlier, decisions about the composition of the Council have been taken with the goal of establishing consensus among organized interests toward such equality policy. In parliament, the support is reflected by the designation of policies that almost all parties can accept. By restricting the niche for these activities, this widespread agreement can be continued.[5] If the legislation moved toward positive action and the inclusion of women's policies, as advocated by the Socialist People's party and, to some extent, the Social Democratic party, it would undermine this consensus. The maintenance of unified support guarantees a certain stability in the policy of gender equality, making it more independent of variations in left and right party strength and, possibly, also of economic fluctuations.

The price paid for this stability is that the DESC and the policies that occupy it offer few remedies for women who have been disproportionately affected by the attempts to reduce public expenditures. The welfare state extended many services, benefits, and jobs to women. A number of feminist scholars, including myself, have argued that the resulting radical changes in women's position in the labor market and in the family were fostered by an alliance between women and the state, rather than through fundamental changes in gender relations. As a result, women became dependent on the welfare state as consumers, clients of public services and transfers, and public employees. In the same process they also became vulnerable to cutbacks in areas like public service and social welfare (Borchorst, 1994a; Hernes, 1987; Siim, 1993). Because of its limited scope and mandate, Denmark's policy machinery, the DESC, is not able to safeguard women's interests in this regard.

What has been the effect of 20 years of the DESC and equality policy? Activities represent only part of the first step taken on a long road, with gender equality remaining a distant goal. In fact, the wage gap has widened, and sex segregation of the labor market remains unchanged. Women's unemployment is comparatively higher and longer-lasting than men's; this is especially true for mothers of small children. The number of women managers is still very modest, particularly in the private sector of the economy.

One area that has undergone a noticeable change is the composition of public committees. In 1985, women made up 13% of the representatives; in 1992 this had risen to 35%. The work of public authorities for gender equality is less impressive. The Council concluded in 1993 that in most places, this effort is moving too slowly, and many areas have not made a plan for gender equality. Results within the sphere of local governments are particularly meager (Ligestillingsrådet, 1993).

The DESC is limited in its role by the equality laws themselves. First of all, the legislation is passive rather than activist: It prohibits discrimination but does not set forth strategies for ending gender stratification. Laws have not defined equality nor incorporated provisions for distinguishing direct and indirect discrimination. Efforts were made in the 1988 Act on Equality to extend the concept of equality, but the Danish legislation remains generally framed in gender-neutral terms, with affirmative action permitted only through exemption.[6] The lack of definitions of key central concepts in legislation and other generally vague formulations constitute a major obstacle because the intent of the laws tends to be weakened when they are implemented.

Another barrier to effective policy is the enforcement provisions of the legislation. The duration and expense of court processes reduce the number of complaints of infringement. The burden of proof, which in most cases lies with the plaintiff, is also heavy, despite the Council's efforts to provide information. A final barrier is the lack of tangible sanctions for violations. Fines have been negligible in the few cases in which they have been imposed.

Gender equality has occupied a persistent role in the regulation of the EU. Its equal opportunity unit, like the DESC, survives in a niche, isolated from policies determining the balance between state, market, and family. In some ways the EU has yet to catch up to Denmark's lead; the participation of women in decision-making bodies is substantially lower than in Denmark (Borchorst, 1994b). Women's status in Denmark is almost always at the forefront among the EU member states, but Denmark trails other Scandinavian countries in several respects.

The Danish Equal Status Council and the Women's Movement

Statements and strategies of the DESC are largely influenced by women's organizations. Their role has become even stronger since 1988. Although a rivalry exists between these organizations, they share similar perceptions of how to embrace women's interests. The five members representing women's organizations and the women's studies representative rarely disagree on central issues that are taken up by the Council.

Since their establishment in the 1870s and 1890s, the women's rights organizations have devoted considerable resources to addressing public authorities in order to obtain representation on commissions or committees or to put forward their viewpoints (Haavio-Mannila et al., 1985). To them, establishing a women's policy agency meant fulfilling some of their goals. They were able to gain a foothold within the political system from which they could permanently articulate women's interests and influence policy. As they have devoted considerable resources to state activities, the distance between formal and real gender equality has become much more evident to them.

The differences between the two branches of the feminist movement—the older women's rights organizations and the newer women's liberation groups—are not as large as they were 20 years ago; to some extent their interests have merged. Former Redstockings have joined women's rights organizations, and these organizations have adopted ideas and procedures of the new feminist movement. While in the 1970s the strategies of the two branches could be broadly termed equality and liberation, they are somewhat mingled today (Dahlerup, 1993; Siim, 1991).

Thus, the women's movement has changed considerably during the last 20 years. First of all, it is no longer a mass movement. The women's liberation organizations have been dissolved, but their ideas and principles have permeated the culture, with a number of activities in specific areas (Dahlerup, 1986). Regarding the relationship to the state, many feminists seem to have modified their initial distrust. A number of former activists are dealing with women's issues as bureaucrats in public or semipublic agencies, and some of them apply feminist principles, such as the creation of women's groups, consciousness raising, and feminist pedagogy (Dahlerup, 1993). On the other hand, criticism of prevailing equal opportunity concepts is still voiced by former Redstockings.

It has often been claimed that state adoption of feminist goals has the effect of deradicalizing feminism and coopting its leaders. Women's movement activism has declined since the DESC was created, and I believe a number of factors account for that decrease. First of all, there is no single issue such as abortion that could mobilize widespread participation. Second, there is no strong resistance in the form of an antifeminist movement in Denmark. Although the small Christian party articulates a pro-family rhetoric, it also accepts equal opportunity. Criticisms of the strong emphasis on paid work as a strategy to obtain gender equality have been voiced by women who seemingly accept the basic ideas of the feminist movement. Finally, it may be that differences among women have become more pronounced, making a unified movement impossible. The DESC, by embracing the interests of well-educated women more than those of unskilled or marginalized women, may reinforce a separate women's culture with "sisters in suits."

Although Danish women seem to organize separately less than they did in the 1960s and 1970s, they have become politically mobilized in other contexts, such as unions and social movements. The number of women in political institutions has increased, and women's issues have become increasingly visible in unions and political parties (Siim, 1993). A number of female politicians are devoted to feminist issues, and they also articulate women's interests within the political system. The party system mirrors the partisan differences among women, and party discipline in itself tends to reinforce diversification. Women rarely form alliances across political parties in parliament, except for a few occasions like the government's Action Plan. Still, the informal contacts between female politicians serve to keep women's issues on the political agenda (Dahlerup, 1990).

The questions remain whether it was a gain for the women's movement to get inside the political system and whether any gains were made at the expense of the strength of being outside. Dahlerup (1986) argues that the movement's success in "presenting a radical new way of thinking about women which has influenced public opinion as well as public policy" (p. 2) was premised on the feminists working outside the political system. However, to stay outside the political system was really not an option in the 1960s and 1970s, when the distribution and redistribution of money and power underwent radical changes and organized interests obtained representation in many different areas. Similarly, it has been crucial that feminists both inside and outside the political system fight to defend women's interests during the restructuring of the welfare state.

Conclusion:
Blessings and Constraints

It is striking that the bulk of feminist studies on the Danish and the other Scandinavian welfare states points to ambiguous effects for women, in spite of their unmistakable gains (Borchorst, 1994a; Leira, 1993; Siim, 1993). This analysis also fits the record of the DESC. The Council serves very important purposes: to eliminate obvious gender discrimination, to increase the political representation of women, and to provide a platform for the women's organizations to keep women's issues on the political agenda. On the other hand, the restricted scope of the agency's mandate and the prevalence of gender neutrality as a conceptual foundation of equal opportunity policy imply that vital areas for women's status and well-being have remained outside its realm.

The DESC occupies no more than a political niche, despite continuous attempts to widen this niche. The Danish state's efforts to advance the status of women have not been constant. The dynamics have been shaped more by incremental than by radical approaches; the niche has been enlarged more in terms of in-depth attention to a restricted range of policy rather than by widening the coverage to more areas. The circumstances surrounding the establishment of the DESC gave it a slow start, and this might partly explain why the Danish agency seems weaker than similar offices in Sweden and Norway. The strong role of corporatism and consensus in the Danish political culture determined the composition of the Council, thereby reducing its radical potential. At the same time, the corporatist formula has very likely ensured stability of the Council and a widespread political consensus on its activities.

The notion of equality underlying DESC policy initiatives emphasizes equality of opportunities in a gender-neutral sense. Positive action for women has remained a very controversial issue frequently provoking heated debate. Areas of policy focusing on women's lives directly, such as child care, old age care, and health policies, have made it possible for women to enter the labor force and continue to affect their status as workers. Nevertheless, such policies remain outside formal notions of gender equality. As a consequence, the potential of the Danish Equal Status Council to safeguard women's interests during the ongoing process of restructuring the welfare state has been curtailed. With increasing European integration, one can anticipate that policy decisions will be made more and more frequently at the level of EU institutions. Except for the EU equal opportunity unit, far fewer women are found in decision-making positions in the EU than in Denmark. The EU unit, too, is confined to a policy niche.

Notes

1. Good general sources on the DESC are Andersen and Nielsen (1990) and two DESC publications, *Lige Nu* (Right now), its newsletter; and *Ligestillingsrådets årsrapport*, the annual reports, from 1975-1991.

2. This might be explained by the homogeneity of the population compared to most other Western countries and by the fact that race discrimination was prohibited in separate legislation passed in 1971.

3. Two recently established parties, the Christian People's party and the Progress party, a tax denial party on the extreme right, voted against, as they had done in 1974. Two parties, the Liberal party and the Left Socialists, voted neither against nor for the motion.

4. During the process no one proposed that the women's liberation movement, the Redstockings, should obtain representation. Yet, the small Christian People's party feared that the establishment of the Council would follow a blueprint of the movement and imply public support for its ideology (Folketingstidende, 1974, p. 2423; 1978, p. 8064).

5. Only the Progress party strongly rejects feminism, and it has persistently voted against legislation in this area. The Christian People's party voted against the first laws, but it supported laws on equal opportunities since 1985.

6. The DESC has assigned the social partners responsibility for determining when such special exemptions for positive action are permitted. They have a narrow view of the possibilities of such exemptions.

5

Strong State
and Symbolic Reform

The Ministère des Droits de la Femme *in France*

Amy G. Mazur

Beginning in 1965, Fifth Republic governments have engineered a multilayered array of politico-administrative structures charged with some aspect of feminist policy formation.[1] From 1974 to 1986 and from 1988 to 1993, specific ministries have been allowed to contribute to setting the government's agenda for women's rights policy, to formulating feminist policy, and to overseeing the implementation and evaluation of these new policies. Since 1978, these ministries have increasingly had at their disposal an array of administrative mechanisms.

The record of these offices in producing effective policies has been mixed. As this chapter will argue, the influence of such special offices on women's rights policy in France has been circumscribed, tending to produce reforms that are more symbolic than material.[2] Central to this symbolic reform dynamic has been the near-absence of strong society-based support for specialized women's agencies and much of

---

AUTHOR'S NOTE: I would like to thank the American Political Science Association for funding a part of the research for this chapter.

their work. The result is that women's policy machinery in France has consisted of highly politicized and marginalized state structures. Although they have participated in the formulation and implementation of policies, they have failed to generate the means to ensure the effective use of the new policy instruments to help women.[3]

The analysis in this chapter will focus on the *Ministère des Droits de la Femme* (MDF) or Ministry of the Rights of Woman during the first term of Socialist President François Mitterrand from 1981 to 1986. As most observers agree, a feminist policy agenda reached its zenith in France at that time, under the ministerial leadership of Yvette Roudy. The MDF had a clear mandate from the president and the governing party and a significant allocation of budget, personnel, and policymaking responsibility. The MDF was created in the context of a 30-year pattern of state attention to women's policy. The first section of this chapter will review the array of women's policy mechanisms in Fifth Republic France. The second section will scrutinize the establishment and organization of the MDF, its role and effect in feminist policy formation, and its relationship to feminist and other women's advocacy organizations.

Confronting Women's Issues:
The French Tradition from De Gaulle to Mitterrand

Figure 5.1 summarizes the array of state agencies charged with women's policy issues and the evolution of their influence from 1965 to 1994. This section will briefly discuss the position of each structure on a continuum of policymaking power from low to high.[4] Placement for each office is determined by the following criteria:

1. Position in the cabinet, for example, dependence on parent ministry and representation on the Council of Ministers[5]
2. Budget, staff size, and affiliated structures
3. The formal and informal influence of femocrats on the president, prime minister, and ranking ministers[6]

It is important to note that if these offices were placed on the same continuum with all other ministries in the French executive, they all would be be situated at the lowest level of policymaking power.

Year	*Low Policymaking Power*			*High Policymaking Power*				
1965	CETF							
1967	x							
1969	x							
1971	x			CTF				
1973				x				
1974				x		SECF		
1975				x		x		
1976	DNCF (in Lyon)					@		
1977	x			x				
1978	@		CTF		SEEF	MDFCF		
1979			x		x	x		
1980			x		x	x		
1981		CTF			@	@	MDDF	
1982		x					x	
1983		@	CSEP (MEP)				x	
1984		x					x	
1985		x					x	MDF
1986		x	DCF					@
1987		x	x					
1988		x	@			SEDF		
1989		x				x		
1990		x				x		
1991		x				SEDFVQ		
1992		x				x		
1993		x	SDF			@		
1994		x	x					

Figure 5.1. The Evolution of National Women's Policy Offices in France, 1965 to 1994.
NOTE: x = office continues to exist; @ = office is discontinued.

From 1919 to 1963, ruling governments had frequently included a low-level office concerned with women's employment. Unlike women's offices created since 1965, these bureaus did not have an explicit mandate to improve women's rights. For example, in 1963, the *Bureau de la Main d'Oeuvre Féminin* was charged with the development of policies to promote women workers as an inexpensive and flexible source of labor. In contrast, the primary mission of the *Comité d'Etudes et de Liaison des Problèmes du Travail Féminin* (CETF) created in 1965 was to study gender-based inequities in the labor force and to propose policy solutions to equalize disparities between men and women workers. The political influence of certain elite right-wing women was crucial in convincing Gaullist ministers, often hostile to women's equal employment rights, to create this state structure that promoted gender-based equality.

Attached to the staff of the Ministry of Social Affairs, the CETF coordinated regular meetings attended by representatives from labor, management, agriculture, and the state bureaucracy, but it had no decision-making authority. In 1971, the persistent pressure of the femocrats who ran the CETF led to the decision to upgrade that study group to a committee, the *Comité du Travail Féminin* (CTF). Consequently, right-wing governments in the early 1970s reluctantly recognized women's inferior position in the labor force as a public problem (Lévy, 1988). The CTF played a pivotal role in the adoption of the 1972 Equal Pay Law (Mazur, 1995).

In 1974, the CTF's monopoly on women's rights policy issues was broken by the new *Secrétariat d'Etat à la Condition Féminine* (SECF). In the context of the rise of the feminist movement in the early 1970s and bolstered by his presidential campaign promises to address women's equal rights, newly elected Center Right President Valéry Giscard D'Estaing instituted the SECF as a separate Deputy Ministry of Women's Affairs in his Government. He named Françoise Giroud, a well-known, left-oriented magazine editor, to the post of deputy minister. More than any societal call or demand from Giscard's party, the idea for such an office came directly from the president.

Like the CTF, the new office's charge was to improve women's rights and status. Unlike the CTF, the SECF had a formal position in the cabinet, a ministerial staff, an operating budget to support its staff, and a mission that went beyond employment issues. As a deputy minister, however, Giroud could attend only Council of Ministers meetings that were pertinent to her portfolio. Moreover, tensions between Deputy Minister Giroud and Gaullist Prime Minister Jacques Chirac limited the degree to which the SECF could cultivate government support for material feminist reforms. Still, in less than 2 years, the SECF conducted an intensive study of women's status, proposed

100 policy solutions to correct the deficiencies in women's status in French society (Giroud, 1976), and backed several key pieces of women's rights legislation. Nevertheless, the tentative and marginal status of the SECF was confirmed when, following a reorganization in 1976 that named Giroud as Minister of Culture, it disappeared from the Government.

From 1976 to 1978, while the CTF continued to focus on employment questions, a new type of office appeared: the *Délégation Nationale à la Condition Féminine* (DNCF). Attached to the office of the new prime minister, Raymond Barre, the Delegation had no ministerial rank and few staff members. Furthermore, the new delegate, Nicole Pasquier, a close acquaintance of Prime Minister Barre, requested that the office be located near her home in Lyon. In the highly centralized French administrative system, the work of the already weakened DNCF was further diluted. During this period, Paris-based policymakers looked more to the CTF than to the DNCF for policy cues.

In 1978, with the desire to advance her political career, Pasquier convinced Barre to create a more powerful office in Paris, the *Secrétariat d'Etat à l'Emploi Féminin* (SEEF). Given a ranking position in the government and its own staff, the SEEF overshadowed and often replicated the work of the still autonomous CTF, thus weakening the policymaking power of the CTF. Following Pasquier's departure, the DNCF in Lyon was briefly headed by Jacqueline Nonon, a former bureaucrat in the Women's Bureau of the European Commission. After 3 months, Nonon resigned for lack of resources. Giscard took action to resolve the confusion over the various offices and their status by creating an attached ministry, based in Paris, that was more powerful than the previous deputy ministerial position held by Giroud but still weaker than a full ministry.

The Barre government gave Monique Pellitier, the new *Ministère Déléguée auprès du Premier Ministre à la Condition Féminine et à la Famille* (MDCFF), unprecedented resources: a full-time seat on the Council of Ministers, its own interministerial commission, and enough budget and staff to create regional and departmental delegations for women's status. In the context of a worsening economic crisis and increased concern over dropping birthrates at the end of the 1970s, the president also charged the MDCFF with a pro-natalist family policy targeted at working mothers. At the same time, the SEEF under Pasquier was promoting new measures that would help protect women's equal employment rights. Thus, while one office emphasized women's differences from men, the other advocated women's equality with men. As a consequence, the Giscard/Barre Government sent out conflicting messages on the intent of women's rights policy, garbled by the competition among the three separate specialized offices.

If the Right had harbored any expectations that by formally recognizing women's issues, it would reap benefits at the polls, these hopes were dashed by the victory of Socialist François Mitterrand in the 1981 presidential elections, his dissolution of the National Assembly, and the subsequent landslide victory of the Left in legislative elections the same year. It was with a Socialist president and leftist majority in the National Assembly that Prime Minister Pierre Mauroy appointed Yvette Roudy to the new *Ministère Déléguée auprès du Premier Ministre chargé des Droits de la Femme* (MDDF). In addition to having a seat on the Council of Ministers, the MDDF had a much larger budget than any previous women's office. Furthermore, rather than being a presidential innovation, like Giscard's offices, the MDDF was in large part a product of the struggle for women's rights issues within the *Parti Socialiste* (PS). Indeed, women's rights issues had a clear position on the Socialist governing agenda forwarded by President Mitterrand, known as the Socialist Experiment (Ambler, 1985). As a result, the Ministry had more influence in government policymaking circles than its predecessors.

In 1985, the attached Ministry was upgraded to a full Ministry (the MDF),[7] independent of the prime minister's office, and was put in charge of four administrative subdivisions, as well as the Interministerial Commission for the Rights of Women; the *Conseil Supérieur d'Egalité Professionnelle* (CSEP), which, under the law on *égalité professionnelle,* had replaced the CTF in 1983; and a relatively well-developed territorial network of women's rights offices and women's rights information bureaus. In contrast to past competition between women's offices, all women's rights policy mechanisms were subordinate to the MDF. At the same time, this centralization meant that if the Ministry were eliminated from the cabinet, the affiliated structures and programs could also be easily eradicated. Indeed, when Jacques Chirac became prime minister in 1986, following the defeat of the Left in the 1986 legislative elections, he found it easy to eliminate and/or suspend many policy efforts undertaken by the MDF.

During the cohabitation of a left-wing president and a right-wing prime minister from 1986 to 1988, the right-wing cabinet pursued a neoliberal stance on public policy, a departure from the social democratic agenda of President Mitterrand. For women's policy, this meant eliminating the activist women's rights ministry and accentuating policies that promoted the specificity of women's roles as family caretakers and mothers over women's equality in the workforce. The MDF was downgraded to a delegation (*Délégation à la Condition Féminine*— DCF), losing its position on the Council of Ministers and its formal policymaking authority in the government. The administrative offices of the MDF were left intact, but the operating budget was significantly reduced.

Following President François Mitterrand's successful bid for a second term in 1988, he dissolved the right-wing National Assembly. With a new Center Left majority,[8] femocrats in the DCF and feminist observers were hopeful for a return to the activism of the MDF. However, in the context of the increasingly low priority given to women's rights issues by Mitterrand and the PS and the continuing absence of compelling societal demands for such a governmental office, Socialist prime ministers from 1988 to 1993 assigned the lower rank of deputy minister to the women's policy office, called the *Secrétaire d'Etat des Droits des Femmes* (SEDF). As prime minister in 1988, Michel Rocard did not reappoint Roudy to the newly downgraded ministry, instead naming Michèle André. Many observers maintained that Rocard was not interested in women's rights policy and that André's appointment was more a product of her loyalty to Rocard than her commitment to women's rights. From 1988 to 1991, with fewer resources and an apathetic minister, the SEDF took a far less active line in promoting feminist policies than the MDF had taken.

In 1991, in the context of Edith Cresson's appointment to the prime minister's office, another Socialist woman, Véronique Neiertz, took the women's rights portfolio. Like André, Neiertz was not appointed for her work in women's rights policy. In a 1993 interview, for instance, Neiertz downplayed the need for an active women's rights ministry, stating that she agreed to take over the women's rights portfolio only to serve the PS. Originally named to a Deputy Ministry of Daily Life, *vie quotidienne*, Neiertz was allowed to combine the two portfolios. Thus, the SEDF became the *Secrétariat d'Etat aux Droits des Femmes et à la Vie Quotidienne* (SEDFVQ). Following Cresson's resignation in 1991, Neiertz continued to serve as SEDFVQ under Pierre Bérégevoy until 1993. Femocrats maintain that Neiertz was even less active on women's rights issues than André.

The connection between the Socialist party and a ministerial level office for women was demonstrated in 1993: The SEDFVQ lost its position following the landslide victory of the Right in the 1993 legislative elections. After April 1993, under Gaullist Prime Minister Edouard Balladur and Socialist President François Mitterrand, the administrative services were left in place but without a separate ministry or a delegation in the political executive. The women's rights administration, the *Service des Droits des Femmes* (SDF), has remained formally attached to the Ministry of Social Affairs through one upper-level civil servant in the minister's cabinet, situated one level below a delegation and consisting of one department among 19 attached to a ministry that is simultaneously in charge of social affairs, health, and urban issues. Although the minister, Simone Veil, has been known to support women's rights, these issues have composed a minute part of her agenda. Nonetheless, in Spring 1994, Veil reactivated the Higher Commission for Equal Employment (CSEP), which had been virtually ignored by Neiertz, and she mobilized the SDF to prepare a report for the United Nation's 1995 Conference on Women in Beijing.

In the Summer of 1994, many observers asserted that this attention by the right-wing Government to women's rights issues stemmed primarily from its desire to demonstrate to the international community that France was taking seriously the 1995 UN conference in Beijing. For most femocrats and advocates of feminist policy, the precarious position of the women's policy mechanisms in the 1990s will translate, even more than in the past, into a highly constrained government approach to feminist policy issues. As such, after nearly 30 years of action, the future of these highly politicized and ever-changing structures remained uncertain.

The Ministère des Droits de la Femme, 1981 to 1986

ESTABLISHMENT

The MDF, like all women's policy machinery in France, must be placed within the context of the Jacobin tradition of state-society relations embraced by the French political elite since the 1700s. This tradition defines the state, *l'état*, as the prime guarantor of the democratic *République*, the general will (Rousseau's *volonté général*), *grandeur* or international stature, and French national identity. In this view, interest groups are an obstacle to the state's ability to follow the general will of the people. For the French political elite, social change should occur through an active state or *dirigisme*. This strong state ethos has developed in tandem with the instability of elected governments and the permanence of the bureaucracy and the bureaucrats who run it (Suleiman, 1974, 1979, 1987).

In the name of Jacobinism, the centralized state apparatus has taken a pivotal role in guiding democratic change and minimizing the role of organized interests in that change. After first making interest groups illegal with the Loi Chapelier in 1790, the state has (since 1901) required interest groups to register to be officially recognized. Once registered, interest groups enjoy certain rights and significant subsidies from the government. Students of French policy formation under the Fifth Republic hold that even after concerted efforts to decentralize, the strong but "administratively fragmented" state continues to use its "tactical advantages" (Wilsford, 1989, p. 128) to make public policy and limit the role of organized interests in policy formation (see also Hall, 1990; Hoffmann, 1987; Wilson, 1987). Strong administrative bastions in policy areas such as labor, education, health, and agriculture have blocked the efforts of new ministries that cut across established policy sectors, like the MDF, to make concrete reforms. Moreover, it has been difficult to break the hold of more established agencies and their top-level bureaucrats on policy formation, in an effort to accommodate the needs and rights of specific groups—for example, women, ethnic and racial groups, homosexuals, and people with disabilities—that do not fit into class-based interests.

Yet, although decisions to create the MDF and other offices for women's policy were in large part a by-product of Jacobin logic, the establishment of the MDF differed from the creation of similar agencies. With its strong organizational ties to the PS, the MDF had much more leverage within the political executive than similar offices under Giscard. The Socialist women's rights ministry was inextricably linked to feminists loyal to the PS and close to Mitterrand since the mid-1960s. Yvette Roudy and Marie-Thérèse Eyquem founded the *Mouvement Démocratique et Féminin* (mdf, distinguished from MDF, the Ministry of Rights of Woman), a small group of non-Communist feminists on the Left. In 1965, they convinced Mitterrand to include the mdf in his efforts to unite the non-Communist Left under one party. Mitterrand invited the mdf to formally join his new party, which was the precursor to the PS, and in 1966 he named Eyquem minister of *promotion féminine* in his shadow government (Mazur, 1995, Chapter 2).

The mdf feminists were allowed to create a women's office when the new PS was established in 1971; they used this office to initiate partywide discussions on women's rights issues throughout the 1970s. It was in this way that the work of the PS feminists fueled the feminist agenda of the Roudy Ministry, Mitterrand, and the party. In the PS feminist approach, gender-based equality could be achieved through the pursuit of general equality, as long as a feminized Socialist party worked toward women's equality through elected office (see, e.g., PS, 1978). The PS feminists saw an active women's rights ministry, made responsible for women's equality policy in the Socialist Government, as the linchpin of this program.

In representing the views of the PS feminists, the MDF did not incorporate many ideas of the new French feminist movements of the 1970s. The highly fragmented and radical *Mouvement de la Libération des Femmes* (mlf) rejected the PS's reform politics because of what many new-wave feminists saw as the patriarchal system of power underpinning mainstream politics (Delphy, 1984). The mlf had neither reached out to the PS feminists nor called for a women's ministry (Picq, 1983). The PS feminist ideology coincided with demands of some feminist groups, in particular the reform-oriented *Choisir* and the *Ligue du Droit des Femmes* (LDF), both of which were formally registered with the state. For the most part, however, the PS feminists shunned direct connections to feminists outside of their orbit.

Family policy and women's rights policy were separated into two portfolios under the Socialists in 1981. The Roudy Ministry discussed family responsibilities only when these impinged on women's rights to work. As Roudy stated, "Married or not, mother or not, a woman is at first a person in her own right" (quoted in Stetson, 1987, p. 97). The title of the Ministry's publication, *Citoyennes à part entière* (women citizens with full rights) displayed this stance on women's rights. The highest priority of the new MDF was equal employment for women, with a heavy emphasis on equal training opportunities. The decree that created the MDF made its leader responsible for "measures aimed to respect women's rights in society, to eliminate all discrimination against women, and to increase the guarantees of equality for women in politics, the economy, society, and culture" (Décret no. 81, 664, 12 juin 1981).[9]

According to the first newsletter, the Ministry's three orientations were employment and professional training, information, and legislation. The legislative agenda of the MDF included a new equal employment law, public funding for abortions, and an antisexist law that would "eliminate sexist discrimination of which women were the object in culture and education" (*Citoyennes*, 1981, p. 2).

In keeping with Jacobin tradition, the MDF was established more by the feminist politics of the governing party than through any society-based demands. Influence from the United Nations or the European Community (EC) also did not appear to be an important factor in the decision to create the MDF. Even though the call for women's policy machinery by both organizations obviously reinforced arguments for a separate women's ministry, PS feminists stated that these international cues were not decisive in the creation of the MDF.

ORGANIZATION

Yvette Roudy took advantage of her political capital in the PS and the relative importance of women's rights issues on the Government's agenda to increase the size, resources, and scope of the Ministry, first in 1981 and then progressively up until 1986 when the MDF was replaced by the DCF under the Gaullist Prime Minister Jacques Chirac. In its first year, the budget of the MDF was 7 million francs ($1.1 million)[10] larger than the right-wing MDCFF. From 1981 to 1986, the budget increased from 9.27 million francs ($1.5 million) to 128.9 million francs ($21.5 million) (*Citoyennes à part entière*, 1985),[11] but never exceeded .01% of the total state budget. In addition to a nine-person ministerial staff, the MDF was composed of four separate administrative divisions in training and employment, women's individual rights, associations and regional coordination, and general administration. In all, the MDF had 200 administrators under its authority (Arpaillange, 1992, p. 3).

By 1986, women's rights offices had been set up in all 22 regions and in 76 out of the 92 departments. Each regional delegation was staffed by one full-time delegate and several part-time administrators and secretaries.[12] The departmental delegates, in contrast, usually worked alone and on a voluntary basis. The mission of all these offices was to oversee the implementation of policies to improve the status of women. Individual delegates retained a great deal of latitude in their specific missions. They were not invested with any formal authority, however, and limited funding further constrained their work. A report on the operations of the MDF from 1985 to 1986, made by the *Cour des Comptes* (the National Accounting Office), stated that the coordination between the central and territorial agencies was very poor (Arpaillange, 1992). Sloppy administration at the national level, according to the report, delayed the transfer of funds to the territorial agencies, often for as long as 3 months. The assessors also found that the continuity of these offices was greatly disturbed by the highly partisan nature of appointments. For instance, in 1981, Roudy had replaced delegates appointed by Pelletier in 1978 with PS regulars and loyal supporters.

The composition of Roudy's ministerial cabinet in the first years of the Mitterrand experiment reflected the personalized and ideological approach of her leadership. Positions that in the past had been held by formally trained civil servants were filled by left-wing and feminist activists close to the PS feminists. Even the civil servants who worked in the central administration of the MDF tended to be self-proclaimed feminists affiliated with the PS. The ideological affinity among the employees explains remarks made by several staff members that in the first 2 years of the MDF, they worked together in an unconventional manner, similar to the consciousness-raising groups of the feminist movement.

Under the impetus of Roudy, the status of the MDF rose, and in 1985 it became a full ministry. Ironically, however, while Roudy was securing increased resources for the Ministry, the place of feminist policy on the list of Socialist priorities began to fall in 1983. After 1983, the deteriorating economy and rising opposition forced Socialists to trade their redistributive Keynesian Socialist Experiment for a more practical and technocratic policy outlook (Daley, 1995; Ross, Hoffmann, & Malzacher, 1987). Accordingly, Socialist policymakers increasingly ignored MDF demands for costly feminist policy initiatives. Many Socialist ministerial staffs shed their more ideological and idealist members in favor of more traditional members of the bureaucracy (Birnbaum, 1985). Similarly, the number of activists within Roudy's cabinet and the ministerial divisions of the MDF steadily decreased. So, as the Ministry became larger, many politically active members left on their own; others were asked to leave when it became clear that they did not fit into the Government's new approach. By 1986, most of the feminist and PS activists in Roudy's ministerial cabinet had been replaced by conventional upper-level civil servants.

POLICY IMPACT

Although Roudy articulated an ambitious agenda of policy formulation and implementation, the MDF had little long-lasting impact. The Ministry's limited resources, its marginal position in the state hierarchy, the lack of authority given to its affiliated structures, the politicized nature of its mission and staff, and the precarious position of women's rights issues on the PS's agenda constrained action to high-profile gestures. The MDF sponsored and coordinated public information campaigns, conferences, and studies, rather than permanent programs that could withstand partisan shifts in Government. For example, the MDF launched experimental training and education programs for young girls with great fanfare, but it was not successful in getting the Ministries of Labor and Education to follow up with permanent policy for training and education.

Even the major pieces of legislation initiated by the Ministry followed this symbolic reform dynamic. Roudy first proposed an *égalité professionnelle* law in 1981 as a fundamental reform of equal employment law for women. By the time of its adoption in 1983, the *loi Roudy* had been stripped of the authoritative stipulations necessary for accomplishing the goal of equality in the workforce (Mazur, 1992). Instead, the new law established a formal, but not obligatory, process by which management and labor could analyze inequities between men and women in the firm through *rapports annuels* (annual reports). It gave only limited incentives to employers to design *plans d'égalité*, programs to address these disparities. The law also modified existing antidiscrimination laws and gave the right to trade unions, but not to feminist groups, to bring discrimination cases.

Initially, the MDF sought to promote the *loi Roudy*. In 1984, it launched a public relations campaign, issuing implementation directives to all levels of the Work Inspectorate and the women's rights field offices. The Ministry also sent out a detailed pamphlet to firms on how to prepare annual reports and equality plans (MDF, 1984). At the time, femocrats thought that all of the necessary steps had been taken to ensure effective implementation. By 1985, however, it became clear that the weaknesses contained in the 1983 law kept the new *plans d'égalités* and the annual reports from being taken seriously by management, *comité d'entreprise*, (workplace committees), and the trade unions.

The law created a national-level council, called the *Conseil Supérieur d'Egalité Professionnelle* (CSEP). The CSEP was to be composed of representatives from state, labor, management, agriculture, and women's groups, as well as individual experts. Lacking any formal enforcement or implementation powers, the Council made its primary mission to discuss and study equal employment policies for women. Only the minister of the MDF was allowed to convene the Council, thus attaching the fate of this weak implementing agency to the political fortunes of Roudy and her successors. A small administrative office was set up to coordinate the work of the CSEP and to oversee the new égalité professionnelle programs. In 1985, this *Mission pour l'Egalité Professionnelle* (MEP) was staffed by eight full-time employees. The CSEP's work came to a halt during cohabitation from 1986 to 1988.

According to a source close to the MDF, Roudy had predicted in 1984 that 300 equality plans would have been signed by 1986. In the summer of 1993, only 30 plans had been completed, affecting 4,000 women (Jobert, 1993). Throughout its 10-year life, only one women's group has become involved with the implementation of the new law. Trade unions have also been apathetic in promoting the new annual reports and equality contracts as well as pursuing cases of discrimination against women. Thus, as of the summer of 1994, implementation of the *égalité professionnelle* law had failed to generate a significant institutional trail in state and society, with the femocrats in the MEP the most attentive promoters of its implementation.

The second major item on the MDF's legislative agenda, an antisexist bill, did not make it through the legislative process. Intended to extend the definition of sex-based discrimination to include bias in the media and to give feminist groups the right to take discrimination cases to court, the proposal provoked a public uproar. Enough opposition developed around the potential of the law to censor the media that the Socialist government withdrew the bill by 1983.[13]

Many of the policies pursued by the MDF have been abandoned by subsequent ministries and agencies. Also, femocrats have indicated that without a vocal minister to push the formulation and implementation of feminist policy, ministers and administrators in other sectors will not follow through on women's rights proposals. For instance, in 1990, a staffer in the MEP tried to convince the Minister of Labor to better integrate equal employment programs for women into general employment policy. Michèle André, secretary for women's rights at the time, opposed the idea, and the suggestions were easily ignored. Policy measures proposed by the current SDF may well be ignored in the same way.

RELATION TO WOMEN'S ORGANIZATIONS

Students of feminist policy formation in advanced industrial societies have shown that a developed network of groups and state actors is crucial for the implementation of effective policy for women (e.g., Freeman, 1975; Meehan, 1985; Steinberg, 1988). The general weakness of organized interests in France has translated into a dearth of groups capable of working with a ministry to develop such a policy network. The absence of a network of sympathetic insiders in the women's agency and active outsiders in trade unions, women's advocacy groups, or feminist movements has meant that women's policy machinery has not moved beyond a symbolic role.

The MDF was especially selective in its consultation with women's groups, calling on only a small number of groups closely related to the PS. The more established women's associations, like *Femmes Avenir*, affiliated with the Gaullist party, *Union des Femmes Françaises*, linked to the Communist party, and *Union Féminine Civique et Sociale*, created as a part of the Catholic socialist movement, were remote from the activities of the Roudy Ministry. In the 1990s, these organizations are still active, but they are organizationally weak and unimportant players in the equality policy process. The feminist groups and movements that emerged in the 1970s were not only fragmented and weak but also in the main were suspicious of the ability of a state agency like the MDF to help women. Furthermore, by the early 1980s, after the final passage of the abortion law in 1979 and the legal division of the mlf into two hostile wings in the same year, the political influence of organized feminism was at a low point.[14]

Institutionalizing resources for women's issues in the state contributed to the weaknesses of organized feminist and other advocacy groups for women. This occurred despite the availability of subsidies in the MDF budget, which in principle could have strengthened an autonomous women's advocacy network. Each fiscal year the Ministry would decide which organizations would receive funding. Many groups felt that these subsidies, under the MDF, had ideological strings attached. Much of the money went to the so-called independent women's rights information centers, *Centre d'Information de Droits des Femmes* (CIDF). The de facto independence of these associations was questionable; the CIDFs were closely linked to the women's rights administration itself. For example, the MDF used the staff of the national information center in Paris to supplement the work of the ministry (Arpaillange, 1992).

As a result, rather than a partnership between organized feminism and the MDF, a patron-client relationship developed. The Ministry favored groups loyal to its version of socialist feminism. When the MDF funded apparently autonomous groups, they often became dependent on this funding for their livelihood and vulnerable to the declining interest in the women's policy agenda at the cabinet level.

With the change of Government to the Right in 1986, for example, the DCF discontinued the funding of many groups considered to be too radical for the right-wing government. As a result, many feminist groups financed by the Roudy Ministry were forced to disband. For instance, *Agence Femmes Informations*, a press service for women's issues, created with funding from the MDF, went bankrupt after 1986 when the DCF cut its subsidies.

Governments have continued to support some women's projects. State funding of *SOS Femmes Battues*, an antibattering group, and the *Association Européenne contre les Violences Faites aux Femmes Au Travail*, an antisexual harassment group, has greatly contributed to helping women in need. The experiment with direct aid to nongovernmental advocacy organizations under the Roudy Ministry, however, was not successful in creating a solid foundation for sustained influence of women's policy machinery in France.

Conclusion

The various forms of French women's policy machinery are certainly a by-product of the Jacobin political culture, which has legitimated a system of strong state and weak interest groups in policy formation. Up until the election of the right-wing majority in 1993, governments of both the Right and the Left included women's offices at the ministerial level. Similarities between the structure of the MDDCF under Giscard and the MDF under Mitterrand suggest continuity in these agencies. Furthermore, women's ministries were linked to the placement of women's rights issues on the presidential agendas of both Giscard and Mitterrand. At the same time, it was the Socialist Government that gave more resources and a more favorable ideological environment for the promotion of an equality-driven women's policy program.

The record suggests that these offices are largely dependent on the perceptions of mainstream political elite about the relative importance of women's rights issues in French politics. As Socialist politicians have become more concerned with economic retrenchment than with social justice, women's rights issues and the PS feminists within the party that supported them were marginalized from party activities.

Thus, after Socialists returned to power in 1988, prime ministers did not appoint Roudy or any other PS feminists to the women's ministry. Subsequent left-wing and right-wing Governments have increasingly realized that the presence of such a women's ministry yields few advantages in elections. The inability of femocrats to develop and sustain support from more politically powerful groups in French society keeps women's agencies dependent on decisions of the chief executive.

Despite the marginal and politicized nature of these offices, a women's rights administration with over 200 agents throughout the country has developed since 1974. Indeed, the presence of offices at all territorial levels makes it difficult to do away with this institutionalized attention to women's status. Still, the future of the women's rights administration is unclear. As the *Cour des Comtes* report states, "The fragility of the structures of the SEDF . . . has contributed to giving this young ministerial department an uncertain image that goes against the pursued objectives of its founders seeking to promote women's status" (Arpaillange, 1992, p. 3).

Even with more developed structures, given the declining political interest in women's rights issues and the lack of organizational support for state feminist action, it is questionable whether women's policy machinery in France would ever go beyond its symbolic role in the policy process.

Notes

1. This chapter will use the terms *feminist policy,* and *women's rights policy* to refer to any government action that has as its main purpose the improvement of women's position in society.

2. Symbolic policies, according to Elder and Cobb (1983), are policy statements without "actual policy outputs" (p. 22). In contrast to material policies, with measurable outputs such as administrative activity in implementation and enforcement (Anderson, 1990, p. 15), symbolic policies involve an "intensive dissemination of symbols" (Edelman, 1985, p. 26).

3. Skocpol (1988) argues that policies become effective only when they generate long-term institutional feedback in state and society:

Through the official efforts to implement them, policies transform the capacities of the state, affecting possibilities for future efforts at policy implementation. . . . social policies affect the social identities, goals, and capabilities of the groups that subsequently struggle or ally over policy-making. (p. 22)

4. The research for this chapter is based on open-ended interviews conducted from 1988 to 1994 with women's ministers, femocrats, and other pertinent policy actors.

5. The Council of Ministers, composed of ranking ministers and the prime minister and presided over by the president, formally sets the parliamentary agenda. Only government offices given a seat on the Council can independently propose legislation to parliament or draft executive decrees.

6. In France, the political executive is bicephalous: the president, elected every 7 years, appoints the prime minister. The prime minister heads the majority in the lower house of parliament, the *Assemblée Nationale*, which is elected every 5 years. For more on the design of government under the Fifth Republic, see Ehrmann and Schain (1992).

7. Because the change was more in form than substance, the acronym MDF will be used from now on to describe characteristics and efforts of both the MDF and its predecessor.

8. The Socialist party did not have enough seats for a working majority in the National Assembly and so had to build a coalition with centrist deputies.

9. All translations are by the author.

10. From 1981 to 1986, the rate of exchange between the dollar and the franc averaged 6 francs to the dollar.

11. This figure does not include the operating budget for the ministries services, which came out of the prime minister's budget up until 1985.

12. These numbers were taken directly from 1986 staff listings for the territorial offices.

13. For more on the antisexist bill, see Stetson (1987, pp. 183-190) and Picq (1983).

14. For more on the political impact of second-wave feminism in France, see Picq (1987), Duchen (1986), Guadilla (1981), and Jenson (1989).

6

Making Equality

The Women's Affairs Offices in the Federal Republic of Germany

Myra Marx Ferree

Two words in German express the current politics of state feminism; both are controversial. One, *Gleichstellung* (making equal), goes beyond making a claim for equal rights to actually charging the state with responsibility for producing gender equality. The other word, *Frauenbeauftragte* (a person, presumably female, responsible for women) refers to a now-popular means of addressing this feminist goal, women's affairs offices. Indeed, the term *Gleichstellungsstelle* (GSS, or equality job) is often used as a synonym for *Frauenbeauftragte* (or FB). The number of such women's affairs offices at all levels of German governments has grown to approximately 1,100, including 400 in the former German Democratic Republic, or GDR (Wilken, 1992).

AUTHOR'S NOTE: The research for this chapter was supported by a grant from the German Marshall Fund in 1990-1991. I am grateful for the hours of time that many FBs and other feminists spent with me explaining the system, and I hope that I have done justice to their perspectives. I also thank Beth Hess, Dorothy McBride Stetson, and Celia Valiente for their comments and editorial help.

95

The proliferation of such offices is viewed with ambivalence by German feminists. On the one hand, the very notion of "making equal" evokes concern that women are being asked to conform to a male model of values and behavior. Some feminist activists, especially in the former West Germany (the Federal Republic of Germany, or FRG), define women primarily as mothers and offer a politics of "special treatment" to help women with their distinctive burdens. For these feminists, the concept of *Gleichstellung* goes too far in asking women to be like men yet does not go far enough in accommodating women's presumably distinctive ways.[1] They are skeptical of the value of moving "onto the terrain of the state" at all (Reinelt, 1994, p. 84).[2] At the same time, the office of the FB is caught between the demand that it make equality and the demand that it deal with and for women. For some activists, particularly in the former East Germany, the notion of creating equality without changing men appears absurd. In their view, changing policy only as it affects women repeats the error that characterized their former socialist state (Ferree, 1993).

In this chapter, I examine the origins of the FB office in the 1980s, its organizational structure and effectiveness, and the consequences of unification in 1990 with the GDR and its tradition of *Gleichstellung*. As the unchanged name of the new political entity, the Federal Republic of Germany, indicates, the political rules of the West now apply. Nonetheless, a substantial gulf in social, economic, and political conditions remains, creating different challenges for equality offices in the two regions.

Establishment of
Federal Women's Policy Machinery

The Federal Republic of Germany calls itself a social market economy, meaning it has a long tradition of state intervention in the economy to achieve social goals. Unification into a single Prussian-led German state in the 1870s was followed by path-breaking social welfare measures (such as disability insurance and old-age pensions) but also by tight regulations on freedom of assembly (especially for women and apprentices). Both sets of measures were intended to control social unrest. The rise of the National Socialists (Nazis) in the

1930s expanded state control into a totalitarian and genocidal system, leaving a legacy of authoritarianism with which both postwar Germanies had to contend.

The Western zones of occupation that formed the Federal Republic (FRG) chose a path emphasizing decentralization, shifting many government functions, particularly education and social services, to the *Länder*, or constituent states. Consequently, much policy directly affecting women has been made only at this lower level. The GDR (formerly the Russian zone) remained highly centralized, with a national ministry for women, a Communist party-dominated national organization of women, a quota of women in the legislature, and laws mandating support for working women and single mothers. The climate of the Cold War precluded finding value in anything in the East, so such national policy machinery was actively rejected in the West. The egalitarian policies of the GDR were portrayed as undermining women's special role in the family and as defeminizing women (Moeller, 1993). More so than in other Western European countries, FRG policymakers saw full employment for women and support for child care as dangerously communist.

One exception to the rejection of national gender equality policy is the Equal Rights Clause of the FRG's Basic Law, its constitution, adopted in 1949 after fierce debate. The campaign for its inclusion was led by Elisabeth Selbert, a noted jurist and Social Democratic party activist, joined by many women politicians and newly formed women's organizations (Böttger, 1990; Moeller, 1993), most notably the *Deutsche Frauenrat* (German Women's Council). This umbrella organization called itself a women's lobby and picked up where the liberal women's movement of the pre-Nazi years left off (Cornelißen, 1993). Unfortunately, the potential power of the Equal Rights Clause was greatly diluted by another clause of the West German Basic Law, which expressly committed the state to defend and preserve the family (Moeller, 1993). The constitutional court resolved potential conflict by deciding that functional differences in the family and in employment could justify different treatment of women and men. Thus, until the mid-1970s, the court accepted different rates of pay explicitly set by gender as consistent with equal rights, and it gave husbands the legal right to forbid their wives to take paid employment (Berghahn 1993).

The relative weakness of federal policymaking for women in Germany reflected not only characteristics of the state, but also a deeply divided women's movement. One portion consisted of the *Frauenrat* (women's lobby), which was loosely linked to women's caucuses of the political parties and unions. The other strand emerged from the student protest movement about 1968, distancing itself from both the women's lobby and other political organizations.[3] In the name of autonomy, these feminists stressed three principles:

1. separatism in the sense of self-organization, apart from men, in groups where women could define their interests and share support;
2. independence from any larger political entity that might force them to subordinate their interests to some "higher good," as the Nazi and Communist regimes had; and
3. egalitarianism as the antithesis of organizational hierarchy and as a prerequisite for self-actualization.

Equating these principles with feminism led the autonomous women's movement to remain aloof from state policymaking processes and slowed the acceptance of feminist policy goals by the establishment women's lobby *(Fraunrat)*.

Although the FRG lagged behind other Western European nations in setting up national-level policy machinery to address women's concerns, some small steps were taken to include women. In 1972, when the federal executive was in the hands of the Social Democratic party (SPD), a three-person staff in the family division of the Ministry on Health, Family, and Youth was charged with looking at women's policy issues. And in 1974, as the UN Decade for Women brought growing international awareness of women's subordination, the Federal Executive launched a formal inquiry into the status of women and established a larger women's policy group, the *Arbeitsstab Frauenpolitik,* in the Ministry for Health, Family, and Youth. Led by a long-time union activist on women's issues, Marlies Kutsch, this policy group was an important source of funding for the first shelter for battered women, founded by autonomous feminists in Berlin in 1977.

In 1979 the federal parliament mandated equal treatment for women in paid employment (the European Community conformity law) to bring the FRG into minimal compliance with European Community

(EC) directives of 1975 and 1976. Because it imposed no meaningful penalties for violators, and the constitutional court still interpreted gender equality as permitting what it called functional differentiation, the law had no immediate practical effect (Berghahn, 1993; Cornelißen, 1993; Gerhard, 1990). Despite the absence of legal pressure, the federal women's policy group helped unions negotiate some affirmative action plans with employers (Dobberthien, 1988). The *Arbeitsstab Frauenpolitik* began to formulate a more meaningful antidiscrimination law, but control of the government passed from the SPD to a conservative-liberal alliance in 1982, before that law could be finalized.

This alliance, led by Christian Democrats, again took up concern with women's policy in 1986, by appointing Rita Süssmuth to head the Ministry for Health, Family, and Youth. At her insistence, they added "and Women" to the title and transferred staffers working on women's issues from other ministries into her department. Influenced by autonomous feminism, Süssmuth had previously directed a research institute aimed at advancing gender equality. As minister she became a very visible spokesperson on women's policy issues, until she was "kicked upstairs" to the post of president of the Bundestag. In 1991, following unification, this large and relatively powerful ministry was split into three, and a less politically experienced East German, Angela Merkel, was appointed to head the new Ministry for Women and Youth. This ministry turned again in the 1990s to the still-unfinished task of drafting national antidiscrimination legislation.

At the national level, therefore, women's policy machinery remains weak, and concern for women's rights is still held hostage to the constitutional mandate to protect the family. Moreover, the constitutional mandate to protect life has been interpreted as covering the fetus, so legislative reforms of abortion law have been twice overturned by the constitutional court (in 1974 and again in 1993). The alliance of the Christian Democratic Union (CDU), Christian Social Union (CSU), and Free Democratic party (FDP), which has been in power since 1982, has actively opposed even the small steps toward liberalization that have occurred. Following the CDU-CSU victory in the October 1994 Bundestag elections, Chancellor Kohl appointed an East German antiabortion activist, Claudia Nolte, to head a newly reconfigured Ministry of Women, Family, Youth, and the Elderly. As

Nolte has no administrative experience and is only 28 years old, her appointment signaled a dramatic weakening of the already tenuous position of women's affairs at the national level.

Frauenbeauftragte:
Origins, Organization, Activities

At the level of the constituent states, policy development has been more mixed. States with SPD governments were quickest to set up offices for women's policy, led by North Rhine-Westphalia in 1975. In 1979 the states of Hamburg and Hesse established women's affairs offices that provided models for the subsequent flowering of local Frauenbeauftragten. In the 1980s many states followed suit, justifying the FB offices as affirmative action programs required under the EC's first Action Program for Equal Opportunity. In 1985 the SPD-Green coalition government in Hesse gave state secretary rank and a multimillion-dollar budget to its FB office, and in 1988 Schleswig-Holstein's SPD-Green coalition raised the office to ministerial rank. By 1993, all states had some sort of women's affairs office, and a few (Berlin, Hesse, and North Rhine-Westphalia) had passed antidiscrimination laws. Where the office has ministerial status, it is usually headed by a prominent woman politician and controls sizable civil service staffs to do policy research, allocate and oversee grants to state and local women's groups, and develop legislative proposals.

Parallel to this process, by the late 1970s the perspectives of autonomous feminists began to influence women across the political spectrum, including many who were active in political parties and other mainstream organizations (Nave-Herz, 1994). The women's lobby began to want more substantial social transformation, and autonomous feminists developed increasing numbers of projects to shelter battered women, provide health care, support rape victims, and so on. The autonomous movement wanted access to state and local funding for projects, and the women's lobby was looking for worthwhile areas in which to exercise and expand its political leverage. This mutual need was an important precondition for the rise of local FB offices in the 1980s.

Also, the lack of a federal mandate for affirmative action made it difficult for local activists to pressure private employers to hire or promote women. This left city governments, themselves large employers, as the most accessible targets for efforts to improve the status of women. Thus the position of *Frauenbeauftragte* was invented in part as an affirmative action officer for the state or city government itself. The first city (Cologne) and state (Bremen) governments (both SPD) established independent offices specifically charged with the goal of *Gleichstellung* in 1982. In 1984, the Hamburg FB produced the first affirmative action plan for women in government employment (Goericke, 1989). The guidelines sounded better than they would prove in practice, because they only said that "equally qualified" women candidates "should" be preferred, without defining how equal qualification should be measured or offering potential sanctions.[4] But these guidelines provided a model for other states and cities, particularly in creating an expanded role for the FB to develop them and oversee their implementation.

Growing awareness of women as voters interested in equal opportunity made the political parties increasingly responsive. Competition for the women's vote between the SPD and the CDU was heightened by the emergence of the Greens, a consciously alternative party with an explicit commitment to environmentalism and feminist issues. Women were a target constituency, as the CDU worried about the loss of younger women voters to the SPD, the SPD felt competition from the Greens, and the small, liberal FDP worried it might drop below the 5% vote required for parliamentary representation (Cornelißen, 1993).

In the early 1980s, therefore, pressure from the EC and from women's groups combined with competition among political parties to make some form of affirmative action policy a priority. The number of women's affairs offices expanded rapidly nationwide, growing from 40 in 1985 to approximately 250 in 1987 and to 600 in 1989. To coordinate their efforts across party lines, a National Network of Local FBs was founded in 1985 (Vollmer, 1988; Wilken, 1992). North Rhine-Westphalia, a strongly SPD state, mandated that every town of over 10,000 population have a FB office. The FB model has become so popular that many universities and other large government agencies appoint their own. Yet movement pressure has often been needed to create an FB office in an individual city or town; in 1987 three quarters of the local FBs named women's groups, especially those associated with the SPD and unions (and in a quarter of the communities, autonomous feminist groups), as instrumental in creating their position (Goericke, 1989, p. 71).

The institutionalization of local women's affairs offices should not disguise the variety of the organizational forms they continue to take (Wilken, 1992). Although almost all such offices have been charged with developing an internal affirmative action plan for the local government, little else is specified beyond vaguely calling for outreach and education for women in the community. Within the limits of available resources, the FB has considerable latitude to define her own position and to negotiate her job description with the chief administrative officer and/or the legislature making the appointment (Goericke, 1989; Schlapeit-Beck, 1988; Wilken, 1992).

The level of resources varies widely, especially according to the political party in power (Cornelißen, 1993; Krautkrämer-Wagner, 1989). Social Democratic governments tend to establish the position with at least the minimum required to do the job, for example, a full-time professional position and some clerical assistance. Mid-size to large cities and states provide more resources and typically larger staffs (e.g., the 13-person office in Cologne). Where the Green Party is in coalition with the SPD, the FBs tend to have more staff and budget resources and also more authority to look into files, to issue independent reports, and to review decisions before they are finalized. Yet a significant minority of all local FB offices rely on unpaid volunteers (community activists or legislators) and can do little besides providing an open door to women with specific complaints and formulating an internal affirmative action policy in broad strokes (Goericke, 1989). Such positions are seen by feminists as "alibi jobs" or sheer tokenism, intended to obscure rather than remedy government's failure to create gender equality (Wilken, 1992). In small towns with conservative governments, nearly all women's affairs offices are powerless alibi positions (Goericke, 1989; Wilken, 1992). The most typical FB offices, however, are part of the administrative structure of the Länd or city government, are staffed with full-time civil service jobs, and report directly to the head of administration (Goericke, 1989; Schlapeit-Beck, 1988; Wilken,

1992). Although not all offices meet this standard, the following discussion of the role of FBs in policy formulation and implementation will focus on this type of full-time, paid position.

Role in Policy Formulation and Implementation

In all jurisdictions, the FB has a special charge to draw up and oversee the implementation of affirmative action plans for women in the civil service. Many see this as an opportunity to make government hiring a vanguard and model for other organizations. In reality, the plans are still largely restricted to making suggestions about what should be done rather than changing the rules for hiring and promotion, and their effect has been small. For example, between 1970 and 1990, the proportion of women among civil service employees with supervisory responsibilities remained virtually unchanged; 10.5% in 1979 and 11% in 1990 (Kurz-Scherf, 1992, p. 41). But because most affirmative action plans were put in place only after hiring was being cut back due to the recession, many FBs claim that keeping women's share of employment stable is a sign of victory.

Aside from promoting affirmative action in the civil service, the role and policy interests of FBs vary widely, yet all see some part of their job as sensitizing other government departments to the women's dimension in their mission. The extent to which the FB has authority to find out about or participate in the decisions being made in other departments differs among jurisdictions. Individual city governments set the rules for whether the FB has the right to examine files, to be notified of pending decisions, or to speak to the city parliament on behalf of her views. Very few FBs have even a temporary veto over proposals that they see as having a negative impact on women (Goericke, 1989, p. 86). Most have a right to be informed about what other departments are doing, but this can lead simply to an unmanageable blizzard of paperwork. Unless the FB has a strong sense of priorities and directions in which she wants to influence other departments, she can be made just as ineffective by too much information as by too little.

Setting priorities for what decisions and policies have a significant women's dimension is not easy. FBs who see women as mostly mothers of young children give special scrutiny to parks, playgrounds, and public transportation. Others emphasize affirmative action issues, seeing women primarily as current or potential employees of the city, for example, as teachers, nurses, social workers, and clerical workers. Others, seeing women as victims of sexual assault and abuse, look to public safety measures, such as streetlights and the staffing of subway stations, and social welfare programs, such as public housing for battered women and counseling for sexually abused girls. Only a few of the very largest offices can afford to devote attention to multiple domains with any degree of effectiveness.

The FB's success in meeting her goals is greatly affected by the working relationship she develops with her direct superior. Because the job is largely undefined and the responsibilities potentially enormous, having a boss who supports her general direction and backs up her specific decisions is crucial. This relationship is complicated by a number of organizational factors, as well as the specific personalities involved. First, the typical FB has to have good working relationships with many departments, so that they will inform her about pending decisions and perhaps allow her to participate in discussions or offer additional proposals. Because the FB reports directly to the chief administrator and needs to have his (very few women run city halls) confidence and support, the departments may see her as his spy or his agent within the bureaucracy. Distancing herself from him, either by criticizing him or by emphasizing the separate nature of her agenda, may create confidence that she will not "carry tales." At the same time this strategy can undercut the FB's perceived legitimacy to speak with the voice of his authority. Most of the FB's power derives from the chief executive's willingness to implement her recommendations, penalize those who refuse to cooperate, and endorse her definition of the problem. Such borrowed power is diametrically opposed to the principle of autonomy that feminists hold dear, so it is remarkable that a number of individuals schooled in the autonomous women's movement have moved into FB positions and used them quite shrewdly.

Second, bureaucratic accountability is a problem. Few FBs have a special exemption from the general principle that the administration speaks with a single voice. Just 21% had such a right in 1988 (Goericke, 1989). With these exceptions, a FB who has not been able to implement her agenda within the system is legally barred from publicly criticizing the decision that was made. As a member of the administration, she has to defend its actions or keep silent, at the risk of losing her job. As a member of the women's movement, she may be the most accessible target women have for expressing their anger and criticism.

Another problem in finding a role in administrative policymaking arises with regard to the budget of the office. A big budget usually connotes status within a bureaucracy, and FBs can build the size of their budgets by taking on responsibility for funding women's projects in a variety of areas like culture, social services, education, and employment, thus increasing their status and legitimacy within the government and increasing their influence with their peers. Bigger budgets also allow for more discretion (and possibly radical priorities) in deciding what to fund. Many autonomous women's projects fought for a FB, hoping that she would build up and control such a discretionary budget.

Funding responsibility comes with two significant costs. First, it tends to define the FB as the target of all proposals from women's groups. No FB has a budget that could hope to support all the various activities in which women are engaged. Seeing the FB budget as the place for women to turn diverts pressure from other departments, legitimates the low level of funding that these departments offer to women's compared to men's programs, and directs women's legitimate rage at the FB rather than city government when worthy projects are not supported. Second, it places the FB in the role of judge vis-à-vis women's proposals. Particularly for those FBs who are trying to create a women's public and who need the cooperation and support of diverse women's movement groups, being forced to alienate many of their potential allies by denying funding for their pet projects is awkward. Thus, although most FBs have at least a small pot of money to distribute in grants and subsidies, a few FBs strategically choose not to take responsibility for funding women's projects.

In sum, the position of a FB is only partly defined by a formal organizational chart and has little institutionalized power. Her integration into the bureaucracy, her budget, her authority in relation to her supervisor, her public voice, and her definition of responsibilities with regard to her amorphous public constituency all shape her potential effectiveness. It is thus impossible to provide a single assessment of the impact of FBs as an institution at the local level. Some have combined personal political skills and favorable administrative conditions into a powerful recipe for successful influence. Others have been marginalized and toil thanklessly on a Sisyphean mountain of unmet needs and irrelevant paperwork.

Relation to the Women's Movement

Most FBs' responsibilities include both affirmative action internal to the civil service and outreach into the community to make government more responsive to women's needs. In the former case, the FB's constituency is relatively well-defined, including women employees of government and potential candidates for jobs. In the latter, all women in the city are her potential constituency. The FB must herself define when and how they are to be reached, which of their diverse needs are relevant to her job of making equality for them, and what such *Gleichstellung* implies for how she does her work.

These definitions span a spectrum of engagement and self-conscious feminism. At the one end are those FBs who see their position as meeting the needs of individual women who come to their office hours. They expend considerable energy in guiding these women through the labyrinths of the bureaucracy, attempting to mediate complaints about mistreatment by other offices, and making referrals to other agencies such as housing, health, welfare, and so on. These efforts can be called a form of social work, a term used pejoratively in much of the women's movement. A second position is to try to aggregate the individual problems that women present and derive general needs from these one-on-one encounters. These FBs attempt to avoid direct social work as inefficient, instead using office hours to identify recurrent issues so that they can develop informational brochures, set up lectures and workshops, and present noncontroversial policy initiatives that they perceive to be widely useful to women, such as reentry courses or curb cuts for strollers. Most are geared toward informing women of their options and encouraging women to take their own initiatives.

A third, more activist approach is to reach out into the community with a specific agenda and encourage women who have experience or interest in this subject to come in during office hours. The agenda chosen often reflects the FB's previous experience in the women's movement. Those coming from the autonomous feminist movement typically have a strong interest in the issue of violence and may solicit input on antiviolence measures, ranging from better lighting in parking garages to free taxi rides after dark. Activist FBs with experience in mainstream women's organizations generally prefer measures to increase women's occupational status, such as networking in corporate settings and training girls for jobs in technical fields. Whatever their agenda, FBs who define outreach in this way use the local media to promote their activities and to encourage women to work with them. Although they get their share of women who present complaints or problems, they discourage work on individual cases and are particularly sensitive to the charge of doing social work. They have a focused vision of the policies they think will contribute to making equality for women.

At the most movement-oriented end of the spectrum are those FBs who define their responsibility as representing women as a collectivity. Although virtually all FBs sometimes bring women in the autonomous movement and in conventional women's organizations together, these movement-oriented FBs feel particularly responsible for forging a women's public (*Frauenöffentlichkeit*) that can be mobilized around women's issues and thus keep women on the political agenda.[5] They see women's organizations and autonomous feminist groups as already providing mechanisms for making women's interests politically relevant, and thus they define their role as channeling resources to these organizations, creating legitimacy for them, and encouraging their mutual support. These FBs use their offices to place issues on the agenda of the movement and to stimulate a response from the women's public, to encourage and reward the achievements of the women's movement, and to direct money and participants to movement groups.

It is clear that many FBs have had an impact on the women's movement. Women in these jobs who actively envision policy changes are able to create an opening for government and the women's movement to participate in achieving them. To some extent they have overcome the estrangement between the women's lobby and the autonomous feminist projects that arose in the 1970s. Frequently they are the point of contact between individual women in diverse projects and organizations, as well as a point of entry for women interested in the policy process. Competition and conflict between state offices for women and nongovernmental women's groups are not unusual, but a reasonable level of ongoing cooperation with a mobilized women's public characterizes the more successful offices (Schlapeit-Beck, 1988; Wilken, 1992). Although some feminists continue to criticize these offices on principle, others from the autonomous movement have entered these jobs, defined them effectively, and carried them out with significant effects in their local communities. The FB has been important in developing a sense that autonomous feminists and members of women's caucuses within organizations are part of the same movement and in channeling communication and resources between them.

Consequences of Unification

When the GDR entered the FRG in 1990, it already had experience with equality offices. In addition to an ambiguous 40-year history of national policy machinery for women under state socialism, local FB offices were established in the brief period of independent reform between the fall of the Communist government and unification, as part of a consciously feminist policy initiative. The driving force of this new feminism was the *Unabhängiger Frauenverband* (UFV; Independent Women's Association), an active participant among the movement groups that precipitated the end of the GDR (Ferree, 1994b; Hampele, 1993). The UFV was an umbrella organization lending credibility to grass-roots groups that successfully struggled for representation on the roundtables that shaped this transitional period; it also sent its own delegate to the national roundtable and put its own minister in the transitional cabinet. The UFV aspired both to have a voice in government policy and to establish local grass-roots projects that would allow women to discuss their experiences and address concerns directly but with the financial support of the state.

In the transition year between December 1989 and December 1990, the UFV successfully won substantive concessions. Among these was a law mandating a *Gleichstellung* office in every community of over 10,000; UFV members frequently became the staff. Space and funds were provided for women's shelters, women's studies programs, women's centers, and other women's projects around the country. But the UFV failed to win seats in the interim parliament, and after unification in 1990 its credibility and influence faded. Although the transitional law creating local equality offices was picked up by the new states of the former GDR, by then a confused and weakened UFV was trying to find a new direction in the largely unfamiliar political and economic milieu of the FRG.

The equality offices in these five former GDR states are thus in a peculiar position. On the one hand, their incumbents have been a statutory part of the bureaucracy from the beginning of reform and are more firmly interwoven in the local administration than their FRG counterparts. On the other hand, they and their colleagues are just beginning to learn the political rules of the new political system. In addition, they were immediately confronted with an economic crisis of enormous magnitude, affecting women particularly severely. Within 2 years of unification nearly half of the jobs in the former GDR ceased to exist. The official unemployment rate stood at 15% in 1993; the true number of people without work was approximately twice as high, and women accounted for roughly two thirds of the jobless. Women over 50 and mothers of young children are at particular risk of being pushed out of the labor force.[6] Accommodation to West German ways means a shift away from opportunity and self-sufficiency for former GDR women. Women who thought paid employment was a self-evident part of their lives are being encouraged to stay home and leave the jobs for men. Men are being preferred for jobs in occupations that had been virtually all female in the East, while women find themselves excluded because they have children or simply because they are women (Einhorn, 1993; Ferree, 1994a). For example, the proportion of women in management positions dropped from one third in GDR days to nearly zero in just 2 years (Maier, 1992).

Therefore, local and state equality officers must fight a forest fire with teacups; given the enormity of the problem, their tools of persuasion and education are woefully inadequate. Still, they have had some effects. They successfully spread the word of the vicious circle confronting women who lose their jobs. If unemployed women take their children out of child care, the FRG will class them not available to work and hence not unemployed, and the child care center itself may close for lack of demand. With both information and money, *Gleich-*

stellung offices have helped keep many child care places in the former GDR open. They have prevented worst-case scenarios from coming to pass in other areas. For example, although women have lost ground relative to their previous status at the Humboldt University in Berlin, they still make up 13% of the faculty, much higher than is typical in the West (5%) and higher than the expected retention rate (Ferree & Young, 1993; Nolte, 1994). They have also maintained funding for shelters and other feminist projects that might well have fallen victim to the state's fiscal crisis.

Such successes would not have been possible without cooperation between East and West, but although the West German women's movement rushed to embrace its sisters in the former GDR, the actual process of building any mutual support is far more difficult than either side anticipated. Membership in the national network of local women's affairs offices was easy to extend; coming to a common understanding of the mission of a *Frauenbeauftragte* is much harder. On one hand, the theoretical and practical struggles of FRG feminists over the past 20 years make them confident that their analysis of the situation of women is correct and slow to recognize that the situation they know is not the one that GDR women have experienced (Ferree, 1995). On the other hand, the perspective of GDR feminists is still shaped by their ambivalence toward the policies of the former GDR and their shock at and incomprehension of the FRG system.

The vision that the equality officers in the East have of feminism necessarily differs in some important ways from that of their colleagues in the West. FRG feminists are still struggling over issues of reentry for women who leave the workforce to raise children. In the FRG, unlike the former GDR, women interrupt their careers for 10 years or more, and fewer than a third of all women 30 to 50 years old work full-time (Maier, 1993).[7] FRG feminists tend to advocate making special allowances for mothers as the most effective form of affirmative action. In the old GDR, women did not drop out. They expected policies that allowed them to combine paid work with child rearing but criticized the government for extending special benefits to women alone rather than restructuring work hours for everyone. GDR feminists thought such special treatment led to a marked increase in discrimination against women at work; they argued that it merely added to women's work, rather than changing gender roles, because the state never tried to bring men into domestic labor or female-only jobs. In their experience, affirmative action for only women is a dangerous course, one that will institutionalize an inferior "mommy track" and entrench a double day of paid and unpaid labor for women alone (Ferree, 1993, 1994b). In the abstract, many GDR feminists would like programs that would create equality by changing occupations of both women and men, for example, by drawing men into conventionally female occupations such as nurse and child care worker. In reality, the loss of women's jobs and the takeover of female sex-typed occupations by men is so great that such measures would be absurd. Also, the enormous costs of unification forced cutbacks in the West, and women's projects and programs were often targeted for elimination, throwing FRG feminists out of work and increasing resentment of special benefits flowing to the East.

Overall, therefore, unification has provided a stress for feminists in both East and West that is difficult to ignore or to wish away with fine words about sisterhood. There are real differences in experience and perspective that will need to be dealt with in the coming years, and there is more competition for fewer resources than at any previous time. Whether the women's movements in both parts of the country, both inside and outside of the government, will be able to rise to the occasion remains an open question. Some grounds for hope appeared on International Women's Day (March 8, 1994) when UFV groups and equality offices in the East joined women union activists, politicians, autonomous feminists, and FBs in the West to orchestrate a national day of protest.

Conclusions

What has the move to institutionalize *Frauenbeauftragten* at all levels of government brought to women and to the women's movement in Germany? At a minimum, it offers a structural mechanism for channeling communication and resources between the autonomous feminist movement and women's caucuses and organizations and between East and West. It has helped to place and keep affirmative action on the political agenda, despite the pressure of unification issues to displace all other subjects. It has produced a number of visible women politicians in ministries at the state and federal levels who are not afraid to speak out as women on behalf of women's issues, from abortion rights to unemployment. It has contributed to the construction of a women's public that is attentive to such issues and that continues to make the parties concerned about addressing women as potential voters. It has helped the movement win some substantive victories, from creating antidiscrimination laws and women's studies positions to keeping child care centers open in the former GDR.

At the same time, the political institution of the *Frauenbeauftragte* has not—at least not yet—produced conspicuous gains in civil service hiring, its original mandate. Nor has it been able to prevent massive cuts in the budgets of autonomous women's projects in both East and West as a consequence of unification or to stem the tide of unemployment sweeping over women in the former GDR. It has not been able to put effective sanctions into antidiscrimination laws or remove provisions that allow mothers, but not fathers, who lose their jobs to be held accountable for child care arrangements in order to be eligible for unemployment. It has not yet been able to create a common understanding between the women's movements in East and West on what sort of future for women and men is worth striving for.

Whether this is a half-full or half-empty glass, therefore, depends on which elements one chooses to stress. Given the long-standing pro-housewife stance of FRG policy and the initial estrangement of autonomous feminists from government and even from the rest of the women's movement, it seems a notable achievement of the past 15 years that the glass is there at all.

Notes

1. For expressions of such specific reservations, see discussions in Weg and Stein (1988). See also the critique of this general point of view in Pinl (1993), which cites the main theoretical documents of the movement expressing this position.

2. By using Claire Reinelt's (1994) term, *the terrain of the state,* I wish to invoke her view of the state as a differentiated arena or a set of playing fields on which feminists can engage with a variety of other interests and groups.

3. In Germany, *feminism* is a term usually applied exclusively to the autonomous portion of the women's movement, not to all who would call themselves part of this movement. Women who are part of male-run organizations, such as unions or

political parties, will often not claim the label feminist even if their career has focused on working for women's equality.

4. In fact, Berghahn (1993, p. 80) points out that the constitutional status of any sort of affirmative action is still uncertain, as a lower court ruled in 1991 that it was impermissible to allow the North Rhine-Westphalia mandate for affirmative action to be used to outweigh the 2 months of official seniority that an otherwise equally qualified male candidate had by virtue of his army service.

5. A women's public, in some ways analogous to issue public, is modeled on the term *Gegenöffentlichkeit,* a counterpublic or counterculture, which places a different set of demands on politicians and the political process than it is used to dealing with.

6. For a more detailed discussion of the gendered impact of unification see Bialis and Ettl (1993) and Ferree (1994a).

7. FRG culture, unlike norms in the former GDR, also validates the conflict between employment and motherhood. A majority of West Germans (55%) think that employed mothers cannot give their children as much security as other mothers. In contrast, only 36% of other Europeans and 29% of East Germans agreed (Institut für Demoskopie Allensbach, 1993, p. 42). This structural and cultural incompatibility is a central issue for the women's movement in the West, whereas women in the former GDR took for granted their ability to have one or two children and a full-time job (Maier, 1993).

7

An Emerging Advocate

The Equal Opportunities
Commission in Great Britain

Joni Lovenduski

The Sex Discrimination Act of 1975 created a new state agency in Great Britain, the Equal Opportunities Commission (EOC), to oversee the law's implementation. The EOC opened for business at the end of 1975. Although equal employment policy in Great Britain is made by a number of agencies with numerous committees and officers in branches of government and industry, and representative associations are responsible for equality between women and men, the EOC is the major authority in charge of enforcing and developing equality legislation. The EOC covers England, Scotland, and Wales and works in conjunction with the Northern Ireland Equal Opportunities Commission (NIEOC). The NIEOC fulfills the same duties as the EOC, while operating within the different legal circumstances of Northern Ireland.

The only other state organization with a national brief to oversee women's interests is the Women's National Commission (WNC). The WNC is a small, low profile, advisory agency currently located within the Department of Employment. Between 1987 and 1994, the major opposition party, the Labour party, has maintained a Shadow Ministry for women,[1] pledging to institutionalize this portfolio along unprecedented superministry lines. There has been no equivalent top-level women's ministry in the Conservative Government. Junior ministers in the Employment and Health Departments are given specific assignments on women's policy issues as part of their portfolio.[2] For example, in the Employment Department, a Junior minister is given the responsibility to oversee the work of the EOC and serves as the conduit of accountability between the EOC and the electorate. Following the 1992 General Elections, in which a reduced Conservative party's majority in the House of Commons was returned, the Department of Employment was reorganized to house a Sex Equality Branch to coordinate government policies in this area.

The discipline of British party politics has successfully impeded any impulse for networking across government and opposition agencies between policy actors interested in promoting policy that improves the status of women.[3] As a result, the EOC has been the focal point for networking on women's policies at the national level. The EOC is the only state agency with a large established staff to manage its strategic law-enforcement powers, with a leading role in formulating British sex equality policy, and with links to the main organizations that treat women's issues, including local government agencies and women's interest and professional groups. Although formally independent, its operation has been visibly affected by the changes in the political climate since its founding. Nevertheless, as this chapter will show, a linear, positive development of sex equality policy may be traced to the work of its staff, who have used their expertise to expand the economic and social rights of British women.

The EOC was established with all-party support by the Sex Discrimination Act of 1975. Despite such auspicious beginnings, its initial activities were characterized by caution and timidity. The first chairman (sic) of the EOC was Betty Lockwood, formerly the Labour party's national women's officer. Instead of bringing Labour's traditions of supporting women's equality with her to office, Lockwood brought the secretive, defensive styles of working that were characteristic of Labour's headquarters staff at the time. Feminists politically active in the 1970s, referred to as new-wave or second-wave feminists, were excluded from the Commission's activities as much as possible. Long-established women's organizations fared little better. Administrators, lawyers, and experts pushing for more effective women's equality policy found it difficult to get jobs at the Commission. Furthermore, many feminist policy actors who were assigned to positions in the EOC departed soon after their appointments, frustrated by their inability to initiate action and by the unwillingness of the EOC to take the decisive action its founding legislation empowered it to do. Outside of the agency, feminists despaired of its caution and sought other ways to further women's rights. By the end of the 1970s, the Commission appeared to many observers to be an embarrassing failure.

But during the 1980s a number of coinciding pressures altered its course. The strategic thinking of the EOC's legal staff became, perhaps inevitably, more imaginative and determined. A new leadership also encouraged, responded to, and developed these initiatives. External pressures on the EOC to take more concrete action resulted from the growing militancy of the older women's organizations and the increased entry of new-wave feminists into mainstream politics. At the same time, equality directives passed in the 1970s by the European Commission of the European Community (EC) offered promising opportunities for action. This chapter traces these developments in an exploration of the establishment, organization, policy influence, and relation to women's organizations of the EOC, the leading agency in the formation of sex equality strategy in Britain.

Establishment

The political processes that led to the creation of the EOC are in keeping with dominant views of the state's role in British society. In Almond and Verba's (1963) study of political culture in five advanced industrialized countries, British political culture was associated with the notion of a deferential civic culture that sustains stable democratic institutions. British political norms and attitudes were once characterized as approximating the right combination of participation in, distance from, and respect for the state (Almond & Verba, 1963, p. 315). This view has since been replaced with the notion that although Britons have a relatively high degree of allegiance to their political system (Norton, 1994, p. 33) and have "no desire for radical changes," there is nevertheless "no great popular confidence in the political institutions" (Kavanagh, 1980, p. 170).

This predilection toward a democratic political culture has been a major factor in the slow gradual development of British democracy and the parallel emergence of the British nation-state. Unlike countries that have experienced uneven democratic development, the modern state in Great Britain has evolved alongside representative institutions without abrupt regime changes. Indeed, the alleged neutrality of the upper civil service in Great Britain is a result of this gradualism in state and society (Rose, 1984, pp. 136-137). At the same time, the highly centralized state apparatus, reinforced by parliamentary politics and an insular, relatively powerful, upper civil service, has made it difficult for disadvantaged groups such as women—groups that are not clearly aligned with the major political parties or peak occupational associations—to influence policy formation structures (Lovenduski & Randall, 1993, pp. 18-19; Meehan, 1985). The establishment and slow takeoff of the EOC is, therefore, simultaneously a product of a political culture that sees the British liberal democratic state as a legitimate agent of social change and of state-society relations that tend to close out groups outside the arena of party politics or tripartite relations between state actors and organized occupational interests.

At the end of the 1960s, the Government turned its attention to the enactment of comprehensive legislation for sex equality. This legislation was developed during a decade when there was considerable parliamentary support for action aimed at bringing about equality for disadvantaged groups. Two Race Relations Acts were adopted in the 1960s, and a third bill was passed in 1976. Moreover, the House of Commons adopted private members' bills to liberalize abortion law and to decriminalize homosexual acts for consenting adult males in 1967. The Equal Pay Act (EPA) of 1970 was also adopted during this reform period. Designed to be fully effective by 1975, it was passed with support from both government and opposition, and its few critics were those who believed it did not go far enough.

With support from the Trade Union Congress (TUC), the political parties, and numerous women's advocacy organizations, the logical EPA's corollary, the Sex Discrimination Act (SDA), was announced in 1974 and became law in 1975. More radical than its previous discussion had envisaged, the SDA nonetheless passed with little opposition. One of its innovations was provision for the EOC, an agency of implementation and enforcement that was given wide powers. The untroubled passage of the EPA and the SDA has been attributed to the climate of social reform in the 1970s, the role of pressure groups, the roles of individual women members of Parliament (MPs), and to various external factors; in particular to pressures to comply with the provisions of the 1957 Treaty of Rome for the European Economic Communities, the Equal Pay (1975) and Treatment (1976) Directives of the European Commission, and various International Labour Organization Conventions (Meehan, 1985; Randall, 1982, p. 185). Also important was experience gained in the shaping of race relations legislation and the influence of U.S. equality legislation, which had greatly impressed the Home Office officials responsible for drafting the bill (Byrne & Lovenduski, 1978).

During the campaigns for the SDA, women's groups displayed enormous activism. The first consultative document, *Equal Opportunities for Men and Women,* published by the Conservative Government in 1973, generated responses from 300 groups. The Labour electoral victories in 1974 saw a growth in both Government and group activity related to sex equality policy. The National Council for Civil Liberties, which then housed an active equality unit, held a series of conferences around the country to prepare concrete proposals. Women MPs were also active. The Equal Pay Campaign chaired by MP Thelma Cazalet-Keir had linked at least 30 women's groups and professional organizations (Bagihole, 1994, Chapter 1; Lovenduski & Randall, 1993, Chapters 5, 6).

The 1975 SDA gave individuals the right to pursue equality actions through the courts. Recognizing that a rather haphazard and piecemeal approach to implementation would result from leaving action to be taken as and when individuals chose, Parliament gave the EOC an important strategic role. Through its powers of enforcement and investigation, the EOC was enabled to design a coherent strategy for the advancement of sex equality in employment, education, training, and access to goods, facilities, and services (Lovenduski, 1986, pp. 256-264).

Organization

The organization of the EOC was not specified in the Sex Discrimination Act nor was the relationship between the commissioners and the staff. Thus the Home Office, the EOC's parent ministry, followed normal Whitehall practices when it appointed the first 15 commissioners. Following custom, nominations for such public appointments were sought from the trade union and business peak organizations and from Government departments. Leading posts in key agencies went to nominees of the political parties. Feminists had no discernible input into these arrangements.

The Whitehall-based EOC nominations reflected party and regional divisions and the two sides of industry, represented by the TUC and the Confederation of British Industry (CBI). Both TUC and CBI delegates were tied by loyalties to their nominating organizations rather than by a commitment to the work of the EOC (Byrne & Lovenduski, 1978). The two leading places among the commissioners were taken by party political nominees, one from Labour and one from the Conservatives, people who seemed to be in the pockets of their respective party leadership. The politics of commissioner appointments, therefore, meant that most of the 15 commissioners were in favor of the status quo in industrial relations. In many matters to do with employment policy, the views of the unions and employers coincided. As the analysis of the policy influence of the Commission will show, this tripartite structure strangled the EOC. Beneath the commissioner level, the original structure was divided into operations and services sections, each of which was headed by the equivalent of a civil service principal officer. At first, however, all major decisions were taken by the commissioners, who were reluctant to delegate power (Byrne & Lovenduski, 1978).

At the time it was established, the EOC was a typical British QUANGO (Quasi Nongovernment Organization). This form of organization was favored for public agencies that needed to operate with some visible degree of independence from particular Governments. Margaret Thatcher came to power in 1979 and pledged to rid the country of its excessive number of QUANGOS. However, by 1993 they had proliferated to the number of 5,521 executive QUANGOs, one for every 10,000 people in the United Kingdom (Hall & Hall, 1994). The accountability of such organizations has never been straightforward.

By QUANGO standards, the EOC's budget has never been large. It was 1.6 million pounds (about $2.4 million) in 1979, 3.2 million pounds (about $4.8 million) in 1984, and 5.5 million pounds (about

$8.25 million) in 1993.[4] These are modest amounts for work that involves costly litigation. Originally the EOC was funded by and responsible to the Home Office and accountable to Parliament through the home secretary. John Major's first Government in 1991 moved the EOC to the Department of Employment (which is where its feminist supporters had wanted it to be located in the first place). The thread of accountability to the electorate is thus a fine one, running to the electorate via the cabinet and Parliament through a junior member of the Government. A more complex set of relations links the EOC to employers and employee organizations, to women's organizations, to sections of the European Commission, and to other branches of government. These operate variously through powers of nomination to the commission, networking by commission officials and senior staff, and the provision of expert services by the EOC to particular organizations such as firms and associations.

Formally the Government-appointed commissioners are responsible for strategy but, as in most QUANGOs, the leadership depends upon the quality of ideas generated by its staff for key policy initiatives. The EOC's early organization was hierarchical, modeled on what were, even then, rather old-fashioned ideas about how the civil service worked. This was a manifestation of the caution of senior staff, whose lack of confidence in the Government's commitment to sex equality inclined them to make haste slowly. Until the 1980s, the operational work of the EOC was organized under five functional managers responsible for legal issues, employment, goods, facilities and services, and research/policy coordination. Such factors as a lack of relevant expertise among commissioners and the inexperience of the early management teams led to notably poor administration and performance.

Vera Sacks, for instance, quotes the comments of a commissioner serving between 1978 and 1982, who reported that in those years the commissioners were continually discussing internal dissension and rarely dealing with matters of policy. Sacks (1986) recounts the commissioners' detailed involvement with day-to-day decisions, such as the consideration of expenditure requests from its various sections, concluding that "they [the commissioners] appear therefore to be supervising very closely rather than delegating within an agreed policy framework" (p. 563). The result was a lack of coherence and direction, evident from the absence of overall policy statements against which to measure progress. After 1988, the organization was streamlined into sections on law enforcement, development, public affairs, and organization. These changes were designed to enable strategic planning.

Inevitably the EOC experienced tensions in its relationship to feminism similar to those applying to women's policy offices in other countries and political contexts. As a government agency, it could never be organizationally congruent with feminist ideas. Although there is now evidence of considerable teamwork and good working relationships among the staff, the continuing civil service basis of their employment is antithetical to the avoidance of hierarchy, and it does little to facilitate the collectivist spirit and grass-roots orientation favored by many feminists. In any case, such an orientation would probably take the EOC well beyond mainstream employment issues.

The experience of local authority women's committees and equality units is instructive here. A recurring theme of interviews Vicky Randall and I conducted with women's officers and equality officers in British local authorities at the end of the 1980s was an emphasis on issues other than employment. True, they spoke of child care provision of all kinds, but they were particularly concerned about issues such as housing and male violence against women. This trend away from a focus on equality in employment appeared to grow over time in the job; that is, local consultation and outreach work gave officers a view of women's lives that emphasized concerns other than employment. Interestingly, these local authorities were often expressly organized along feminist antihierarchical principles, but with results that were far from positive. Our scrutiny of their impact indicated that the lack of hierarchy and the failure to respect conventions about seniority and experience made it extremely difficult for such officers to manage effectively the politics of the local authority policymaking structures (Lovenduski & Randall, 1993, Chapters 5, 6). Thus, the local authority initiatives illustrate possible disadvantages to organizing equality agency work according to feminist collectivist or nonhierarchical principles.

Policy Activities and Influence

The early work of the EOC proved disappointing to many observers. Held back by its tripartite structure of labor, management, and traditional state representatives, the agency failed to generate grass-roots support networks. In the 1970s, with organized labor's influence in government, tripartism was a particular impediment. One result of this was that the Commission was reluctant to use its wider powers of law enforcement. To feminists, this was a manifestation of the kind of establishment politics that had always excluded women from decision making. Their objections appeared to be vindicated as the first networks to emerge were elite-oriented, with almost no base in grass-roots women's activities. Under the leadership of Labour's Betty Lockwood and later Baroness Platt (Conservative), the EOC sought to establish and maintain good contacts with government agencies and ministries. Undoubtedly this was done in the knowledge that executive support was and is essential if a policy is to be effective in Britain, yet it is clear that during the 1970s the cabinet gave little priority to equal opportunities.

This shift in priority was partly due to James Callaghan's succession to the leadership of the Labour party. Under Prime Minister Callaghan, Barbara Castle, employment secretary and a vocal advocate of women's rights at work, was forced to resign. However, it is not clear that the Government had ever wanted the EOC to be a real political force. The placement of its headquarters in Manchester was an early signal that it would not be taken seriously. The Government could more easily ignore an institution placed 200 miles away. The EOC did little to help itself overcome these initial political disadvantages. For example, it was particularly constrained by the bureaucratic style it adopted. This style, which in Britain encourages the neutrality of officials, made a setting in which commissioners jealously guarded their policymaking prerogatives. Delegation to staff was limited, and infrequent Commission meetings made the decision process a slow and laborious one. Press ridicule alarmed commissioners and some of the EOC's most senior officials, who sought to inhibit the initiatives of its salaried staff and to distance themselves from involvement with feminist and women's organizations.

Thus, for political, institutional, and personnel reasons, it was difficult for new-wave feminists—who had sought to establish a movement outside of established trade unions, political parties, and women's groups in the 1970s—to become established in equality policymaking networks dominated by the EOC. The only notable exception to this pattern was the influence of the research commissioned by

Christine Jackson, the EOC's first research officer. Under her guidance, the ideas of feminists active at the grass-roots level found their way into reports and documents that would later be taken up by EOC staff. Nevertheless, by the end of the 1970s, Britain's autonomous feminist movement had written off the EOC, leaving the frustrating task of influencing its policies to older women's groups and women's caucuses in different sections of the labor movement and in the professions.

As a result of the problems of the EOC in these early years, the feminist movement did not become integrated into equal opportunities policy networks until the appearance of the local women's committees during the 1980s. By this time, a major shift had occurred that pushed the EOC to seek a role in the emerging equal opportunities movement. Since the mid-1970s, women's groups and race-based groups had been promoting equal opportunities by developing programs, pressuring government, and so on. This network emerged largely outside of the EOC's orbit. By the end of the 1980s, however, as the early promise of a municipal equality strategy faded, the EOC was playing a central role in an equality movement that attracted a substantial number of newer feminist organizations. There were many reasons for the change, including the accumulation of expertise, skill, and ability by Commission staff, the appointment of commissioners with women's movement experience and strong feminist commitments, and a growing ability to use the rules of the political game.

Moreover, the equality legislation was variously amended and strengthened by EC law, which compelled member states to legislate for sex equality in accordance with five directives on equal pay and treatment. Resources were made available to those charged with the promotion of sex equality in public and private institutions and organizations, and, by and large, those resources were used. EOC officials believed the government wanted them to do the job they had been appointed to do, and they behaved accordingly. Even during the years of Margaret Thatcher's Government (1979 to 1990) when the political rhetoric of the governing party stressed rolling back the state, cultivating personal autonomy, and deregulating the labor market, the EOC was able to develop its work; its budget was maintained, and its role changed from being mainly an advice and information agency to that of an active legal protagonist.

Thus, at the height of Thatcherism, the law on equality was greatly strengthened by amendments and court decisions. These developments were the effect of four changes in the EOC. First, the political barriers to its work, erected by the trade union movement, disintegrated as trade union power collapsed in the face of sustained Thatcher Government assault. Second, personnel changes and developments in the skills of senior agency staff led to more effective strategic planning and action. Third, the law was greatly strengthened by amendments and court decisions. Finally, the EOC became more feminist. The second and third of these were, of course, closely related. Given that policy in the agency is made by the commissioners in conjunction with senior staff, opportunities were spotted and cases were selected by staff in the legal department who wanted to make use of the courts. Gradually, the Commission was persuaded that using the law and the courts would be faster and more effective in bringing change than chipping away at Government opinion. An important breakthrough after 1987 was the practice of judicial review, whereby the Commission was able to sue the Government itself for breaches in equality procedures.

A key element of the EOC strategy was making use of the equality policies devised by the EC. Indeed, EOC participation in European equality networks served to accelerate the implementation of sex equality objectives in a number of European Commission initiatives. It is necessary to understand the activism of the EOC in this respect. While the EC brought judicial proceedings against the United Kingdom to correct defects and exclusions in domestic legislation, the EOC used its legal resources to support a series of cases brought to the European Court of Justice that clarified the rights conferred by European law. Changes from both sources became part of the 1983 Equal Value (Amendment) Regulations and of the Sex Discrimination Act 1986, which removed many of the loopholes from the original legislation and established the principle of pay parity whereby men's and women's different work was judged according to criteria of comparable value (Kahn, 1992).

Perhaps the most striking development was the growing feminism of the EOC. Some of this was inevitable, the result of work among women who sought to achieve feminist goals. And although the vocabulary of feminism continued to be controversial, there was widespread support for equal pay and equal opportunities for women and men throughout the 1980s.[5] Personnel changes were also important. Joanna Foster was appointed to lead the EOC in 1988, becoming the first chair with a background in efforts to improve women's employment rights and opportunities. Within a very short period of time, Valerie Amos was appointed as chief executive, responsible for the administrative leadership of the agency. Amos is a Black feminist whose previous employment experience was women's rights work for a London local authority. Supported by Foster, she emphasized the importance of strategic thinking and of law enforcement roles of the agency, confirming and encouraging much of the philosophy of the legal section.

The changes soon became apparent to the new-wave feminist activists involved with women's issues at the grass-roots level. Women seeking help and resources for feminist causes found that support from the EOC was much easier to get and that, from their perspective, the leadership of the EOC had greatly improved. At the same time, women's movement activists were becoming much more inclined to deal with state organizations and to attempt to work with and in established political institutions. During the 1970s, both the separatism and determined structurelessness of the women's liberation movement inhibited such networking, but the 1980s were characterized by a sustained feminist presence in political parties, trade unions, and professional associations as well as a growing feminism among members of traditional women's organizations, party sections, and women's caucuses of all kinds. The EOC was part of these changes.

Dismissed by feminists as an expensive and disappointing irrelevance at the beginning of the 1980s, the EOC was winning many friends a decade later with its more aggressive stance. Under Foster and Amos, it became well-networked nationally, not only with the women's movement but also with other equality agencies, such as the Commission for Racial Equality, the NIEOC, the Fair Employment Commission, and the TUC Women's Unit. Internationally it played a leading role in the European Commission Advisory Committee on Equal Opportunities for Women and Men.

The EOC document, *From Policy to Practice: An Equal Opportunities Strategy for the 1990s*, published in 1988, signified a turning point in the agency's functioning. The report set out a clear set of objectives, expressed as three themes and five "overall objectives" divided into 17 specific objectives. The overall goals were the following:

1. To enable men and women to be effective and responsible employees and effective and responsible family members
2. To remove barriers that prevent women from participating in the full range of training opportunities
3. To reduce the difference between men's and women's earnings
4. To increase fiscal and pensions equality and remove disincentives to employment
5. To develop awareness and acceptance at policymaking and at grass-roots levels of the idea that equal opportunities affects all aspects of men's and women's working and nonworking lives

The document aimed at the mainstreaming of sex equality policy and set out objectives against which progress could be monitored and measured.

Although strategic thinking about litigation was a long time in coming, there is some evidence to suggest that successive Conservative Governments of the 1980s wanted more effective action from the Commission. In May 1986, Margaret Thatcher established a Ministerial Group on Women's Issues to provide a coordinated examination of policy issues of special concern to women, and Joanna Foster's appointment as chair of the EOC in 1988 indicated the Government wanted more from the agency. What they got, as we have seen, was an organization prepared to take on the Government itself, to use its powers as effectively as the law allowed, and to extend that law as far as it could be stretched. In other words the EOC may have become rather too effective for the Government's taste.

After 1988, the EOC went from strength to strength. But in the early 1990s, under Conservative Prime Minister John Major, the EOC may once again have been at cross-purposes with Government aspirations. Until 1993, the position of chair was full-time. Then, Major appointed Kamlesh Bahl to be the EOC's first part-time chair. This coincided with the launch of Opportunity 2000, a voluntary association of businesses pledged to support sex equality in employment. Established with enthusiastic Government support and led by a prominent Tory (Conservative), Lady Elspeth Howe, who was the first deputy chair of the EOC, Opportunity 2000 has been well-publicized since its launch in 1992. Its work overlaps with the EOC's; seen in conjunction with the appointment of a part-time EOC chair, this may indicate that the Conservatives would like a more conservative approach to equal opportunities policy.

It is difficult to assess the outcomes of the EOC's work because so many factors affect the progress of equality between the sexes. Scrutiny of the EOC's operations during the 1990s indicates that it has developed its powers only in areas directly related to employment. But this work on employment law and practice has been quite effective. Of the specific objectives outlined in the 1988 strategy document, those to do with employment show the most progress. Important legal precedents have been won on pay, pensions, taxation, and social security, the direct result of EOC legal action. The EOC became a key actor in the equal opportunities movement, has contributed to the networking of organized women, and has assisted feminist research through funding.

Nonetheless, women's pay stubbornly continues to be about three quarters of men's, child care provision continues to be inadequate, and women continue to represent the majority of Britons who live in poverty. Rates of pay for single parents, 90% of whom are mothers, dropped during the 1980s, and their levels of poverty grew. Occupational segregation, the main source of pay inequalities, remains pronounced. The relationship between work and family life has been little affected by EOC action, and the multidimensional sources of gender inequalities provide a strong rationale for the establishment of a Ministry for Women.

The EOC and Women's Organizations

A well-established universe of women's organizations exists in Britain. In 1964, 3 million women were reported to be members of 120 national organizations. In 1972, an official report listed over 200 organizations wholly for women or with women's branches (Meehan, 1985, p. 54). In 1994, the Women's National Commission's Directory of UK Women's Organizations listed over 240 entries. Many of these have been active in the promotion of sex equality and were engaged in the establishment of the EOC, lobbying for passage of the Sex Discrimination Act. Thus, the initial exclusion of British women's organizations and feminist groups from the work of EOC policymaking is astonishing. Indeed, when the original commissioners were appointed, none had backgrounds in work for women's rights, and only one of the original 15, Caroline Woodruffe from the Brook Advisory Centres, had a professional interest in women. Women's-interest organizations expressed preferences for appointments of individuals knowledgeable about women's employment and with feminist sympathies, but to little effect.

For many years the main connection between the EOC and organized communities of women was the receipt of grants. Even in this area, commissioners were reluctant to establish contact with the overtly feminist groups of the women's liberation movement. As a result, women's organizations developed policies in isolation from the EOC, lobbied government directly about their dissatisfaction with the EOC, and sought equal opportunities policy changes directly from Government after the EOC was established. Women in the Media, the Equal Pay and Opportunities Campaign, the Women's Farm and Garden Association, and the Fawcett Society all recommended wide-ranging improvements in the enforcement of the acts. On November 27, 1980, a day of action was held, organized by Women in the Media and the Fawcett Society and attended by 67 other groups. Its agenda was sent to the prime minister. Relations improved during the 1980s, but for many years British feminists were engaged only as clients, as academic experts on employment, or as members in accepted pressure groups, such as the TUC and the CBI.

One important effect of years of exclusion was to convince feminists they were not welcome in national equality policy communities. This served to reinforce new-wave feminist suspicion of established politics. The British second wave of feminism emerged from the political subculture of the 1960s Left, which had a strong syndicalist current. Wary of legislative strategies and suspicious of the state, its attitudes were undoubtedly important in feminist decisions to keep their distance from the EOC. One effect of this was that discussion of equal opportunities legislation and strategy found very little place in the theoretical literature of second-wave feminists, despite an enormous empirical concern with such issues in the research of the women's studies movement. To this day, many feminists regard the legislation as useless and its reform as a waste of valuable energy.

Arguably the appearance of local authority women's committees during the 1980s was partly a product of feminist hostility to the EOC. Set up as a response to grass-roots feminist activism, these committees implemented equal employment policies in local public sectors where many women were employed. But they also grappled with the other areas of oppression in women's lives, treating issues of safety in the home and on the streets, child care, health care provision, and so on. They networked nationally both as organizations and around particular issue areas and formed a policy community that was significantly more feminist than the EOC. Eventually the EOC became part of that policy community (Lovenduski & Randall, 1993, Chapters 5, 6).

Conclusion

To be sure, British Governments have been ambivalent about sex equality policy. Wide-ranging laws have been promulgated, but they proved too complicated to use properly. A powerful agency was established but located in Manchester where it would be remote from day-to-day government. The original actors in the politics of equal opportunities were the traditional political actors: parties, unions, employers organizations (with personnel officers playing a special role), large women's organizations, and women's sections in established organizations and institutions. Needless to say opponents of sex equality policy among unions and employers, as well as in the political parties, took the original caution and muddle of the EOC to be a signal they could ignore the spirit, if not the letter, of sex equality law. That early failure on the part of the EOC proved difficult to overcome.

Nevertheless, relations have altered over the years. For example, the trade union movement became more interested in equal opportunities policies as the unions lost their once-privileged position in British political life and were required to seek new alliances and new constituencies. The EOC has been instrumental in helping the TUC to develop more women-friendly collective bargaining practices. There has been a similar shift in the politics of the Labour party. The party's strategic thinking, however, generated proposals for a rather different form of women's policy machinery. In the General Election campaigns of 1987 and 1992, Labour pledged to establish a Ministry for Women at the cabinet level. Partly inspired by the Roudy Ministry in France, this ministry will, it is promised, place initiatives on women's rights at the heart of Government and ensure powerful political support for sex equality measures.

Labour is less clear about what it will do with the EOC. One plan is to amalgamate it with the Commission for Racial Equality; another proposal is to enhance its legal functions, but move its other activities into the relevant government departments under the supervision of the proposed new Ministry. More recent documents and pronouncements simply call for it to be strengthened. It has, of course, been the Conservatives who have had the most direct impact on the work of the EOC. Although established during a Labour administration, virtually the whole of the EOC's existence has been under Conservative Governments, hence its leadership has been mainly Conservative appointees. Conservative feminism, such as it is, is of an individualistic kind. The values of self-reliance take precedence over those of collectivist or state action. Under such circumstances the characteristics and agendas of individual EOC chairs have been important.

In conclusion, the tensions and contradictions of the EOC are undoubtedly familiar to students of women's policy machinery and of public administration. Agencies to promote equality are, like all organizations, affected by their political environments. The EOC was established with unprecedented legal powers but faced an immediate change of government and has often been insecure about its continuation, whether because of changing ideas about the implementation of sex equality policies, because of public disaffection with QUANGOs, or because of ideological opposition to state intervention. It is an agency that is formally independent of the Government, but it was established by a Government that determines its funding. It experiences inevitable difficulties in deciding whether it should carry out Government policy, reflect changing ideas about equality, or respond to a constituency of mobilized women irrespective of Government views. The British EOC shares this position not only with equality agencies elsewhere, but also with other British QUANGOS. As Christopher Hood (1982) has written:

> Agencies in this position walk a political tightrope in attempting to avoid, on the one hand, the role of mere spokesman and guardian of these collective interests and, on the other hand, the role of a feeble supervisor with no real standing in the political system. (p. 64, cited in Sacks, 1986)

The agency will inevitably be torn between its formal accountability, its understanding of the imperatives of Government, the traditions of administration, and the many feminisms that are located in Britain. The movement of the EOC from a disregard for feminist concerns to a conditional regard is likely to be about as far as it can reasonably be expected to go.

Notes

1. Opposition political parties in Great Britain compose a shadow cabinet from their members of Parliament, which will serve as the new Government should their party win a majority of seats in parliamentary elections.

2. In Great Britain, the cabinet consists of the top 20 or so ministers, usually the heads of the most important departments, who meet collectively to make major policy decisions. Below these ministerial positions are an additional 80 to 85 ministerial posts, referred to as junior ministers, attached to departments and working as parliamentary whips. In 1993, the Conservative Government had 107 members, of which 22 were in the cabinet (Norton, 1994, pp. 184-192). The Labour party's Shadow Ministry for Women is placed at the cabinet level.

3. Unlike the United States, with its weak and fragmented parties, Great Britain has the two major political parties that wield a great deal of influence over elected and appointed officials. Indeed, the dynamics of a first-past-the-post electoral system that produces the stable two-party system, of a parliamentary form of government, and of a unitary distribution of territorial power all underpin the high degree of influence the governing party wields in all spheres of the policy formation process and the degree to which public policy debates are shaped by party politics. The highly adversarial relationship between the Labour and Conservative parties has kept bipartisan efforts to develop public policy to a minimum. For more on political party strength in Great Britain, see Norton (1994, Chapter 6).

4. The conversion to dollars is based on $1.50 to a pound.

5. British Social Attitudes Cumulative Sourcebook. (1992). Tables N2-6 and N2-28. Aldershot: Gower.

8

Ireland's Policy Machinery

The Ministry of State for Women's Affairs
and Joint Oireachtas Committees for Women's Rights

Evelyn Mahon

Unlike other countries, Ireland has never experienced a challenge to its Catholic hegemony from an economic demand for women in paid labor. As a consequence, Irish feminists are acutely aware of a patriarchal state encroaching on women's daily lives. The Irish constitution's endorsement of Catholicism's values and its definition of women's place as being in the home have made reproductive rights and family law difficult. At the same time, Ireland's membership in the European Community (EC) since 1973, together with the activities of the women's movement, have introduced some positive changes for women. Irish feminists, by challenging the public-private division of the patriarchal state, have successfully pushed for new laws that address domestic violence and marital rape. Liberal feminists in particular have organized to reform laws that discriminate against women.

For many feminist advocates, the presence of women's policy machinery has been an important part of the campaign for women's improved status. The Employment Equality Act created the Employment Equality Agency in 1977. A second structure for women, the

Ministry of State for Women's Affairs (MSWA), was established in 1982 by the Fine Gael/Labour Coalition government. The Joint Oireachtas Committee on Women's Rights (JOCWR), a permanent interparliamentary committee, in 1983 became the third state agency for women. This chapter has two sections, each describing the establishment, organization and activities, role in policy process, and relation to women's organizations of the two women's policy structures. The first section will focus on the MSWA (1982-1987), and the next section will examine in more detail the first three JOCWRs, up to 1993.

The Ministry of State for Women's Affairs

ESTABLISHMENT

The establishment of women's policy structures in the executive and legislative branches must first be situated within the context of the design of the Irish parliamentary system and the particularly strong influence of Catholic church doctrine in constitutional matters.[1] State procedures in Ireland were codified in the 1937 constitution, which can be modified only through national referendum. The original constitution used Catholic principles as guidelines for the country's institutions and social policies, appointing the Catholic church "as the guardian of the Faith professed by the Great majority of its citizens."[2] Article 41 declares that

> the State [defined as the cabinet and prime minister or Government, the legislature, and the judiciary] recognizes the Family as the natural primary and fundamental unit group of Society, and as a moral institution possessing inalienable and imprescriptible rights antecedent and superior to all positive law. (Chubb, 1992, p. 47)

The constitution also guarantees to protect marriage and so forbids divorce. Article 41.2 recognizes that "the primary and natural educator of the child is the family." Article 41 specifically mentions women:

> In particular, the State recognizes that by her life within the home, woman gives to the State a support without which the common good

cannot be achieved. The State shall, therefore, endeavor to ensure that mothers shall not be obliged by economic necessity to engage in labour to the neglect of the duties in the home.

These articles have placed important restrictions on women's policy. Until Ireland became a member of the EC in 1973, there was a marriage law that prohibited the employment of married women in the civil service, banks, and trade unions (Mahon, 1987). Yet, the constitutionally defined position of women in the home has never resulted in positive property or financial gains for them. When it comes to claiming family home ownership, for example, nonearning wives are disadvantaged in comparison to women in the paid labor force. Judicial interpretation of the constitution has brought about some improvement in women's rights, such as the right to import contraceptives for personal use (Mahon, 1987). At the same time, the Supreme Court has declared other legislation expected to advance women's status, such as the Matrimonial Properties Act, to be unconstitutional. In November 1982 Fine Gael and the Labour party together won the majority of seats in the Dail.[3] The two parties combined to form a coalition government, which lasted until 1987. Out of 166 members of the Dail, the lower house of parliament, 14 women (9.2%) were elected in the November 1987 elections, including liberal feminist activists such as Nuala Fennell. Recognizing the political importance of women, the Fine Gael Taoiseach, Prime Minister Garrett Fitzgerald, established the Ministry of State for Women's Affairs (MSWA) and named Fennell as minister. Later she was given responsibility for Family and Law Reform in the Department of Justice.

ORGANIZATION

There were high expectations for the Ministry on the part of liberal feminists. However, as a ministry of state, the MSWA was a junior ministry in the department of the Taoiseach with a very small staff and budget.[4] As a result, Minister Fennell's role was circumscribed by the jurisdiction of other, more senior ministries. Some departments did send policy proposals for Fennell's perusal, but this depended on their interest in women's affairs. Fennell found that her freedom as minister was also curtailed by senior members of her party. As she asserted in an interview, Fine Gael leadership prevented her from commenting on issues as a feminist, expecting her to follow the party line.

Although the potential scope of the MSWA was quite broad, involving all aspects of women's lives, Fennell's formal charge was narrow, and other departments were formally involved with many different women's policy issues. For instance, equal employment policy was the responsibility of the Department of Labour, the abortion issue was part of a national referendum debate (thereby outside of the cabinet's control), contraception was the closely guarded concern of the Ministry for Health, rape reform was in the domain of the Ministry for Justice, and a parliamentary committee had been set up to consider marriage breakdown. The MSWA was left with family law policy and whatever other areas the minister could pursue without impinging on the briefs of other ministers. Fennell's own interest in family law reform also underpinned the main focus of the MSWA.[5]

The 1987 elections produced a Dail with a conservative majority, led by Fianna Fail, and a specific women's affairs ministry was eliminated from the new cabinet. Fianna Fail had never favored a segregationist approach to women's policy. Instead, the prime minister appointed Marie Geoghegan Quinn, chair of the Joint Oireachtas Committee of Women's Rights from 1983 to 1987, as minister of state for European community affairs with special responsibility for women's affairs.

POLICY ACTIVITIES

Despite considerable limitations, the MSWA (1985) prepared a baseline report on the position of Irish women: published in 1985, *Irish Women: Agenda for Practical Action*. This became Ireland's national report for the UN Decade for Women and the Nairobi conference the same year. In 1987, the Ministry declared the following achievements:

The provision of family planning services, including the ability of adults to freely purchase nonmedical contraceptives

The Status of Children Act, which eliminated discrimination between marital and nonmarital children

The 1986 Domicile and Recognition of Foreign Divorces Act, which removed the requirement that a married woman had to take the domicile of her husband

The Irish Nationality and Citizenship Act, which ended the differentiation between men and women with regard to the acquisition of Irish citizenship by foreign spouses

Higher social welfare benefits for married women, in compliance with the EC Directive on equal treatment of men and women[6]

In addition to these legal changes, there were a number of broader policies instituted while the MSWA was in existence. A new pilot scheme on family mediation was begun. The civil service introduced job sharing, career breaks, and an equal opportunities policy. The Government issued a statement on positive action, and the Gardai (police) and the Prison Service were no longer exempted from the provisions of the Employment Equality Act. The Government launched a program called Action in Education, 1984-1987, to eliminate all aspects of sexism in education. More specifically, the MSWA introduced a special award scheme for mature female students, promoted the extension of cancer screening facilities for women, and facilitated the opening of a sexual assault treatment center and a refuge for battered wives in Dublin. The MSWA also implemented a Woman into Enterprise scheme and funded research on the topic. The Government assisted by giving a special allocation to the Women in Industry campaign in 1986.

The Ministry also established the Interdepartmental Working Party on Women's Affairs and Family Law reform, which had the task of identifying discrimination against women and initiating measures to remove the causes of the noted inequities. The publication of this group's report in 1985 gave visibility to these issues, helping to stimulate subsequent legal changes. This review of women's policy issues during the 1980s demonstrates that although many commentators were dismissive of the Ministry's achievements, it actually was involved with a large number of initiatives (Fitzgerald, 1991).

RELATION TO WOMEN'S
ORGANIZATIONS AND MOVEMENTS

The constitutional and political limits placed on the MSWA made working with the Ministry a problem for feminist groups and women's advocacy organizations. This was so despite small grants the Ministry made available to women's organizations.[7] The women's movement in Ireland in the 1970s and 1980s was divided into two groups: a liberal reform current and a socialist radical current. Under Nuala Fennell's leadership, the liberal reformists thought that the best way to improve women's position was to bring about legal reforms, following the pattern of the National Organization for Women in the United States. These women are best characterized as a woman's rights group in a liberal tradition. The second current consisted of independent action groups, popularly called women's liberation groups, which sought to mobilize public opinion but did not seek to work with state actors. Many evolved into pressure groups, such as Irish Women United, Contraception Action Campaign, and Women's Right to Choose Group (Mahon, 1987).

If one accepts the definition of feminism broadly as "all ideologies, activities, and policies whose goal it is to remove discrimination against women and to break down male domination of society" (Lovenduski & Randall, 1993, p. 2), then both groups are feminist. They did, however, adopt very different strategies of action in relation to the state. The liberal feminists looked upon the state as a key player in improving women's condition through legal changes (Mahon, 1987). The liberation groups, on the contrary, have tended to view any attempt to work with the state as co-optation.

It is no surprise, then, that the more radical wing viewed Minister Fennell as revisionist and politically coopted. As a result, radical feminist groups refused to work with her or the MSWA. This suspicion was not just limited to radical feminists. The restrictions placed on her office and her responsibilities to her political party alienated her even further from popular feminist support. Feminists from both parts of the movement criticized Fennell for not taking a position on contraception and divorce reform. For example, Fennell noted in an interview that the Council for the Status of Women, a nongovernmental organization (NGO) set up to monitor equal pay policy, was also very critical of her, refusing to work with the Ministry. Perhaps the group felt that the establishment of the MSWA would mean that they would no longer receive subsidies from the Taoiseach's Office. Fennell also received negative criticism from women journalists.

The Joint Oireachtas Committees
on Women's Rights

ESTABLISHMENT

Since 1983, there have been four Joint Oireachtas Committees on Women's Rights (JOCWR). The following analysis will focus on the establishment, organization, and activities of the first three JOCWRs, until 1992. But first, it is important to discuss the role of interparliamentary committees in general policy development in Ireland. Like the traditional Westminster parliamentary model it emulated, Ireland's parliament had never developed a strong committee system to shape and process government policy. Irish cabinets and civil servants have resisted the emergence of an authoritative parliamentary committee structure (Chubb, 1992, p. 202). Until the 1980s, parliament or Oireachtas only had a few select committees, and these were not allowed to question government policy (Gallagher, 1993, p. 139). Moreover, committee reports are generally not available to the general public, and few are ever debated in the Dail. Indeed, unless the chairperson can develop a media profile, many feel that committee work earns politicians few benefits.

Oireachtas Committees have no permanent existence and have to be reconstituted at the beginning of each new parliament (Gallagher, 1993, p. 140). Because the majority of Dail members have a good chance of being in the cabinet, Teachtái Dálas (TDs; members of parliament) are reluctant to use the committees to inquire into and criticize Government affairs. TDs' limited time and resources further reduce the committees' power to scrutinize Government. To criticize aspects of Government policy, opposition party TDs are more likely to speak directly in Dail sessions, rather than in committees, as the Dail provides immediate and more widespread publicity. Yet, committee work has increased the expertise of the backbenchers. Those who subsequently become ministers are often influenced by the ideas and issues they heard during committee sessions. Thus, the Oireachtas Women's Rights Committee can be seen as a training ground for women's policy experts in government.

Interest groups that are active on a national level can make submissions to appropriate joint committees or relevant departments or make a prebudget submission to the Government. When such submissions are made on a topic under committee review, a Joint Committee examines the group's evidence and publishes its own report and recommendations. Issues are discussed between members of the committee and the relevant ministers. This does not take an adversarial form; it constitutes an exchange of ideas. Through its research, the committee is able to pinpoint grievances not often accessible to ministers or TDs. As part of an interparty Government committee report, the submissions, as interpreted by the committee, provide legitimacy to the demands of feminist and other groups.

Researchers on Oireachtas committees are divided over their effectiveness. Some have suggested that the scope of committees has been too large and their members too busy to be effective (O'Halpin, 1986). Others argue that the committees improve executive accountability (Zimmerman, 1988) with prior TD committee membership strengthening and informing their subsequent activities as ministers (Arkins, 1988). Nonetheless, these interparliamentary committees continue to have a limited role in public policy formation.

The first JOCWR was established on July 7, 1983, under the Fine Gael/Labour Government. Its creation was unaffected by external influences from either the UN or the EC. Fine Gael, unlike Fianna Fail, favored reform of the Dail, as well as the introduction and use of special committees. When Fianna Fail returned to power in 1987, therefore, only three of those committees were reconstituted, including the JOCWR.

ORGANIZATION

The JOCWR is an all-party committee. It elects its own chair, a member of the opposition, who to date has always been a woman. Like all parliamentary committees, the JOCWR is disbanded before each Dail election. Each committee has new members, a different approach, and a set of interests reflecting the new composition of the Dail. After the dissolution of the Dail in 1992, a Ministry of Equality and Law Reform (MELR) was established. As a result, it appeared that the JOCWR might not be reconvened. Several women TDs, however, argued for its retention, and it has continued to operate with the same brief.

The JOCWR was initially composed of 11 members of the Dail and 6 members of the Senate. The Joint Committee has had an illustrious membership, with many of its early members subsequently becoming ministers. The first Committee was chaired by the present Minister for Justice, Maire Geoghegan Quinn. It also included C. J. Haughey, who became Taoiseach; Labour Senator M.D. Higgins, now Minister for Arts and Culture; and Mary O'Rourke who later recommended that education be the first topic addressed. The first Committee was charged with the following three tasks (Dail Debates, July 7, 1983, p. 2510):

1. Examine or propose legislative measures that would materially affect the interests of women
2. Consider the means by which any areas of discrimination against women can be eliminated and by which obstacles to their full participation in the political, social, and economic life of the community can be removed
3. Consider specific economic and social disadvantages applying to women in the home, bearing in mind the special nature of their contribution to the community, to recommend effective policy and administrative changes to help eliminate these disadvantages and report to the Houses of the Oireachtas thereon

It was also given powers to send for people, papers, and records, and it could engage the services of specialist consultants (subject to the approval of the Department of Public Service). The committee has a small budget for research. A clerk and a clerk typist are appointed to each Committee. The overall style of chairing is inclusive and accommodating rather than adversarial. Frequency of attendance and contributions at Committee meetings have varied among members, with a core of activists inside each different JOCWR. Until 1988, the verbatim minutes of the meetings were recorded officially.

Early meetings of the JOCWR were devoted to a discussion of priorities. The Committee's usual approach was to investigate issues and formally publish its reports. Any person who felt aggrieved could write to the Committee, bringing any injustice to their attention. The chair could then decide to investigate the matter further or to invite a more formal delegation to discuss the issue with the Committee. On rape legislation, the JOCWR asked for submissions from the Rape Crisis Centre, the Law Society, and the chief superintendent of the police.

Since its inception, discussions of the JOCWR have tended to pursue a liberal feminist approach to rights and equal treatment in all areas, consistent with the logic of Article 41, which affords similar rights to "women in the home."[8] Although the overall philosophy of the four Committees could be characterized as liberal feminist, not all of their members would describe themselves in these terms. Some initiated special privileges for mothers whereas others opposed attacks on the rights of mothers to paid employment.

Because the Committees are all-party committees, they have avoided topics that might divide members along party lines. Major issues, such as abortion-related referenda and the divorce referendum, were never discussed by any JOCWR. In 1983, a Joint Committee on Marital Breakdown was initiated, thus giving the JOCWR a valid reason to avoid a contentious discussion on divorce. Chairs of the Committees sought a consensus on issues they addressed; this goal might have proved impossible with these difficult reform issues.

POLICY ACTIVITIES

The first Committee laid out a specific agenda and published four major reports on the following topics: education (1984); social welfare (1985); the portrayal of women in the media (1986); and sexual violence (1987). The second and third Committees adopted a number of focal issues on which they commissioned research.[9] The second published a series of reports on changing attitudes of women in Ireland (researched by M. Fine Davis). The third committee published a report on motherhood, work, and equal opportunities, based on research on equal opportunities in the Irish civil service (Mahon, 1991), and a report entitled "Gender Equality in Education in the Republic of Ireland (1984-1991)," researched by J. Gleeson. These reports were based on work conducted by professional researchers, as well as oral and written submissions from appropriate groups. For instance, during the Committee's first-year examination of education, the following individuals made submissions: Sylvia Meehan, chairperson of the

Employment Equality Agency; The Council for the Status of Women, AIM Group; Conference of Major Religious Superiors; Irish Federation of University Teachers; and Teachers Union of Ireland.

The format of the JOCWR's reports is similar. Each gives a summary of the overall findings of the Committee on the topic and issues a series of recommendations based on them. The published reports are then forwarded to Government departments and to all members of the Dail and Senate. Their publication usually attracted considerable media attention, helping to disseminate their ideas. None of the reports of the Oireachtas Committee, however, have been debated or discussed in the Dail.

The actual effects of the JOCWR reports are difficult to assess. If the explicit criterion for determining the Committee's influence is the introduction of new legislation or new policies in Government departments based on report recommendations, then it is impossible to argue that the Committee was solely responsible for legal changes in these areas. The JOCWR's work, however, did serve as a catalyst by legitimating the demands for policy changes among Government members. The following is an examination of three areas of committee activity—education, social welfare, and sexual violence.

Education

The first JOCWR identified education as a priority. Members agreed that many of the inequalities between the sexes were rooted in the educational system. They addressed four aspects of education: coeducation, curriculum reform, educational facilities for female students, and the position of women teachers. The key recommendations of their report included the following:

All new schools should be coeducational.[10]
School curricula should be widened to facilitate greater career choices for
    girls.
Teacher education should include all aspects of equality.
Sexism should be eliminated in the preparation of students for the teaching
    profession.
Sex education should be introduced in both primary and secondary
    schools.

On the subject of coeducation, the Committee opted for only a gradual change, with the retention of the right of parental choice.

To the Committee, the Department of Education did not appear to have any specific means for implementing a policy of coeducation, were one established. Nonetheless, it recommended that the department harness the goodwill of the Conference of Major Religious Superiors, who favored involvement in coeducation, when a new school was to be built or two schools amalgamated. In terms of curriculum reform, the JOCWR argued that girls and boys should be encouraged to take up nontraditional subjects. Greater flexibility and cooperation between management and teachers to allow for the interchange of pupils and staff would promote this goal. The Committee also advocated that sex education be a part of a life skills course in primary and secondary schools.

The Committee's references to the Ministry for Education, rather than being stridently negative, noted positive developments. It pointed out that the minister for education, when introducing the Program for Action in Education 1984-1987 in the Dail, encouraged schools to offer subjects equally to both sexes. Although welcoming such encouragement, however, the members of the JOCWR felt that words alone would not be sufficient to achieve equality; extra resources might also be required. The JOCWR went on to remark that the minister for education said that assistance would be available from the department for schools to plan sex education programs. They also praised the Program for Action in Education, introduced in 1984, which set the elimination of sexism and sex stereotyping as a priority and provided appropriate guidelines to publishers of school textbooks.

With respect to job opportunity, the Committee drew attention to the very low participation rate of women in apprenticeship training programs. Considering change in attitudes to be vital, they urged the Departments of Labour and Education to ensure that adequate training schemes were available to women. The obstacles to adult education for women, including costs and lack of day care and suitable classroom accommodation, were also put on the agenda. The Committee raised the issue of the treatment of married women at interviews for promotion and the poor representation of women in principal positions. They recommended that the Department of Education issue guidelines for interviews to prevent discriminatory and sexist questioning at interview boards. The Committee also argued in the report that a 50% representation of women on interview boards was desirable. In the interest of developing a consensus on this particular issue, the JOCWR only recommended increased representation of women, as opposed to male/female parity.

The Second Report of the Third Joint Committee on Women's Rights (on the subject of education) reviewed developments since the publication of the 1984 report. They found that the Department of Education had taken several initiatives to reduce sexism in schools and in teacher training. The department had also issued a policy statement on gender equity in 1990. The report noted the establishment in 1991 of a National Council for Curriculum Assessment, which included gender equity in its terms of reference. The introduction of a new junior certificate was also seen as a positive development. Although there has been a diminution of gender differences in enrollments in subjects at the second level, progress toward coeducational schools was slow, with 48% of second-level students still attending single-sex schools. The second JOCWR report also showed research findings that girls may not perform as well in coed schools as in separate schools.

The Committee noted the failure of the Primary Curriculum Review Body and the Primary Education Review Body to address the issue of gender equity. Other results showed that in-service teacher training on gender equity was still inadequate, reflecting the low level of general expenditure on this. There was still a need for child day care facilities, and the number of girls in apprenticeships remained very low. The provision of sex education in schools continued to be controversial, incurring some hostility from the Catholic church; nevertheless it remains on the political agenda.

Social Welfare

The recommendations of the JOCWR on social welfare combined equal treatment for women with special help for mothers. To promote equal treatment, the Committee recommended payment of an allowance to a deserted husband similar to that already paid to a deserted wife and the introduction of parental leave. They sought the introduction of regulations prohibiting discriminatory questioning of applicants, such as questioning mothers as to their availability for work.

In general, mothers with young children were refused unemployment assistance, and those who qualified for unemployment benefits only received them for 6 months (men receive benefits for a year). The EC Directive on Equal Treatment was designed to eliminate these discriminatory practices. However, the Committee feared that the introduction of this directive's principle might result in lower total family incomes for some families, and they recommended safeguards to protect against that. They also recommended retroactive payments for women under that new legislation.

The Committee noted that the majority of Irish women, engaged in home duties and not in the paid workforce, were excluded from insurance-based benefits. A number of woman-based recommendations were thus made in this report, including lowering the age of eligibility for the single woman's allowance to 55, from 58.[11] The JOCWR recommended the extension of existing maternity benefits to cover all mothers, not simply insured workers. With regard to deserted wives, the JOCWR report made a number of recommendations, like replacing the term *deserted wives* with *abandoned spouses* and the abolition of the 3-month waiting period before payment of the deserted wife's maintenance through the Department of Social Welfare. The report also recommended the introduction of a system of credits for women and men who temporarily left the workforce. Many other general recommendations were made, such as helping men to be present at childbirth; the provision of child care at maternity hospitals; a better appeals system; better social welfare offices; and greater local decision-making powers to eradicate delays in social welfare. A number of other recommendations concerned the care and support of the elderly.

Some Committee recommendations were implemented. The Social Welfare (No. 2) Act, introduced in 1985, gave equal treatment to men and women in matters of social security, in accordance with EC Directives, although without retroactive payments. In 1994, however, the Department of Social Welfare was ordered to make these retroactive payments, as a result of a European Court of Justice judgment. Dental, oral, and optical benefits were extended to the wives of insured men. The category *deserted wives* has now been replaced by the term *lone parents*. Payments to lone parents, now made through the Department of Social Welfare, have been improved. Although a majority of recommendations have been implemented by the Department of Social Welfare, day care facilities and pensions for women in the home are only just now reaching the policy agenda.

Sexual Violence

Instigated by a written submission from the Rape Crisis Centre calling for amendments to the Criminal Law (Rape) Act of 1981, the first JOCWR made its fourth report on the subject of sexual violence (1987). The following organizations made submissions for this report: the Rape Crisis Centre; chief superintendent from the Gardai (police); the Law Society (representing lawyers); and the Sexual Assault Treatment Centre. The Rape Crisis Centre group argued that the 1981 Act had a number of defects, failing to

> define rape in its broadest sense to include oral sex, sodomy, and the use of inanimate objects,
> protect the anonymity of the victim,
> restrict the admissibility of irrelevant evidence as to the complainant's past sexual history,
> protect the complainant from feeling that she was on trial, and
> criminalize rape in marriage.

Following the cues of the Rape Crisis Centre, the JOCWR report advocated new legislation to address these issues. Other recommendations included free legal aid for victims of sexual assault, the hearing of rape cases to be held *in camera,* the prosecution of rape cases in the Circuit Court or High Court, and the introduction of guidelines for sentencing for all sexual offenses and other serious crimes. It made a number of recommendations in relation to the sexual abuse of children. The published minutes of the meetings for this report reveal that the police, represented by the Gardai, and lawyers, represented by the Law Society, had reservations about the need for law changes, with both groups intimating that existing law was adequate. However, in meetings with the JOCWR, the representatives for the two groups agreed with the changes recommended by the Rape Crisis Centre. Evidence of a complainant's past sexual history was the most contentious issue; the lawyer and police groups thought such evidence was relevant and did not agree with the Rape Crisis Centre's view that it should be inadmissible.

Publication of the Law Reform Commission's (LRC) consultation paper on rape in 1987 boosted the influence of the Committee report. The LRC's findings overlapped considerably those of the Oireachtas Committee. In due course, the Criminal Law (Rape Amendment) Act of 1990 contained virtually all of the recommendations of the Committee's report, including the expanded definition of rape (under Section 4) to encompass penetration by any object. The legislation also abolished marital exemption to rape and the age requirement in terms of capacity to rape.

The Dail proceedings show the very active role played by Monica Barnes (chairperson of the second and third JOCWRs and member of the first) in arguing for the passage of the reform bill through the Dail. She drew extensively on feminist research on rape as contained in submissions and in the published report. The Rape Amendment legislation is a very good illustration of the JOCWR's effectiveness, provided its themes are discussed in the Dail or are relevant to proposed legislation. Such effectiveness is dependent, however, on inclusion of reports as part of official Dail discussions.

RELATION TO WOMEN'S ADVOCACY ORGANIZATIONS

Once the first JOCWR had adopted its general program of activities, it then advertised in the newspaper advising the public of its activities and seeking submissions on chosen topics. Concerned individuals, relevant organizations, and women's advocacy groups replied. Many of them were asked to speak formally to the Committee. Through invited submissions, feminist or advocacy organizations could make a direct contribution to the Committee's work. The advocacy groups that became involved depended on the topics under the Committee's consideration. For instance, when discussing education, the teacher unions were consulted, as well as the Employment Equality Agency and the Council for the Status of Women.[12] The advocacy group Campaign Against Sexual Exploitation made a submission when the discussion topic was images of women in the media. The Committee also held discussions with newspaper editors. Other interest groups have increased their power and position in recent years. The more successful develop strategic plans and have an effective public relations approach to their campaigns.

Conclusion

The JOCWR's report on sexual violence, the subsequent Dail debate, and the final legislation suggest how the Committee might approach future legislative concerns. The similar influence of the MSWA in certain areas of women's legislation indicates an important role for these women's policy structures. However, the limits placed on these offices in their choice of women's issues appears to be crucial. It is regrettable that major issues remained outside the JOCWR's and MSWA's scope. The particularities of Irish state-society relations meant that divorce and abortion, major issues in feminist movements elsewhere, were not on the agenda of the women's policy machinery in Ireland. Instead, it has fallen to nongovernmental agencies and pressure groups to address them. A referendum on divorce and accompanying legislation are planned for 1995.

Despite their inability to influence crucial areas of women's policy, the successive JOCWRs and the MSWA were very important in procuring legislative reforms for Irish women. As the legislative changes indicate, these reforms went beyond their paper record to concretely help women. These changes were undoubtedly brought about with the help of pressure groups, but these women's policy agencies, even in their restricted form, expedited social change for women in Ireland.

Notes

1. Like the British parliamentary system after which it was modeled, the Irish system gives authority to make policy and laws to the cabinet and the Oireachtas, composed of the Dail and the Senate. Lower-house members of the Dail are called TDs (Teachta Dala). As the popularly elected chamber, the majority party of the Dail chooses its party leader as prime minister (Taoiseach). The Taoiseach in turn selects the ministers (Chubb, 1992).

2. This provision was deleted in 1972.

3. Fine Gael is a center right party oriented toward more liberal positions and belongs to the Christian Democratic group in the European Parliament.

4. Ministries of State are usually placed under the jurisdiction of a full ministry. Lacking a full ministry on women's policy, the MSWA was attached to the prime minister's office.

5. Fennell had been a founding member of AIM. This group campaigned for changes in family law. In 1982, prior to the creation of the Ministry, women's rights legislation had been enacted to reform family and criminal law (Mahon, 1987).

6. It is difficult to specifically credit the MSWA with these achievements, but the publicity Minister Fennell drew to these issues and the existence of the structure contributed to mobilizing action in areas of women's policy that required legal change.

7. Small community women's groups continue to receive funding from the Department of Social Welfare.

8. For example, in the evolution of social welfare law, they recommended some specific payments to women who had not been in the labor force.

9. Information on the second and subsequent JOCWRs is limited because minutes were not published.

10. In 1988-1989, 53% of girls and 42% of boys attended single-sex postprimary schools.

11. This allowance was introduced because women who never worked found it impossible to get unemployment benefits or assistance. Some had taken care of their elderly parents and when the latter died, they had no income.

12. The Council for the Status of Women is a national federation of women's groups and the strongest pressure group for women in Ireland.

9

The Latecomers

Italy's Equal Status and Equal Opportunity Agencies

Marila Guadagnini

Italy did not set up its first state agencies aimed at promoting equal status for women until the 1980s, several years after most other European countries. The government chose a committee rather than a stronger solution, such as a Department for Women's Affairs. It also favored a plurality of agencies, rather than a single cross-sectoral structure. Multiple agencies were considered better, provided there was a clear-cut differentiation in jurisdiction, because many agencies would allow for a better comprehension of each issue, greater impact, and, at the same time, close cooperation among agencies.

The two principal agencies are

1. The *Commissione Nazionale per la Paritàle le Pari Opportunità* (Equal Status and Equal Opportunity National Commission—ESONC),[1] attached to the prime minister's office

2. The *Comitato Nazionale per l'attuazione dei principi di parità di trattamento ed uguaglianza di opportunità tra lavoratori e lavoratrici* (Equal Status Committee for the implementation of equal treatment and

equal opportunities for men and women in the workplace—ESC), which is attached to the Ministry of Labor and Social Security

The ESONC has the tasks of furthering equality and equal opportunities between sexes in the fields of communication and culture and of promoting women's presence in politics and power positions. The ESC is more specifically committed to issues dealing with equality in the workplace and access to it. This chapter will look at the establishment and organization of both agencies. In examining the role of Italy's women's policy machinery, the chapter will pay most attention to the ESONC, because of the broader scope of its activities. But it will also look into the ESC's new responsibility in the area of affirmative action labor legislation. The last section summarizes the distant relations between the women's policy machinery and the women's movement.

Establishment of ESONC and ESC

To understand the process leading to the agencies' establishment requires a description of the conception of the state in Italy and an outline of the relations between the state and feminist and other women's organizations. Of special interest is the period between the emergence of the new feminist movement in the mid-1970s and the creation of the agencies in the 1980s.

Italy is characterized by a centralized state structure (albeit strained by regional divisions and loyalties) and a fragmented ideological context in which conflictual politics tend to predominate. For a number of reasons, the role of the public administration is less meaningful than in other European systems. Its organization is highly hierarchic and sclerotic, and responsibilities for the same subject are spread among many offices (Zincone, 1983, p. 5.5).

According to the constitution, parliament has the principal decision-making power. Parliament is divided into two branches, the Chamber of Deputies and the Senate, which have similar tasks. Adopted after the fall of the fascist regime, the constitution emphasizes the principle of active participation by citizens and workers in the political, economic, and social organization of the country. Participation should mainly take place through two channels, parties and unions.

Although neither parties nor trade unions have public legal status, in practice collective bargaining regulates labor matters. Trade union representatives draw up collective work contracts—agreements with the entrepreneurs' associations—and lay down work conditions that guide all individual labor relations. Therefore, collective bargaining has a de facto power to bind workers in particular categories, whether or not they are members of the unions that signed the agreement.

Parties and the party system play a decisive (now declining) role in both interest articulation and decision making and have a substantial role in appointments to jobs in public and semipublic structures. Since the end of World War II, the highly fragmented party system has caused unstable (albeit, at the same time, substantially unvaried) government coalitions, characterized by the lack of alternation. Until 1994, the Christian Democratic party was constantly in power, either alone or in coalition with other parties, notably the Liberals, the Republicans, the Socialists, and the Social Democrats. The major left-wing party, the Communist party (PCI), was regularly barred from government on the grounds of its alleged antisystem attitude and its close ties with the former Soviet Union. The continuity of the governing coalitions was ensured, until 1994, by a proportional electoral system, which created a parliament reflecting the deeply rooted ideologies of the stable and loyal electorate.

Italy's closed and conflictual political system accounts for the orientation of the ideological left-wing feminist movement of the 1970s, which opposed authority and institutions and promoted expressiveness, personal transformation, consciousness, and changes in the system of values. Fringe groups penetrating unions and political parties tended to reject any form of representation and stressed the need for a distinct and separate identity for women as women within institutions. In fact, it was not equality but female specificity that formed the breeding ground of the movement, in and out of trade unions. With "difference" as its trademark, the movement was more interested in reproduction and sexuality issues than in labor issues, and it did not try to achieve positions of political and social power. Rather than seeking to become a pressure group, the movement in the 1970s stood aloof from decisional mechanisms (Zincone, 1983). It was only later that a younger generation of feminists opted for greater involvement in the established party and union structures, thus bringing feminist values and perspectives into them (Guadagnini, 1993).

Italy has many women's associations that still have a mass membership. With their number increased by the new groups established in the 1980s, there are now 80 leading associations. Their kaleidoscopic texture ranges from traditional groups to ideologically oriented (Catholic and leftist) ones to professional organizations. In the mid-1970s, women's associations gathered into *Consulte femminili* (advisory committees) attached to local administrations. Because of their ideological cleavages and heterogeneous goals, these associations had no actual power and did not represent an organized network. They had only informal relations with feminist movement groups. A notable exception is *Unione Donne Italiane* (UDI), the largest women's association, created in the aftermath of World War II and linked in its first years to the PCI. The UDI joined with the women's liberation movement in the struggle for divorce and abortion reform.

A development of significance in the process leading to the creation of ESONC and ESC was the adoption in 1977 of the Equality Act No. 903, which bars discrimination in access to work, vocational training, allowances, positions, and tasks.[2] On the surface, the Act appears to be the outcome of women's mobilization in unions and society in the 1970s women's movement. In fact, it was enacted mainly to bring Italian law into line with European Community (EC) directives on equal treatment and pay.

In the preceding years, feminists in the unions had addressed their efforts to the achievement of civil and reproductive rights rather than equality at work. Thus, feminist union women in Italy appear to have set different targets than their counterparts in other countries, who were working toward both protection of working women and equality in the workplace.

The union commitment to equality has been ambiguous. Although supporting protection of women workers (and, in particular, maternity protection), equal pay, creation of public child care facilities and home-workers policy, unions held back when it came to equality and equal opportunities for women in the workplace.

Equality Act No. 903 was proposed by the Minister of Labor (at the time, a woman, Tina Anselmi), and it was very quickly passed by

Parliament. Because neither union nor feminist activists felt they were involved in the discussion leading to its enactment, the law was deemed to have merely symbolic value. The Act was not followed up by effective enforcement solutions, and very little progress was made. The Act's most notable innovations concerned the abolition of compulsory pension plans and the creation of a common list (both men and women) of the registered unemployed. This change resulted in a considerable increase in the number of gainfully employed women. Most of these, however, held unskilled jobs.

In practice, the 1977 Equality Act had a number of limitations. The burden of proving the existence of discrimination before the judiciary rested upon the woman worker. The criteria for proving the existence of discriminatory practices were usually at the discretion of the magistrate. The exception was so-called numerical hiring: Employers were required to accept people who appeared at the top of the employment office's list of names. Sanctions were very lenient: moderate fines for the employer and no damages for the injured party, therefore, no proper remedy for the correction of a pattern of discrimination. Finally, Act 903 did not provide for affirmative action (Beccalli, 1985). In short, institutions and resources for enforcement capable of fostering equality and repressing discrimination were lacking.

The widespread awareness of these inadequacies in implementation—there was practically no follow-up, and court orders were few in number and limited in scope—led to the establishment of the ESC in the Ministry of Labor on December 3, 1983 (Ballestrero, 1985). The agency was not the result of demands from interested and powerful groups, but rather the result of international pressure and favorable trends in public opinion. At the same time, it seemed to be a partial response to a proposal developed by a working group of the National Commission for Family Issues.[3]

Establishment of the ESC led to the prime minister's decree to create the more inclusive ESONC. The family issues commission had been working on a proposal to adapt a structure modeled after the Equal Opportunity Commission in Britain to the Italian political and legal system (Ballestrero, 1985, p. 124). A debate ensued concerning the choice of the Committee's seat, that is, whether it should be attached to the prime minister's office or the Labor Ministry. The majority, firmly convinced of the importance of labor issues, opted for the Labor

Ministry. This location would also provide a direct link between the Committee and the ministry's network of central and peripheral structures, called *Ispettorati del lavoro* (labor inspectorates), which were fully equipped to monitor implementation of the Equality Act. In order to fulfill the alternate request for an agency with a broader mandate, on June 12, 1984, Prime Minister Craxi, Socialist party leader of the five-party coalition, established a second national body, the ESONC, with the task of dealing with all women's issues, except for labor issues. Initially set up by decree, the ESONC was subsequently ratified by Statute No. 400 of August 23, 1988, which gives it the status of a permanent body with precise and definite tasks, jurisdiction, composition, duration, and financial resources. The initial establishment of both of Italy's national equality agencies in 1983 and 1984 was prompted by EC directives and EC activities, along with UN initiatives to celebrate the International Decade for Women.[4]

Organization and Activities

Members of the ESONC are appointed every 3 years by the prime minister. The ESONC consists of 29 members, representing women's associations (7), political parties (11), unions (3), entrepreneurs and cooperatives (4), and renowned scholars and intellectuals (4) (Commissione Nazionale, 1994). Since 1984, the ESONC's composition has reflected the composition of governing coalitions. Therefore, until 1993 only the choice of chairwoman reflected partisan shifts: from a Socialist representative, Elena Marinucci, during Socialist Bettino Craxi's five-party coalition, to a Christian Democrat, Tina Anselmi, when the office of prime minister was held by members of the Christian Democratic party. The Commission appointed after the 1994 elections (which witnessed the rise of a new center-right government coalition) was chaired by Tina Lagostena Bassi, a representative of Prime Minister Silvio Berlusconi's Forza Italia.

ESONC operates through plenary sessions (9 to 10 a year). Working groups are set up within its framework, some permanent, such as Women and Mass Media, Women and Immigration, and Women and Institutional Reforms. The Commission sits in Rome, in Palazzo Chigi, the building that also houses the prime minister's office. Equipment and personnel are also shared. The secretariat consists of nine staff members having different functions. The ESONC has an independent budget (2 billion lira or $1.3 million in 1992 and 1993).

Statute 164/1990 set the formal goals of furthering equality and equal opportunities between women and men, pointing out existing instances of discrimination, and supplying solutions to these problems. The ESONC acts as an advisory and supporting body to the government in general, and to the prime minister in particular, through proposals pursuing adjustment of laws and rules governing social, economic, and cultural policies to the equality principle. ESONC is both the Italian representative within the EC Equal Opportunities Commission and the prime minister's supporting agency vis-à-vis other countries on women's issues.

ESONC also carries out its own activities. These include the following:

> The promotion and coordination of equality agencies within the state administration and public bodies
> Measures to create a suitable cultural environment, where the achievement of equality may become an irreversible process
> Surveys and research studies on current achievements
> Initiatives to further women's active participation in political, social, and economic life, especially in the economic and political decision-making centers, a weak point of the equality process (Commissione Nazionale, 1994)

The ESONC coordinates equality agencies at a national level and furthers the creation of equal opportunities commissions at a local level. Between the late 1980s and the early 1990s, a network of equality agencies appeared, which comprises such structures as the ESC attached to the Minister of Education; the Commission for the Protection of Women's Health, within the Research Division of the Health Ministry (1992); and the special division for equality operating within the *Osservatorio del pubblico impiego*.[5]

Several agencies operate at regional, provincial, and municipal levels, as well as within businesses and the public administration sector. They have the tasks of furthering the expansion of an equality culture, of safeguarding women's rights, and of acting to stop any form of discrimination and injustice. Between 1989 and 1992, such equality agencies were founded by the regions and by 43 out of 94 provinces. On average, only one out of five municipalities, most of them in northern Italy, followed suit.

The ESC in the Ministry of Labor initially had only a few limited tasks. It was to formulate proposals and express opinions on general questions of equality in order to improve existing legislation. The ESC was also to set out codes that would define rules of action toward equality targets and to point out direct or indirect examples of discrimination. The ESC had authority to carry out investigations at the workplace through *Ispettorati del lavoro* and to act as a sort of ombudsman in connection with disputes over the violation of equality rules.

The ESC's tasks and role have recently been strengthened by the Affirmative Action Act (No. 125), adopted in 1991. It now has the power to select, finance, and monitor affirmative action programs. Thus, Act 125/1991 has introduced substantial legal innovations in the labor field, providing a new means of safeguarding equality for working women, as well as some financing and training. The goal is to remove all obstacles hindering the achievement of equal status and equal opportunities by permitting measures in favor of women. The ESC provides incentives in the form of partial or total cost reimbursement. It also shifts the burden of proof when "the party, upon whom it rested originally, supplies evidentiary facts, also inferred from statistical information," in connection with employees' hiring, wages and salaries, task and position allocation, transfers, promotions, and dismissals; in such cases there is a conclusive presumption of sexually discriminatory acts or behaviors.

The statute further provides for the appointment of a *Consigliere di parità* (equal status advocate) at the provincial level. Such advocates were provided for by the 1984 employment act in regional and municipal employment commissions. The equal status advocates, nonvoting members of employment commissions, had an advisory role to watch over the application of equal status principles. The 1991 Act granted the advocate more powers to act *iure proprio* (in her own right) as attorney in fact during judicial proceedings on behalf of a woman who is clearly a victim of discrimination or to start discrimination actions in the event of collective labor disputes, wherein the victims are not clearly and directly discernible. Finally, the statute secures enforcement by imposing a number of sanctions—limited in scope, however—providing for suspension of financial benefits and exclusion from public procurement, in order to prevent employers from indulging in discriminatory acts (De Cristofaro, 1993).

Despite the new powers given in 1991, the organization of the ESC has undergone no material changes, compared to 1983. The Committee is made up of the labor and social security ministers, as well as representatives of leading worker's unions (5), employer's associations (5), the cooperative movement (1), national women's organizations operating in the field of equality and equal opportunities (11 members), and the *Consigliere di parità*, a member of the Central Employment Commission. In addition, a number of experts and government and ministerial officials without voting rights may take part in the Committee's meetings.

Role and Effect of
ESONC and ESC on Policymaking

ESONC

The first period of ESONC's activities (1984-1989), chaired by socialist member of parliament (MP) Elena Marinucci, differs slightly from its second period (1989-1994), chaired by MP Tina Anselmi of the Christian Democrats. Both periods were strongly affected by the activity of international organizations (the United Nations and EC), and, in particular, by the guidelines set out in a number of "equality action plans."

In 1984, the ESONC was set into motion in an enthusiastic climate leading up to the UN Decade of Women Conference in Nairobi. Preparations gave impetus to the research studies and surveys on women's condition and stimulated activities in three main sectors of activity: sensitizing and forming culture, promoting women's political participation, and networking equality agencies at a local level. The ESONC published a great deal of literature in the 1980s.[6] These writings highlight the Commission's priority of informing women of their condition and rights and dismantling cultural prejudices and stereotypes.[7]

The ESONC also paid special attention to women's political participation. The presence of women in elective representative bodies, at a
national and local level, has been quite limited compared with many
other European countries, in particular the northern ones. Despite the
equality principles enacted by the Italian constitution, the percentage
of women elected to parliament hovered at approximately 6% between 1948 (first legislature) and 1983 (ninth legislature).

In its 1986 action plan, the ESONC set out appropriate guidelines for
disseminating information in the schools and for using mass media to
sensitize public opinion, political parties, and unions to the need to
increase women's representation. It recommended acting through
electoral legislation or through the parties' inner structures to create
incentives leading to equal opportunities for women candidates.

During the 1987 parliamentary election, the ESONC, together with
a number of women politicians, launched a campaign for more equal
gender representation in elective bodies. Pressure on political parties
to increase the number of women candidates, along with a request
asking voters to support women candidates, resulted in a larger
number of women elected (from 67 in 1983 to 104 in 1987). Between
1989 and 1990, initiatives were carried out mainly through debates,
roundtables, and meetings with party leaders to obtain ampler guarantees for in-party administrative elections.

During 1992 elections, ESONC promoted a series of announcements
and commercials that read "More votes to women, more value to
politics." The campaign involved 6 magazines, 22 dailies, RAI (Italian
Radio and Television Broadcasting Corporation), 85 local television
stations, and 87 local radio channels. Radio broadcasting was provided free. However, the initiative proved to be rather controversial;
a male candidate charged that it discriminated against men and was
therefore unconstitutional. Nevertheless, the campaign's legitimacy
was acknowledged by judicial decision. Due in part to a change in
electoral laws,[8] the election outcome was disappointing: The percentage of women elected increased slightly in the Senate, but it decreased
dramatically in the Chamber of Deputies, going from 104 women
representatives down to 82, out of a total of 945 MPs.

Since then, the ESONC has pledged its efforts to foster women's
active participation in politics in the context of a period of major
institutional change in Italy. The new laws governing mayoral elec-

tions and introducing a majority system for election to the Chamber of Deputies have required renewed commitment by the ESONC to prevent such reforms from further reducing the proportion of women among MPs.

In the 1994 parliamentary elections, 75% of deputies were elected within single-member constituencies with the majority system, whereas 25% were selected on a proportional representation system based on preset, fixed lists *(liste bloccate)*. In the course of the debate on the electoral law, the ESONC urged parliament to introduce rules to guarantee women's representation. These proposals for a quota system triggered controversial reactions. Opponents included several prominent women—feminists, as well as center to center-right MPs. Nevertheless, a rule was enacted requiring candidates to be listed in alternate order by gender on the proportional representation fixed lists; that is, where the candidates' ranking order may not be altered by a preference vote. The outcome was a positive one: The number of women elected to the Chamber of Deputies went up from 82 (8.6%) in the previous polls to 124 (13.1%) in 1994. In the Senate, where such a rule was not adopted, the number of women decreased.

A rule designed to guarantee women representation was also introduced in the new electoral law for municipalities. The presence of women on local councils in Italy has always been low (the percentage of local women councilors was only 8.5% in 1991). According to the 1993 rule, neither sex may exceed three quarters of the candidates on the lists presented in small (fewer than 15,000 inhabitants) municipalities; this figure falls to two thirds in larger towns. It is impossible to evaluate the concrete impact of such a provision, because polls have only been held in a few municipalities since its adoption. A rule preventing either sex from being represented by more than two thirds of the candidates was adapted for the 1995 regional elections.

Through its chairwoman, ESONC has played a role in equal employment policy. The ESONC chairwoman, Tina Anselmi, was chosen as the parliamentary *relatrice* (proponent) of the bill that led to the aforementioned Affirmative Action Statute 125/1991. (The ESC played a major role in drafting the bill; see next section.) She also proposed the laws on "affirmative actions in favor of women entrepreneurs" and on maternity leave. Both laws have been adopted too recently for an adequate evaluation of their effectiveness. However, according to a number of recent studies, their implementation has been quite limited.

ESC

The ESC has the power to submit proposals to the minister of labor concerning the field of women's work. Immediately after its establishment in 1983, it inserted a number of measures in Act 863, an omnibus employment act of 1984. Specifically, it succeeded in having the institution of the equal status advocate included in the Act, thus establishing an institutional figure within regional employment commissions, the bodies regulating the labor market at the regional level. In this way hiring practices were subject to control for their compliance with equality principles.

The ESC also played a decisive role in proposing the 1991 affirmative action law. A working group within the ESC put forth the first proposal for such a bill to the labor minister, Socialist Gianni De Michelis. After his review, the proposal received the approval of the Council of Ministers and was considered in a number of sessions of the parliamentary Labor Committee. The final text was promoted by ESONC Chairwoman Anselmi. ESC's role in proposing legislation continues. It has recently drafted an opinion on sexual harassment that is under review by the Labor Committee in parliament.

Although its role was significant in promoting the act that created the *Consigliere di parità* and affirmative action law, between 1984 and 1991 the ESC had a merely advisory role. In practice, equal employment policy has been produced primarily through collective bargaining, not government agencies, especially since the late 1980s. Some progress has been made. In 1986-1987, for example, renewal of national labor contracts provided for professional training for women, supported by both national and EC funds; affirmative action projects; and *commissioni paritetiche* (joint committees) to investigate and propose affirmative actions.

The 1991 Affirmative Action Act considerably strengthened ESC's responsibilities and resources for implementation. But these remain small, given the needs. In launching affirmative action programs, ESC allocated 9 billion lira ($6 million) to finance 49 projects in 1991 and 74 projects in 1992. Many of these projects are being developed in northern and central Italy. Although it is too early to do a complete evaluation of its new role, the ESC has not developed into the robust defender of equal rights that many expected. So far, ESC's activity has been generally regarded as limited in scope, due to inadequate financial resources and to the weak support given to the promotion of affirmative actions by trade unions and employers.

The ESC's impact would be significantly increased if it could inject its agenda effectively into the collective bargaining process. Since ESC was institutionalized as a permanent agency, its main activity has been to establish working procedures setting its machinery into motion, according to the tasks entrusted to it by Act 125/1991. ESC has so far avoided dealing with the controversial bargaining issues; it is already split by inner disagreements, not only among the different social partners, but also among the union members and members of different political parties. In the future, however, ESC may have an influence on bargaining, because it now includes a mechanism for confrontation and discussion between the social partners that would contribute to the legitimization of equal opportunity policies.

Apart from their roles in initiating legislation, both ESC and ESONC face impediments to their policy impact. These include the institutional context, cultural factors, and the ideological and organizational features of the women's movement. With respect to the institutional context, strong organizations (unions and parties) "filter" the requests for policies. This filtering inhibits any innovation on behalf of equality in the absence of a critical mass of women united and clear about the strategy to be adopted. In Italy, union executive positions are still male-dominated.

The culture remains strongly traditional, despite processes of secularization that led to enactment and ratification by referenda of divorce and abortion reform laws. The deeply rooted Catholic tradition sustains beliefs in a strict separation of gender roles. The culture of equal opportunities and affirmative action, which addresses women as individuals, runs counter to this culture. It also clashes with Italy's welfare state policies, which have often been instrumental in strengthening the family as a collective body, not granting women rights as individuals.

A further weak point for institutional equality mechanisms comes from the poor support given by women's advocates themselves. The many cleavages that split the women's movement affect unions and parties, and, more generally, the chance for women's advocates to develop appropriate networks and to mobilize on emancipation-related issues, such as the creation of agencies fostering women's status.

Relation of Agencies to the Women's Movement

If the establishment of women's policy machinery is expected to lead to a merger between the grass-roots feminist movement and a state- and party/union-supported feminism elsewhere, this is far from being the case in Italy. Equality agencies have no funds to assist feminist or women's organizations nationally or at the local level, nor do they yet serve as conduits for networking among women's advocacy groups in unions, parties, and associations.

Feminism lingered in the background during the process that led to the establishment of the equality agencies, and feminists looked upon them with diffidence. There were three components of the women's movement in the 1980s. The divisions among them were so great that it is hardly possible to talk about "a" women's movement (although this phrase is being used here for the sake of brevity).

The so-called cultural wing sought to penetrate cultural life and created women's centers that were to be run by women in an autonomous way, although financed with public funds (Tatafiore, 1992). Approximately 20 new magazines were published between 1981 and 1991, ranging from specialized feminist publications (*Memoria, DWF*) to information bulletins (*Il paese delle donne*), to publications containing political proposals (*Reti, Sottosopra*) and others (*Lapis, Tuttosopra*). Cultural centers were active in Rome (*Centro culturale Virginia Woolf*) and in other Italian towns, with financing from local governments. There were about 100 cultural and women's centers in the 1980s. Networks of scholars and researchers were also set up, such as *Società Italiana delle Storiche, Associazione delle Letterate,* and *Fondazione Donne e Scienza.* An interdisciplinary women's study center (*CIRSDe*) was created within Turin University in 1990, gathering more than 80 scholars. The coordination center *Produrre e Riprodurre* was also founded in Turin during the same period. It developed from the experience of *collettivi femminili* (women's groups) active in the unions, which also founded the *Sindacato Donna* (women's union). The last 10 years have witnessed intense activity on the part of groups and associations of women opposing violence against women.

A second component of the movement was composed of the flourishing women's associations, especially in the professions, such as the Italian Federation of Women in the Arts, Professions, and Business (FIDAPA), Women Entrepreneurs and Managers Association (AIDDA), *Donne in carriera,* and others (Rossi Doria, 1994). These organizations worked for emancipation-oriented policies promoting women's status.

The third component of the movement is represented by women in parties and unions. Within such entities, the dichotomy between equality and difference divides women on the strategy to pursue in their working lives and in institutions. This results in a conflict between equal opportunity policy and a feminist strategy that aims at penetrating institutions by maintaining a women-specific identity and reshaping organizations and institutions according to the female identity. This debate involves and affects women's policies within unions and left-wing parties.

In 1986, PCI women adopted the *Carta delle donne comuniste* (Communist women's charter), eradicating the party's traditional emancipation-oriented policy. "Women's power from women" was the slogan of the charter, which aimed at creating feminine solidarity as the source of women's political power and at changing politics from within. The charter was inspired by the theoretical framework developed by *Libreria delle donne* (Women's Bookstore). Being against the women's rights orientation of feminism, as well as the creation of equality commissions, this group suggested that women should abandon their separatist strategy in favor of a novel involvement in cultural and political institutions. According to this group, the only feasible way to build up suitable relations among women, to change the existing order, was that of *affidamento tra donne* (trust among women).

At the same time, Communist women MPs have strongly supported the adoption of equal opportunity legislation and the creation of equality agencies. The difficulties met with by women within the PCI highlight the problems connected with the feminism/institutions relationship. The turning point in 1989, which led to the birth of the

Democratic party of the Left (PDS) and subsequently to a separate group, *Rifondazione Comunista* (Communist Refoundation), caused different opinions to overlap with the party's internal divisions. In *Rifondazione Comunista*, the promotion of the Communist ideology is given priority over women's issues, whereas PDS follows (not without internal disagreement) a reformist policy in addressing women's issues, thus coming into line with the European left-wing parties.

The ultimate objective to be reached in order to improve women's condition is represented by the very penetration of political institutions. In this perspective, the most appropriate strategy may be that of making use of the existing state agencies and promoting cooperation among the different components of the movement. The local government level may be the most useful one. Cooperation among feminists, women's organizations, and equal opportunity commissions has indeed been more effective at a local level. An example is the many centers set up over the past few years, among them the *Alma Mater* center for women immigrants recently opened in Turin, which is not only a point of reference but also encourages entrepreneurial initiatives.

Conclusion

If we want to take stock of the first years of activity of Italy's equal opportunities agencies, it is hard to separate their roles from the political and social context. Focusing on the ESONC, it cannot be denied that despite its limited influence on policy making, it did have a cultural impact. The Commission has distributed much information through local agencies and associations, telling women about their rights. Both national and local commissions often supplied support and stimulated research studies on women's condition in a country where women's studies are not acknowledged by universities.

The members of ESONC include renowned personalities who are deeply committed to women's issues. However, because the criteria for the appointment of members still involve party membership and the parties' power ratios, ESONC is affected by the same evils that beset the political system in general: Its ideological segmentation limits its scope to either very general interventions (rights awareness, abolition of stereotypes, and so on) or very sectorial ones. Their interventions do not reach the inner core of patriarchal society, namely, the role of women in the family. They are hindered in taking on issues, such as the reorganization of the labor market, that would lead to role sharing within the family. The other agency, ESC, has been important in the formulation of equality legislation. This has been due to demands of international agencies rather than through alliances with domestic advocates. ESC has not been able to infiltrate the collective bargaining process, which remains the effective site of equality policy implementation.

Finally, the Italian women's policy machinery at the national level has not yet been able to contribute to a resolution of many of the major issues of women's status. Their weak to nonexistent links with women's organizations and feminists makes the commissions of little assistance in furthering the feminist policy agenda. The issue of rape law reform is a good example. This issue has been on the agenda of the women's movement since the late 1970s and has been discussed in parliament since 1980. Only in May 1995 did women draft a common bill on rape. It remains to be seen what role ESONC will be able to play in pushing for a prompt adoption of the law.

Notes

1. This Commission was known, at first, as *Commissione Nazionale per la realizzazione della parità tra uomo e donna* (National Commission for the achievement of equality between men and women) and subsequently as *Commissione Nazionale per la parità e le pari opportunità tra uomo e donna* (Equal Status and Equal Opportunity National Commission).

2. The Italian constitution ratifies the principle of equality among all citizens, without regard to sex, in all fields and, in particular, under the law (article 3), in the family (article 29), in the workplace (article 37), as to political rights (article 48), and in the access to public and elective office (article 51). Implementation of such principles through legislation has involved a long and complex process and required the abandonment of the women's "protection" postulate in favor of the "actual equality" one, through the adoption of ad hoc measures.

3. The working group, made up of jurists, economists, lawyers, magistrates, and representatives of unions worked between 1981 and 1982. Its proposal was discussed by the larger Commission, composed of representatives of unions and traditional women's associations, but no feminist groups.

4. Italian legislation as a whole is largely influenced by EC legislation, in particular by the following directives: 75/117 on equal pay; 76/207 on equal

treatment in the access to work, training, and work conditions; 79/7 and 86/378 in the field of social security; 86/613 on the application of the equality principle between self-employed men and women, as well as on maternity protection, and 92/85 on physical maternity protection.

5. It was created on July 25, 1986, by ministerial decree, with the task of collecting data on the presence of women within the public administration and, in particular, on equality of access and career mechanisms, as well as on the employment situation in the south of Italy.

6. The Commission has published approximately 30 works.

7. An important example is *Codice Donna* published in February 1985 and updated in 1990, a collection of women-specific rules and laws, as well as an easy-to-consult guide to women's rights, known as *Pagine Rosa*. This publication lists both women's rights and paths to follow to obtain compliance with them.

8. Until 1992, members of the Chamber of Deputies had been selected by a proportional-cum-preference vote: Voters selected a party and expressed preference for up to four candidates at the same time. With the 1992 election, the number of preferential votes was reduced to one. This had a negative effect on women (Guadagnini, 1993).

First, this change nullified a mechanism that had favored women in the past. Before 1992, party leaders used to "package" groups of candidates, usually in groups of three. When a woman candidate was packaged with one or two strong male candidates, she had a good chance of being elected. Second, allowing only one preference vote creased increased competition among candidates within each part. The strong candidates—with greater financial resources, political links, fame, and so on—were favored. Women were not.

In 1993, more substantial changes were introduced. Only 25% of the seats in the Chamber of Deputies were filled by the proportional system, and the remaining 75% were allowed on a first-past-the-post mechanism. For the 25% proportional group, parties present "preset" or fixed lists of candidates, and voters cannot express any preferences at all. A rule favoring women has also been included: Fixed lists must contain the same number of women and men, set out in an alternate order (man, woman, man, woman, etc.).

10

Administrative Accommodation
in the Netherlands

*The Department for the
Coordination of Equality Policy*

Joyce Outshoorn

Interviewer: Does it make a difference that there is a women's policy unit?

Femocrat 1: Absolutely. I think that if the club didn't exist, everything would break down quite quickly. And it starts by just being there, the fact the joint exists also keeps things going . . .

Femocrat 2: If the unit didn't exist you'd miss a motor within the government bureaucracy, a motor that gives impulses, innovation . . . and in second resort you'd miss a conscience.[1]

These comments were made by two femocrats who worked in the *Directie Coordinatie Emancipatiebeleid* (Department for the Coordination of Equality Policy; DCE). Despite their different backgrounds and different tenure in the Department, they agreed that the women's policy unit made a difference. The DCE has been in existence since 1978 and has become a regular feature in The Hague's (the Dutch capital) bureaucratic landscape. Located in the Ministry of Social

Affairs and Employment and headed by a state secretary, the Dutch equivalent of a junior minister, the Department is the most important Dutch government agency for women's policy. Although civil servants are responsible for women's policy in other ministries and there is an official advisory council for women's affairs, it is the DCE that coordinates all policy in this area.

Policy machinery to advance women's status has been present in the Dutch state since 1977. Often criticized by the women's movement, these state agencies have been the object of feminist debate and research.[2] For example, in 1982, two femocrats at the DCE argued that the establishment of a policy network or iron triangle in which the women's movement and women's policy offices cooperated was crucial for the success of women's equality policy (Dijkstra & Swiebel, 1982).[3] This chapter will examine the degree to which such a policy network developed around women's equality policy. It will focus on how the Dutch state responded to women's movement demands by creating the DCE and trace the role of this office in the formulation and implementation of women's equality policy. The analysis will look, first, at the establishment and organization of the DCE; second, at its role in policy formation; and third, at the DCE's relations with the women's movement in the Netherlands. The question of whether the development of such a network is a sufficient condition for successful policy in contemporary Dutch politics will be treated in the conclusion.

Establishment

The administrative incorporation of the feminist question must be first placed in the context of the Dutch style of accommodating conflict. Beginning in World War I, Dutch policy formation was dominated by *Verzuiling*, vertically organized groups based on religion and class. Although the *Verzuiling* system began to break down in the 1960s and 1970s, the legacy of this pillared interest articulation still underpins the particular way in which conflict and opposition are regulated through compromise and accommodation (Daalder, 1974; Lijphart, 1982). Rather than a single dominant view on state intervention embraced by a handful of state elites, the *Verzuiling* produced a pragmatic consensus on the state's role in society that blurred the division between state and society and between the public and the private. This consensus about state intervention has made it easier for Governments to make women's policy in certain areas, but it prevents Governments from dealing with women's policy issues defined as nonstate. The pillared nature of Dutch society also contributed to the manner in which well-organized interests have been able to directly influence government agencies. This highly institutionalized nexus between government agencies and powerful groups has been an important factor in the decline of parliament and the political parties.

The rise of the welfare state after World War II, grafted onto the legacy of *Verzuiling*, led to far-reaching state intervention. Not only does the Dutch state actively intervene in economic life, but it also deeply influences the lives of its citizens by building an extensive social security safety net against the harmful effects of the market economy. The welfare state also regulated private life by introducing the breadwinner/housewife family model into all social security arrangements. The institutionalization of this family norm effectively turned single women into anomalies and made working mothers anathema. The Netherlands, therefore, had a policy on women long before the second wave of feminism reopened the women's issue in the late 1960s.

The call for change in this policy was placed on the national agenda in the 1970s by the new women's movement, which had begun in the 1960s and was characterized by two main currents; a reform-oriented current that voiced conventional demands and a radical, younger branch using direct action tactics and consciousness raising (Outshoorn, 1986). The reform-oriented current represented by the group *Man-Vrouw-Maatschappij* (Man-Woman-Society, MVM), formally articulated the demand for a new policy for women in 1973. The cabinet, a coalition led by the Social Democrats since 1972, responded in 1974 by creating an external commission, the *Emancipatiekommissie* (Emancipation Commission, EK) to advise government on the content of future policy changes.

This quick government response was a result of several political factors. First, MVM, consisting of well-educated men and career women, had the experience and connections to operate effectively in mainstream politics. MVM leaders, for example, had personal connections to leading members of the Dutch Social Democrat party. Set up as a pressure group for women's equality policies in employment, education, and fiscal and social policy, MVM did not shun conventional politics, unlike the radical branch of the movement. Second, MVM's program matched the orientation of the left-wing cabinet, which had called for the "distribution of knowledge, power, and income." As Socialist Prime Minister Joop den Uyl claimed in his speech at the inauguration of the EK, these ideas captured the goals of women's equality policy. Both MVM feminists and Socialists were optimistic about human nature and believed in the state's role in social change. They also shared the distrust of organized confessionalism with its tradition of relegating women to the home. Finally, International Women's Year (IWY) played a role, making the demands of MVM a godsend for the cabinet, which had forgotten that the United Nations had designated 1975 IWY (Dijkstra & Swiebel, 1982, p. 44). The Government provided funding for a new committee to organize the Dutch contribution to IWY and to distribute money to women's groups. This new committee became the first source of government funding for women's groups.

It is important to note that the cabinet did not prescribe the specifics of the new women's policy. Instead, it assigned this task to the experts and representatives from various women's organizations outside of the established state bureaucracy. As a consequence, important government actors would question the legitimacy of these new policies during later stages of the policy process (Dijkstra & Swiebel, 1982, p. 45). Also, given that 11 of the 16 original members of the EK were from the left and several of these were members of MVM (Prins, 1987, p. 105), Liberal and Christian Democrat women, who felt underrepresented, boycotted the Commission's inauguration. The boycott from the Right, the criticisms from the radical branch of the women's movement about the EK, and the highly symbolic nature of IWY left MVM as the major supporter of the EK.

Despite its inauspicious start, the Commission became a very dynamic body. In its 5-year life, it set the precedent for future cabinets on women's equality policy. Its report (*Emancipatie Kommissie*, 1976), *Aanzet tot een vijf jaren plan* (Design for a 5-Year Plan), with little amendment, became the basic policy document of the government in 1977: *Emancipatie: Proces van verandering en groei* (Emancipation: Process of Change and Growth). By redefining feminist demands into moderate and, particularly for civil servants, comprehensible terms, the EK succeeded in translating women's issues into appropriate items for government intervention, thus creating a feasible basis for future work. The leading principle of the new policy was greater freedom of choice for both women and men in shaping their lives. This goal would be achieved by promoting policies to enable women to make up for lost opportunities, to widen the range of options open to both sexes, and to enhance the appreciation of so-called feminine values and activities.

The EK also engineered the blueprint for the DCE by calling for the creation of a special unit for women's policy to be headed by a state secretary and coordinated by an interministerial committee. This new structure would then set up a women's policy network within regular political and bureaucratic practices. The Commission also emphasized the cross-cutting nature of women's policy and initiated an intersectoral approach to women's policy, in which a central women's policy office at the cabinet level would coordinate and monitor policy activities in the other departments related to women's equality issues. Even though analysts (e.g., Prins, 1989) and women's movement activists criticized such intersectoral coordination for being unwieldy and potentially obstructive to the development of effective policy, the decision to take this approach was dictated by political sense and logical necessity. Women's issues surface in all policy areas for these feminist critics; reducing them to a single ministry would have been at odds with feminist ideas and practice (Swiebel & Outshoorn, 1990, p. 15).[4]

During the parliamentary election campaign of 1977, women from the Social Democrat party campaigned for the appointment of a state secretary for women's policy in the new cabinet. Even though the Socialists lost their position in the cabinet to the Liberal/Christian Democrats, the new cabinet still appointed a state secretary, a Protestant Christian Democrat, Jeltien Kraaijeveld-Wouters, who had not been an active supporter of women's equality policy. Kraaijeveld-Wouters implemented the EK's national machinery proposal with a considerable budget of 46 million guilder ($6.9 million), setting up the DCE in the Ministry of Culture, Recreation, and Welfare in 1978. Given that the cabinet defined women's issues as a matter of raising consciousness and changing people's attitudes, placing the DCE in this ministry was not illogical. Not only did the ministry's portfolio include family welfare, disadvantaged groups, and adult education, but two key civil servants who had worked in its family policy unit were transferred to the new DCE.

Organization

At the end of 1978 the DCE had 15 staff members (Prins, 1989, p. 51). Continuing the tradition of the EK's close links to the moderate wing of the women's movement, several staffers who had started with the MVM were hired from the EK. Other staff members were recruited from outside of the career civil service, with only the department head having a traditional civil-servant background. Appointees also had different occupational backgrounds and diverse university training (Outshoorn, 1994b). Most of them had some experience in the women's movement, which was seen as an asset, as expertise in women's issues was hard to come by. Hiring from outside was facilitated by the common practice within the Dutch civil service of decentralized recruitment: Ministries and their subunits hire their own personnel. External recruitment did mean, however, that many of the new employees were not well-versed in bureaucratic procedure and civil service culture. In 1993, the DCE counted 26 full-time positions, of which 15 were responsible for formulating new policies.

Several of the femocrats who initially had been active in the women's movement applied their feminist ideals to the organization of the DCE by attempting to make the office less hierarchical. Today the DCE is still a relatively informal and nonhierarchical organization compared with other government agencies, with senior staff easily accessible to junior members. However, the open nature of policy discussion has begun to disappear in recent years, with policy having become more technical and newer appointees having less feminist experience.

The DCE did not have an elevated position within the administrative hierarchy of the Ministry of Culture, Recreation, and Welfare. With little formal power and a relatively limited budget, the DCE used indirect tactics of persuasion and enlisting political support to influence policy decisions in the ministry. At the same time, the cabinet position of the DCE state secretary strengthened its ability to influence policy decisions. Even if a state secretary has limited powers—she has access to the Council of Ministers (where policy differences between ministries are settled in the end) only when her policies are on its agenda—she is a member of the cabinet and can provide the essential political backing. Another strength of the unit was that, unlike the EK, it was set up for an indefinite period of time. As long as women's equality issues were high on the Government's agenda, the unit was not threatened, even when consecutive cabinets tried to reduce the size of the government bureaucracy.

The political situation in this initial period has been aptly described by Dijkstra and Swiebel (1982) as one in which equality policy was both "fashionable and a taboo" (p. 42). On the one hand, there was a consensus that *something* had to be done; on the other, there was no clear idea of *what* needed to be done. During the first parliamentary debates on women's policy, the political parties did not take issue with the formulated policy goals and came with few concrete demands. Only the fundamentalist Protestant parties voiced opposition, saying Dutch women did not want to be liberated. This consensus, however, was very superficial and lasted only as long as more controversial issues were avoided or not defined as part of women's policy. For instance, because the abortion issue was being dealt with in a different arena, the fragile consensus around new women's equality policy did not include this highly controversial issue (Outshoorn, 1986, pp. 67-68).[5] Also, the government only took up the divisive issue of equal treatment in the area of paid employment because of pressure from European Community (EC) policy directives.[6]

The DCE entered a new phase after the national elections of 1981. A Socialist/Christian Democrat Government was formed, and during the negotiations it was decided to move the DCE to the Ministry of Social Affairs and Employment.[7] This paralleled an ideological shift in the definition of women's issues (Van Praag, 1985). The new definition held that economic independence was crucial for the advancement of women. Hence, employment and entitlement of women to social security became primary concerns, matters traditionally falling under that ministry. Hedy d'Ancona, one of the founding members of MVM and also a Socialist, became the state secretary. The move of the

DCE also reflected the wish of senior femocrats and the former EK to ally women's issues to a powerful force in the cabinet. The minister of social affairs, along with his colleagues of finance and economic affairs and the prime minister, form what is referred to as the socioeconomic triangle, in which the major policy issues of the cabinet are decided. Access to this channel looked promising, the more so as social security and employment had top priority on the agenda of the new cabinet.

The new state secretary, d'Ancona, soon had her staff writing a new policy document that redefined women's issues in terms of power and also took sexual issues into account. The new cabinet, however, fell after only 9 months, and a Liberal/Christian Democrat coalition took over after new elections were held in 1982. Despite this change, work on the new draft continued, and the cabinet and parliament finally accepted it in 1985 as the new foundation for its women's equality policy (Beleidsplan, 1985).

The new Liberal state secretary, Annelien Kappeyne van de Coppello, accentuated women's choice between work and family and made the constitutional principle of bodily integrity the cornerstone of her policy against sexual violence. But in practice, labor market policy has become the core of women's equality policy, crowding out other issues (Keuzenkamp & Teunissen, 1990). The Beleidsplan provided the foundation for new policy initiatives in all ministries, monitored by the state secretary of the DCE, who visited all ministers regularly to discuss the progress made. In the 1980s, the Beleidsplan, therefore, strengthened the position of the DCE, made for more effective policy in a number of areas, and laid the groundwork for the integration of women's policy into all ministries.

Policy Influence

Because of the DCE's coordinating role, its ability to initiate new policies has been limited. The Department can only develop certain initiatives on its own, because many issues belong to other departments. Thus the major task of the DCE has been to try to intervene at an early stage if a policy proposal involves women's issues. Also, the Interministerial Committee for Equality Policy, which should have been involved with influencing women's policy, has lain dormant

because ministries either sent junior representatives or ignored proceedings. If policy results were disappointing or if the DCE was over-
ruled, its staff could gain the support of its state secretary or go outside
of the executive branch by getting members of parliament (MPs) to
ask questions or by winning their support for specific legislation.

In the 1980s, the parliamentary route increasingly became a viable
alternative for the DCE because by then political parties had developed their own definitions of feminism and had more expert MPs,
most of them women, who were keen to take up women's issues. From
1983 onward, women MPs in the Second Chamber formed a nonpartisan
alliance in the *Kamerbreed Vrouwenoverleg* (Women's Parliamentary
Coalition). Although this did not lead to cross-voting very often
(given the strong emphasis in parliament on party discipline), it did
provide an additional forum for discussion and negotiation for the
DCE. Taking advantage of the favorable climate for equality policy,
the DCE succeeded in strengthening the national machinery. The most
important step was the establishment in 1986 of the Cabinet Committee for Women's Policy, chaired by the prime minister. This committee's interest enhanced the status of the issue, giving femocrats in the
DCE better access to cabinet meetings (Swiebel & Outshoorn, 1990, p.
15). The Cabinet Committee also compensated for the loss of the state
secretary position, abolished after the elections of 1986. Women's
policy now fell directly under the Minister of Social Affairs, Christian
Democrat Jan de Koning. On the one hand this was an advantage. As
minister he had direct access to the cabinet, and he was a political
heavyweight. On the other hand, he had other pressing concerns and
priorities. Indeed, in general, moving the DCE to this ministry proved
to be disadvantageous. Given that the ministry's main focus had
always been labor market policy and social security, women's issues
tended to be marginalized, with women's equality policy becoming
mostly oriented toward employment.

At the same time, the DCE started to increase its leverage by using
its budget to set up joint ventures with other departments, making it
attractive for them to develop their own policy on women. Some
ministries did not need to be persuaded: The Ministry of Education
had already developed a women's program in 1979; the Ministry of
Health, Welfare, and Culture started subsidizing battered women's
shelters in 1982 and had its own special subsidy regulation for women's

initiatives at the local level.[8] The DCE also established a women's rights and law center and several women's health centers as pilot projects for a limited number of years, managing to persuade the Ministries of Justice and Health to take over the funding, so that its own budget could be used for new projects. It also set up in 1985 a *Stimuleringsgroep Emancipatieonderzoek* (Steering Committee for Women's Research, STEO) for which four other ministries also provided finances. For 6 years STEO was a major resource for the institutionalization of women's studies within the Dutch university system.

The ability of the DCE to intervene to produce policy outcomes that helped women generally depended on how the policy was defined and in which policy arena the issue was settled. Using Lowi's (1964) typology, which divides policies into three categories of distributive, regulatory, and redistributive, one can see that the DCE was most successful in distributive policies (Swiebel & Outshoorn, 1990). The DCE devoted much of its budget to creating women's policy machinery, such as the women's bureaus in all provinces and three major cities. The Department funded a variety of small feminist projects, such as feminist films and books; small businesses; and women's service projects, including rape crisis centers, women's education classes, and job centers for returning women workers. One of the most interesting policy innovations subsidized by the DCE has been the "emancipation workers project," which provides financial incentives to large nongovernmental organizations to employ women officers to develop women's policy (Outshoorn, 1992). All these initiatives have provided the Dutch women's movement with a strong state-subsidized backbone, allowing for both continuity in organization and institutionalization of new initiatives. In this way the DCE created its own clientele and its own legitimacy in the movement.

Many other issues that the women's movement either put on the political agenda or was interested in fall into the category of regulatory policy, which regulates behavior of individuals and groups. The political arena for such policy is parliament, making for open and conflictual politics. The legalization of abortion, issues of child custody and access rights, rape, violence against women, incest, pornography, antidiscrimination legislation, and child care all fall into this category. These issues traditionally involve the territory of the Ministry of Justice, which arguably has had little sympathy for feminist concerns. Given that these issues were already in the jurisdiction of another ministry, all the DCE could do was to try to exert influence indirectly over policy decisions. This usually succeeded only when there was strong feminist support and substantial backing in parliament. In the area of sexual violence, for instance, the DCE affected the content of draft proposals. The DCE could also exert influence through funding crisis intervention centers, turning incest and violence against women into distributive policy issues.

Indicative of the limits on the DCE's policy influence has been the drawn-out battle over antidiscrimination legislation. Originally intended to remedy the gaps in the Equal Treatment Act of 1980, the new law was passed in 1994. The original draft, with a strong DCE influence, included a ban on discrimination on the grounds of homosexuality, a move the women's movement strongly supported. But this proposal drew violent and protracted opposition from Protestant quarters, with arguments that the bill was in conflict with the constitutional right of freedom of religion. Later, the Liberals tacked on prohibition of discrimination on the grounds of race and ethnicity, so that the bill became redefined as a general antidiscrimination bill. The Ministry of Justice could therefore claim exclusive control over the bill.[9] The DCE did manage to prevent the women's issue from completely disappearing from the new text, but, reflecting the recent trend away from women's issues, the press did not even mention that the bill was also intended to end sex discrimination.

Redistributive policy takes place in the dominant socioeconomic arena. In the Netherlands, this arena is primarily controlled by the "social partners," representatives from employers associations, trade unions, and Government. Government representatives are usually selected by the Ministry of Social Affairs, but without input from the DCE. In these tripartite negotiations, women's issues are low on the agenda and women are not represented as women (they are also hardly present among the delegates). Neither trade unions nor employers have placed equal treatment, equal pay, or equal entitlement to social security benefits high on their agendas.[10] The major loss the DCE (and the women's movement) incurred in this policy arena has been in the reform of the social security system in the mid-1980s. This operation was necessitated to comply with the EC directive requiring equal treatment of women in the area of social insurance and social security. Other motives for this huge reform were to simplify the system and to cut costs (Sjerps, 1987). Given recent debates about pensions, the EC directives, and further cuts in welfare spending, this arena will continue to be crucial in the 1990s, but it is the one in which the DCE has exerted the least influence.

One can conclude that the DCE has been strong in suggesting initiatives and in agenda setting, but weak on implementation. For example, two of its pioneering initiatives were to design a policy for migrant women (who were neglected in minority policies of the Ministry of the Interior) and to follow the lead of the women's movement in the regulation of sexual harassment at work. Both policies have been poorly implemented, partially because of the DCE's limited jurisdiction in enforcement.

Links to the Women's
Movement and Organizations

Since its inception, the women's movement has been divided on its stance toward the women's policy offices, reflecting wider disagreement over its use of traditional political methods, such as lobbying and working in political parties. This did not mean that the more radical women were shy of conventional politics altogether, as they formed the backbone of the abortion campaign, but the majority preferred grass-roots activity in autonomous groups. Opposition to women's policy offices increased in the late 1970s, as the DCE became more active in defining women's policy. Notably the establishment of the provincial women's bureaus led to hostile reactions from radical feminists, who perceived these offices as an intentional attempt to coopt the movement from the bottom, calling this policy effort a "subsidized revolution" (Outshoorn, 1991b). Even though the femocrats needed the movement as a source of ideas and of legitimacy, the radical feminists did not see femocrats in the DCE as potential allies.

Other feminists were quick to grasp the advantages of subsidies. For them it was becoming increasingly difficult to run the many feminist service projects on a volunteer basis, and government support enabled them to maintain and expand their activities. A price had to be paid, however; in order to obtain funding, projects had to comply to certain organizational and professional standards, which meant in many cases the end of more open feminist approaches. It also led to the emergence of "bread feminists," who earned their salaries from the DCE and, as critics pointed out, "off the backs" of other women. Still, many radical feminists revised their ideas about the potential of the women's policy offices due to the changing political context at the beginning of the 1980s. The younger feminists joined the older branch of the movement in the strategy that has been called the "long march through the institutions."

With the return of the Liberal/Christian Democrat coalition in 1982 and its strong platform on cutting government spending and the provisions of the welfare state, many new feminists realized the time had come to defend women's interests. They forged new ties with women in a broader spectrum of political parties, not only with those within the Social Democrat party, as had long been the case. This also led to cooperation with the traditional women's organizations, whose origins dated back to the period of the Verzuiling and whose leaders had become increasingly aware of new feminist issues. For the first time since 1974, when the abortion coalition first emerged, a new umbrella organization of women's groups was formed in 1982, the Broad Platform for Economic Independence. In addition to mobilizing women on the issue of economic independence, it lobbied parties and parliament. A second platform organization, the Association for Redistribution of Paid and Unpaid Labor, more rooted in the trade union women's movement, also entered the women's equality policy arena. The two organizations merged in 1993, calling themselves the Alliance for Economic Independence and Redistribution of Work. In addition, women's sections have reemerged in all the major political parties, providing additional support for the platform of these new women's campaigns.

In the course of the 1980s, these new women's organizations eclipsed the autonomous women's movement of the 1960s and 1970s. Many of these feminists had become active in other types of organizations, often within networks in universities or within professions (mainly in the service sector) or within the trade unions. Many others became femocrats, staffing the numerous feminist projects subsidized by national or local government or becoming civil servants for women's equality policy at various levels of government (Outshoorn, 1992).

Indeed, DCE subsidies greatly contributed to the professionalization and institutionalization of the women's movement. In the process, feminism lost its earlier ideas about organizing horizontally and autonomously, accepting (often not without painful fights) pay differentials and a certain amount of hierarchy. In this way the criticism of the DCE and the other state-based women's policy structures and bread feminists disappeared completely.

Although the DCE created its own constituency and opposition to government offices for women disappeared, the Department's relationship to women's groups is still problematic. This is partly because women's groups depend on the DCE for funding. Despite the cuts in government spending the budget of DCE is still substantial and is still used to back feminist projects and organizations. Problems also arise because of changes in DCE personnel. From the beginning it has had strong informal ties with the women's movement, and many femocrats have their roots there. In recent years, women employed at the DCE have increasingly come from outside of the movement, although they share common beliefs with movement feminists. Their relationship to the movement is a professional one and tends to focus on the groups the DCE subsidizes, which are seen by femocrats as "the movement" (Outshoorn, 1994b).

The relationship between movement and agency has also changed considerably because of the process of integrating women's issues into policy areas that fall under the competence of other ministries. This process began in earnest after 1986, when the Minister of Social Affairs started pressing for integration. It meant that other ministries had to take responsibility for women's issues. For women's groups working in those other areas, this has implied that they can no longer turn to the DCE for their support but now have to lobby the other ministries. The direct ties, therefore, between movement and women's agency are loosening. As a consequence, the DCE is losing its support in the movement, and the women's movement is becoming increasingly specialized in various policy sectors. Activists in the field of health, for instance, pressure the Ministry of Health, Welfare, and Culture; legal rights activists turn to the Ministry of Justice; and women's studies advocates lobby the Ministry of Education. In this process, these new specialists are losing contact with women activists in other areas. This has led to a decline in movement solidarity because there is no longer one arena in which feminists share their ideas. This trend has accelerated in recent years, when a number of national single-issue organizations that had government subsidies on a temporary basis were forced to integrate into mainstream institutions.

Conclusion:
Back to the Iron Triangle

The EK envisaged the creation of a policy network, and not just a good working relationship between movement and state. To do this two other sides of the triangle had to be forged. First, there had to be a strong government advisory body. The creative EK, whose mandate ended in 1979, did have a successor, the Emancipatieraad (ER) (1981). But it never became very strong; its composition did not reflect any clear choice for either an independent experts committee or a representative body from the various currents of the women's movement (Prins, 1987). Party membership was more important than feminist expertise, and its permanent staff was too small to match the civil servants from the various ministries. There was some competition between the ER and the DCE, and it took time before one side of the desired triangle was formed.

Second, close ties between parliamentarians and femocrats were long in developing. At first the civil servants seemed to observe the role of loyal servants of the executive and only later did they develop informal contacts with parliamentarians in promoting the cause of women. In 1979, with the creation of the Parliamentary Standing Committee on Emancipation, contacts and expertise were improved, thus establishing the second side of the triangle. The women's policy triangle was slow in taking shape and never worked very well. This raises the question of whether, in the case of intersectoral policy, iron triangles are feasible. The femocrats from the DCE were not in a position to influence certain policy areas. In cases when the civil servants of other ministries dealt with the party specialists, the "women's angle" was regarded as subordinate or of secondary importance. This also rendered powerless those women parliamentarians who were not spokespersons for their party on the issue in question. One effective iron triangle that did emerge was in the more specialized area of women and development, where women from the Ministry of Foreign Affairs, MPs, experts, and several women's groups have been cooperating for over 15 years (Swiebel & Outshoorn, 1990).

The development of a policy network can be seen as a necessary condition for advancing women's equality policy, but not a sufficient one. Crucial is the matter of support for the women's policy agenda among the political elite. With pressure from the movement, support was present into the mid-1980s. That support has declined recently, threatening the edifice erected over the years. Several institutions active in the policy network are falling victim to fashionable ideas about small government, the call for bureaucratic efficiency, and faster parliamentary proceedings. The Social Democrat/Christian Democrat coalition, which took power in 1989, reinstated the state secretary for equality policy, putting the Socialist Elske ter Veld in office, but it abolished the Cabinet Committee for Women's Policy. The Parliamentary Standing Committee for Emancipation met for the last time in March 1994, and the ER is slated to disappear in 1997. The new 1994 antidiscrimination law redirects the scope of the Equal Opportunities Commission to include race as well as sex inequities. To counteract the disappearance of the ER and the Standing Committee, the DCE funded an initiative in 1992 to set up a women's lobby, Arachne.[11] It is too early to say if this new bureau will be able to intervene effectively in policy initiatives and fulfill a watchdog function in monitoring policy implementation, which has become more important with the decline of many national single-issue groups.

The DCE itself is being weakened by the policy of integration; most other ministries, with the exceptions of the Ministries of Education and Foreign Affairs, lack the experience, expertise, and interest to take over its tasks. Moreover, the DCE has not managed to establish control over socioeconomic policy within its own ministry, which makes it susceptible to future internal reorganizations. The trend toward decentralization of national government is also undermining the DCE. A number of women's issues, such as child care and labor market policy, have become a part of policy areas that now fall under the jurisdiction of local government or the social partners. With a general feeling among the political elite that women's policy is no longer needed "as we are all equal now," and a less visible women's movement to give support and legitimacy to women's policy issues, the major question for the DCE in coming years will be its survival.

Notes

1. Quotations are taken from interviews I conducted in summer 1993 for my *Femocrats in the Netherlands* project.

2. This work has for the most part been published in Dutch. For English language analyses, in chronological order, see DeVries (1981), Outshoorn (1986), Sjerps (1987), Swiebel (1988), Bussemaker (1991), and Outshoorn (1991a, 1991b, 1992, 1994b).

3. In general, iron triangles consist of representatives from organizations, government departments, and parliament who work together to develop and implement policy in a given area. Although widely used in the analysis of public policy in the Netherlands, the triangle metaphor does not accurately depict Dutch policy networks, which also include one or two official advisory bodies composed of interest-group representatives, independent experts, and specialized civil servants. Because the membership of these advisory bodies seldom overlaps with the actors in the triangle, Dutch policy networks look more like a quadrangle.

4. The DCE later developed several devices to counter the negative effects of intersectoral policy. For instance, all major policy documents (Beleidsplan, 1985; Emancipatie, 1977; Ministerie van Sociale Zaken en Werkgelegenheid, 1992) were intended to establish effective control. The government also created an interdepartmental coordination committee (1978) on which certain ministries were represented, and later the Cabinet Committee for Women's Policy (1986).

5. Abortion has been available since 1972, although it was only legalized in 1981.

6. In 1975, the Netherlands followed the equal pay directive and in 1980 the equal treatment directive through two new Equal Treatment Laws. The legislation established an Equal Opportunities Commission, with semijudicial and advisory functions, but no power to enforce law. For a discussion of the compliance of the Netherlands to EC regulations see Sjerps (1987).

7. The negotiations for a new cabinet are crucial for putting new items on the political agenda in the Netherlands; if one loses here, one can usually forget about the matter until the next election. Once the cabinet program is agreed on, it takes on the character of holy writ for the coalescing political parties, and it is the basis for parliamentary party discipline.

8. This regulation, the *Rijksbijdrage Regeling Emancipatiewerk* or RBR-EW did not cover the cost of personnel and was discontinued by decentralization policy in 1989. In the early 1990s, most municipal councils no longer provided finances for women's initiatives.

9. As a consequence, the Equal Opportunities Commission will disappear in its present form. Its successor will consist of experts on all forms of discrimination, which will lead to a loss of expertise and less attention to sex-based discrimination.

10. Women's groups have been active in the trade union movement since the mid-1970s. Women now make up most of the new trade union membership, making up for the loss of (male) members in declining industrial sectors. Since the mid-1980s, trade unions have started to push for women's interests in collective bargaining, including issues of child care and sexual harassment.

11. This is not a lobby in the American sense, but a clearance point for information on women's equality policy. It monitors proposals and passes out information to interested women's groups, also alerting them to potential allies. It does not lobby civil servants or parliamentarians itself.

11

Women's Equality Structures in Norway

The Equal Status Council

Jill M. Bystydzienski

Since 1949, Norway's centralized government has included an office of some sort to promote equal status between men and women. Before 1972, two small offices were consecutively charged with the oversight of equal pay issues for women:

1. The Equal Pay Committee was created in 1949.
2. The Equal Pay Council appeared in 1959 in response to Norway's ratification of ILO Convention 100 on equal pay for men and women for work of equal value (Equal Status Council, 1993a, p. 19).

Neither of these bureaus was given any significant authority to develop women's policy.

With the creation of the *Likestillings Radet* (Equal Status Council, ESC) in 1972, the Norwegian government began to cultivate a network of agencies responsible for the implementation and formulation of policies involved with the promotion of sex-based equality that went beyond equal pay. All of these offices have been based on the assumption that women's status in society should be made equal to men's. This network included offices at the national, regional, and local levels, in and out of established bureaucratic structures. Thus, rather than delegating women's policy to a single ministry, Norwegian policymakers have sought to "mainstream the goal of equal status into the sphere of every ministry" (ESC, 1993a, p. 20).

The purpose of this chapter is to systematically examine this network of equality offices. The institutionalization of goals related to the advancement of women and gender equality within agencies involved two dynamics: the state, from above, pulling women into the public sphere as objects of policy, and women's movements and organizations, from below, pushing for policies to advance the status of women. A large portion of this chapter will focus on the ESC because its birth coincided with the takeoff period for women's policy, and it has served as an important coordinating body for government agencies and policies in the promotion of women's equality.

The first part of the chapter will place the ESC within the context of Norwegian state-society relations and of the evolution and general activities of women's equality agencies. Part two will focus on the establishment, organization, and activities of the ESC since 1972. The third and fourth sections will examine the extent to which a women's equality network—women within equality offices and other sectors of the Norwegian state working with women's groups and feminist movements—has contributed to policies designed to improve women's position in Norwegian society.

The Evolution of Women's Policy Agencies and the Norwegian State

Like many other Western European countries, Norway combines a capitalist economic system with a democratic welfare state. The state apparatus has become the dominant institution in Norway, with state and society being closely intertwined. A long tradition of participatory democracy has fostered strong support for norms of equality and social justice (Halsaa, 1989, p. 2). As a result, Norwegian political culture has created "a benign view of the state as an instrument of popular will, which is used to control the private forces of market and family" (Hernes, 1987, p. 156). Since World War II, the state has expanded even more. The discovery of North Sea oil in the 1960s further stimulated tremendous growth in the public sector.

The Norwegian state has four components:

1. The electoral system, which encompasses political parties and elected bodies on the local, regional, and national levels
2. The corporate sector, which constitutes approximately 1,200 permanent and ad hoc committees, boards, and councils with representation from economic and other interest organizations, central government, parliament, and research institutions
3. Public administration, comprising the various ministries and agencies charged with implementing policies and legislation developed within the first two areas
4. The public sector, which employs citizens to provide social services

Two important forces have driven the development of women's equality offices in national, regional, and local governments. The first was the gradual expansion of state activities to encompass maternal health, child care, care of the aged and the sick, socialization, schooling, and other areas of reproductive and family life (Hernes, 1987, p. 44). The second influence came from the political activities of the women's movement. Especially during the 1970s and early 1980s, movement activists articulated women's issues and concerns and organized election campaigns that increased the number of women in public office (Bystydzienski, 1988). These two developments led, on the one hand, to a growing dependence of women on the state and, on the other hand, to increasing demands made by women, from inside as well as outside the state, for equality between the sexes.

This new attention given to women's equality issues in the 1970s, however, was not the first occasion the state had taken up the cause of disadvantaged groups. According to Hernes (1987), there have been two waves of state involvement in promoting the interests of outgroups. The first, which took place following the industrial revolution, drew men from agriculture into wage labor and resulted in the political incorporation of working-class men through the labor movement's trade unions and Socialist parties. The second occurred after 1945 when the expansion of the public sector drew women into the labor market, profoundly affecting families and women's roles (Hernes, 1987, pp. 31-32). In the first wave, working-class men gained access to the state due to agitation from below; in the second, the state took the initiative and began to pull women in as clients and consumers of its social services and as employees in the public sector.

As a result of these welfare state policies, women were the recipients of state policy and services aimed at improving their conditions but were absent from the decision-making processes that profoundly affected their public and private lives (Hernes, 1987). The effect of their absence became more evident as the interests of women increasingly became the object of public policy and as more women entered the public sector, albeit at the lowest rungs. Some argued that men alone would not adequately represent women's interest. The sex equality debate, which began in the early 1950s and continued into the 1960s, reinforced this growing recognition that women needed to be involved in decision making (Bystydzienski, 1988, p. 83).

Pulling women into the welfare state as passive recipients had thus created a counterforce of feminists who agitated or pushed from below for a more equal sharing of power between men and women. Women's groups forged an alliance with women's sections in the political parties, focusing largely on the electoral system. Working through the political parties and teaching voters to use flexible voting rules, activists quadrupled female political representation at both the local and national levels in a period of two decades (Bystydzienski, 1988).

The new women's movement simultaneously raised public consciousness regarding women's disadvantaged economic, political, and family status, and increasingly called on the government to respond to women's issues and problems. As more women entered legislative bodies, corporate committees, and civil service agencies, they took the issues formulated by the movement and placed them on public agendas. Gradually, the state became more responsive to women's demands from below, and women began to participate increasingly in shaping social policies. The creation of state agencies aimed at improving the status of women in the 1970s and 1980s was, therefore, a result of the combined efforts of women's groups and movements in society and women insiders within the state.

Following the documentation of women's inferior economic and social position in a series of official reports, parliament expanded and renamed the Equal Pay Council to form the Equal Status Council in 1972 (Bonnevie, 1953; Holter, 1970). Although the ESC concentrated specifically on breaking down economic barriers to sex equality, the state had broadened its mandate to include all forms of gender-based inequities and gave the Council more freedom to set priorities (Halsaa, 1989, p. 32). This expanded scope allowed the ESC to participate in the work of other new government offices involved with sex-based equality. The rest of this section will survey the women's policy agencies founded throughout the state.

In 1977, a Department for Family Affairs and Equal Status was established under the new Ministry of Consumer Affairs and Government Administration (now the Ministry of Family and Consumer Affairs). The task of the Department has been to coordinate government policies in matters of equal status and to be vigilant so that this aspect is not neglected in policies, regulations, and practices of government ministries (ESC, 1990, p. 13). Since its inception, this Department has taken an active role in promoting sex equality.

During International Women's Year (1975) most Norwegian municipalities appointed local Women's Year Committees. The outcome was so positive that many citizens expressed the desire to establish permanent organizations for promoting equal status in their local communities. As a result in 1977, just 3 months after its creation, the Ministry of Consumer Affairs and Government Administration (1985, p. 9) invited municipalities to set up equal status committees. New local equal status committees were based on political appointments and had the same rights and status as other local government committees (ESC, 1990, p. 13). By 1993, 340 out of the 439 official municipalities had established such committees (ESC, 1993a, p. 28). These municipal bodies are coordinated by the ESC.

Following ESC recommendation, the Ministry of Consumer Affairs and Government Administration proposed two Action Plans to promote equality between the sexes. In conjunction with the second plan (1986-1990), the ministry took the initiative in preparing a research program that resulted in the formation of a new Research Council for Applied Social Science. This council's policy has been to conduct research focusing on economic and political changes taking place in Norwegian society and their effects on and implications for men and women (Norwegian Research Council for Applied Social Science,

1988, p. 6). The ministry also has been responsible for enforcing the provisions of Article 21 of the Equal Status Act (see discussion below) by overseeing compliance of all governmental boards, councils, and committees with a 40% sex quota. The ministry routinely reviews lists of nominees for these bodies and is authorized to make changes in their composition (Hernes, 1987, p. 93).

During the 1980s, the Department of Family Affairs and Equal Status established a Committee on the Role of Men. In its publications promoting this committee, the Department argued that without changes in men's roles and the division of responsibilities of housework and child care, equal status between the sexes could not be achieved (ESC, 1990, p. 14). In 1981, the Ministry of Church and Education (now Ministry of Education, Research, and Ecclesiastical Affairs) established a Secretariat for Equal Opportunities in Education. Its founding coincided with the first Action Plan for Equality, which focused in large part on improving the status of women in education. This secretariat was composed of 5 members, all with a background in education and in equal status work; it organized courses on equal status in education for teachers all over the country, supervised the writing of new textbooks, and, through conferences and study groups, encouraged women to move into administrative positions (Ministry of Consumer Affairs and Government Administration, 1985, pp. 3-4). Because of the work done by this Committee, by the end of the decade equal status policies in education were treated seriously and widely implemented (Halsaa, 1989, p. 30).

Another important government agency established to advance the status of women has been the Secretariat for Women and Research founded in 1981 under the Ministry of Culture and Science. The goals of the Secretariat have been twofold: to increase the number of women in research activities and to initiate and promote research on women (Norwegian Research Council for Science and Humanities, 1987, p. 1). The Secretariat has been working closely with the Norwegian Research Council for Applied Social Science in a collaborative effort to achieve a greater measure of gender equality through research, as outlined in part by the second Action Plan for equality between the sexes. In just over a decade, hundreds of women researchers received the opportunity and support to conduct studies on all aspects of women's lives, resulting in numerous publications (ESC, 1993b).

In addition to the ministries discussed thus far, most other ministries have developed programs to deal with aspects of sex equality. For example, the Ministry of Local Government and Labor has, since 1967, appointed what were initially called "women's consultants" to coordinate and initiate measures concerning women and employment at the regional level. By the late 1980s, every region had its own equality consultant (ESC, 1990, p. 14). The Ministry of Environment initiated several pilot projects for "municipal planning on women's terms," and the Ministry of Agriculture developed its own "Action Plan for Equal Status in Agriculture," encouraging women to take advantage of their inheritance rights and to enroll in schools of agriculture (Halsaa, 1989, p. 31).

Recent budgetary crises and the increasing popularity of privatization have underscored a general agreement on the part of policymakers that a further expansion of women's policy agencies is not economically feasible. Yet, it is unlikely that a movement toward market solutions will dismantle the complex web of existing state structures for women. This resistance to undoing 20 years of constructing women's policy institutions is related to the centrality of the state in the lives of all Norwegians and the notion in Norwegian political culture that the state has the responsibility to equalize economic and social differences between groups.

The Equal Status Council

ESTABLISHMENT

In 1965, the United Nations Commission on the Status of Women recommended that all nations develop plans of action to ameliorate the problems faced by women. In Norway, as in the other Scandinavian countries, the social democratic Labor party became the prime mover behind the initiative.[1] In the same year, the Labor party drafted a report titled "Where is the Women's Place?" The title was a reference to the widely discussed film, *Woman's Place*, made in 1956 by Eva Seeberg (Halsaa, 1990, p. 13). In its report, the Labor party documented the great economic, political, and educational disparities between women and men and called for the creation of state mechanisms, including an equal status body and legislation, to improve women's status.

Two years later, before the local elections of 1967, the National Council of Women, an umbrella organization consisting of women's associations, joined with women's sections of political parties, the Labor and Liberal parties, and the Government to form a broad coalition for women's issues. This loose group organized a preelection campaign, pressuring parties to nominate more women and urging voters to choose female candidates (Bystydzienski, 1988, pp. 83-84). The campaign committee was headed by Prime Minister Per Borten (leader of the Center party) and was publicly financed (Halsaa, 1990, p. 13). After these elections, female representation at the local level more than doubled, and a precedent was set for close cooperation between the government and women's organizations.

Prior to the 1972 referendum on Norwegian membership in the European Community (EC), a special women's campaign against membership was formed (Stromberg, 1980, p. 46). This campaign drew many women into the political arena, strengthening the fledgling women's movement and creating a greater awareness of women's problems and concerns. In 1971, the Labor party came back to power, and by 1972 the time was ripe for a concerted governmental response to increasing pressure, both from inside and outside of the state, to do something about gender equality. The Equal Pay Council had not been an effective body, lacking the enforcement mechanisms necessary for decreasing the economic gap between men and women. On the recommendation of the Labor party, the Norwegian parliament voted to transform the Equal Pay Council into an Equal Status Council, whose task was to "work for equal status in all sectors of society; family life, working life, education, and the community in general" (ESC, 1990, p. 12).

ORGANIZATION

From 1972 to 1979, the ESC consisted of 13 members, comprising representatives from various employment organizations, the National Council of Women, and appointees from academic, research, and governmental institutions (Ministry of Consumer Affairs and Government Administration, 1985, p. 1). Council members were appointed by the Government in power. The ESC was initially set up as an independent consultative agency. Its main function was to make recommendations to appropriate ministries, which in turn would propose policy and legislative changes. By the late 1970s, however, the Council's tasks had been increased to include a more active role in shaping policy and in organizing political actions. This new role for the ESC was formalized in the 1979 Equal Status Act.

It took several years of negotiations between the Labor party, trade union representatives, and representatives of the women's movement to produce the 1979 Act (Skjeie, 1991, pp. 20-24). The impetus came from two sources:

1. The United Nations International Women's Year in 1975 and International Women's Decade (1975-1985) led to many governmental initiatives to promote gender equality.
2. The increasingly active new women's movement mobilized public opinion and kept pressing for more effective measures to improve the status of women.

The increasing number of women in elected office who had been active in the women's movement and were committed to working for gender equality also contributed to the formulation of the 1979 Act.

The draft proposal was introduced in parliament in 1978 and was implemented a year later. Although originally designed primarily as a document to regulate working life, the Act was broadened during lengthy negotiations to include equal treatment in all areas except religious communities and personal relationships (ESC, 1989, p. 5). During the negotiations, feminists lost to the trade unions in the matter of comparable worth; the unions would not agree to include a clause permitting equal pay for work of comparable value (Skjeie, 1991, p. 21). Nonetheless, feminist representatives were able to gain a concession in response to their argument that gender-based discrimination is suffered mainly by women and that a gender-neutral wording of the Act would allow equal treatment of unequals, barring measures that might be effective in improving the status of women (Skjeie, 1991, p. 22). The concession resulted in the following language in the first section of the Equal Status Act: "[the] Act shall promote equal status between the sexes and aims particularly at improving the position of women" (ESC, 1989, p. 4).

With passage of the 1979 law, the ESC was reorganized to consist of seven members. It remained an independent agency, with the Government reserving final approval on appointments to the Council. Two of the members are appointed at the recommendation of the Norwegian Federation of Trade Unions and the Confederation of Norwegian Business and Industry. Men and women from all parts of Norway are represented by Council members, and some members are required to have experience in equal status work and in women's organizations (Halsaa, 1989, p. 33). The National Council of Women, however, was excluded from membership in 1979. The restructuring of the ESC broadened its scope and responsibilities. In addition to its previous mandate of serving as a consultative body to the government and as a link between government, women's organizations, the private sector, and public opinion, it assumed the role of an advisory and coordinating body for equal status committees in counties and municipalities. The Council also was given more resources to gather and disseminate information regarding inequality between the sexes and increased responsibility to initiate conferences and plans of action. Throughout the 1980s, the Council played an active role in stimulating public debate, setting priorities, and organizing numerous initiatives. The content of these activities will be examined in further detail below.

The Equal Status Act of 1979 established the Equal Status Ombud[2] and an Equal Status Appeals Board to enforce its provisions and deal with grievances resulting from infringements. When stipulations of the Act were violated, the Ombud was to try to effect a voluntary agreement. If this proved impossible, the Ombud then could bring the case before the Appeals Board. The Act gave this board the power to invoke prohibitions and injunctions (ESC, 1990, p. 13).[3] The Ombud, although retaining independent status and a separate office, was to work closely with the small staff of the ESC.

The Council's increasing influence during the 1980s has to be understood in the context of Norwegian politics during that decade. The Labor party, which had been a staunch supporter of gender equality policies and a major force behind the establishment of the Council, managed to keep coming back to power despite a growing conservative opposition.[4] The 1980s also saw a tremendous increase in the numbers of women in parliament and in the corporate sector. Between 1977 and 1989, the percentage of women in parliament grew from 16 to 36, and from 18 to 35 on the public boards, committees, and councils. Many of the women entering politics had come up through women's organizations and had been involved in the feminist movement.

Despite ideological differences among feminists (most notably along liberal/radical lines) and among women politicians across political parties, broad agreement on issues such as equal pay, improved child care, a shorter work week, an end to violence against women, a ban on pornography, and election of more women to public offices existed among women's groups inside and outside the state (Bystydzienski, 1988). Thus, there was strong support for equality policies among the organizations and groups that worked closely with the ESC.

By the late 1980s, the worldwide economic recession began to have serious effects in Norway, leading the government to reduce its funding of many agencies, including the ESC. A 1989 evaluation of the Council indicated that due to a shortage of resources, the agency was forced to decrease its contact with women's organizations from an annual to a biannual conference and to reduce the number of publications (Halsaa, 1989, pp. 33-34). In the early 1990s, the Council had only one person coordinating all of the local and regional equal status committees (over 360), and its director held a one-fifth position.

ACTIVITIES AND IMPACT ON POLICY

One of the most important roles played by the Council since its reorganization in 1979 has been as coordinator for local equal status committees. These committees have given priority to increasing the number of women in politics and have been active in campaigns aimed at encouraging women voters to support women candidates and at promoting female political candidates in local council elections. The local equal status bodies have had few resources and limited power with which to promote gender equality in politics (Halsaa, 1989, p. 34). However, with the help of the ESC, these committees have been able to work effectively; during the 1980s, the number of women in local politics had increased steadily. In addition to annual conferences for local equal status committee representatives, the ESC has offered workshops where members learn how to organize and mobilize their communities and provided publications (for distribution in communities) that argue the merits of equal numbers of women and men in politics.

The Council also has taken an active role in national preelection campaigns. Before the 1985 election, the Council organized a meeting for independent and political women's organizations to discuss and plan strategies. It secured public financing and campaign office space from the Ministry of Consumer Affairs and Government Administration. The campaign's slogan was: "Let the women in!" (Halsaa, 1989, p. 38). The Council took similar initiatives before the 1989 and 1993 elections. These campaign activities, along with the use of quotas for women on electoral lists in nearly all of the political parties, contributed to the increase of the number of women in parliament between 1985 and 1993, from 24% to 40%.

Through its frequent conferences on inequities between the sexes, the ESC has helped to stimulate debate, as well as new approaches to the problem. At a 1980 conference, representatives of several women's groups reported on the disadvantages women faced primarily in the workforce and in education. The participants drew up a "plan of action" that was later picked up by the Ministry of Consumer Affairs and Government Administration and adopted by the parliament as the first 5-year (1981-1985) Action Plan to Promote Equal Status Between the Sexes (Royal Ministry of Foreign Affairs, 1989, p. 17). This first plan gave particular emphasis to the use of quotas in education, especially in admission to technical and higher education institutions, where women were sorely disadvantaged relative to men. Quotas in government employment were suggested but had to be handled through separate negotiations between the government and civil service organizations, resulting in provisions for equal work opportunities in the Basic Agreement for Government Employees (Halsaa, 1989, p. 29).

Parliament adopted a second Action Plan for the period 1986-1990. This time, however, the conservative coalition government played down quotas and emphasized integrating sex equality into all areas of public policy. Every ministry was asked to develop its own action program by the end of 1987. This required a review of all legislation, regulations, and administrative practices in order to determine whether they contained gender bias (Halsaa, 1989, p. 30). One outcome of the implementation of this policy has been that the Norwegian Aid Agency, under the Ministry of Foreign Affairs, now evaluates all of its programs and projects (mostly in Third World countries) in terms of how they affect the sexes, and especially what impact they have on women.

Through its contact with all women's organizations, including radical feminist groups, the ESC has been a repository for many ideas and a forum for working through disagreements among the different ideological factions of the women's movement. When the debate about gender-specific quotas began in Norway during the early 1970s, radical feminists supported the proposal to have equal numbers of women and men in all organizations at all levels. The more moderate groups were willing to settle for 30% women. Over time, the groups reached a compromise and agreed on the wording "at least 40 percent of each sex," which came to be accepted by four of the major political parties and by officials in education and public sector employment.[5] By 1981, Article 21 was added to the Equal Status Act, which mandated that all public (corporate) agencies should ensure that the numbers of women and men on boards, committees, and councils should be as equal as possible. By 1988, the Article was amended to read that "each sex shall be represented by at least 40% of the members . . . when a government agency appoints or elects committees, governing boards, councils" and so on (ESC, 1989, p. 18). In 1991, women held 38% of all seats in these bodies (Skjeie, 1992, p. 77).

The ESC also has played a role in spearheading equality legislation, mostly by increasing the awareness of those in government, as well as the general public, of persistent inequalities between the sexes in various areas. For instance, even before the passage of the Equal Status Act, the Council had called attention to the fact that the Allodial Act violated the principle of sex equality by giving priority to the oldest male in family farm inheritance. The Act was amended in 1974, confirming inheritance rights on the oldest child (ESC, 1990, p. 14). During the 1980s, the Council put out many publications regarding the need for fathers to be involved in child care and to have access to parental leave. By 1994, parliament extended family leave to 32 weeks with full pay, allowing the mother to take off from work 2 weeks before and the first 6 weeks after the birth of a child. Four weeks of the remaining period are reserved for the father (Van der Ros, 1994, p. 6). Recent legislation has also given parents with children less than 10 years old 10 days of paid leave each year in case of family emergency (ESC, 1990, p. 12).

The ESC has recently begun to reach out to create links between Norwegian women and women of other countries. In 1991, the Council organized a conference in Oslo titled, "Women and Democracy—Participation and Welfare," bringing together women from central and eastern Europe, as well as Nordic countries. The participants discussed involvement in politics and the labor market, women's health and safety, legal rights, women's organizations, and networking. A number of those who attended have since begun to collaborate on research and action projects. A second conference was planned for 1995 (Baalsrud, 1992).

Relations Between Equality Offices and Women's Interests in Society: Co-Optation or Integration

It should be clear from the above discussion that many women have been active in the Norwegian corporate system through state agencies charged with improving the status of women. Women in great numbers also have entered the state through elective offices and the civil service bureaucracy. With the lines between these three sectors blurred, politicians are often members of corporate committees, councils, and boards, and representatives from various organizations and interest groups run for political offices. Some of the independent organizations represented in the corporate sector also have close ties to specific political parties.

Public administration officials prepare and implement decisions made by the cabinet and parliament and meet members of women's organizations and politicians in the extensive system of public committees, boards, and councils (Halsaa, 1989, p. 49). The women in the elected and corporate sectors frequently know each other and, to a considerable extent, cooperate to promote the interests of women. Halsaa (1989) indicates that there is a special "equal status segment" or women's equality network within the state in which women politicians, public administration officials, and members of equal status agencies meet in various ways to define goals and means, with women's researchers playing an important role as providers of expertise (Halsaa, 1989, p. 49). Many participants have links to women's organizations outside the state and are committed to feminist ideals.

The close relationship between women's political activism and the state in Norway raises the question of whether feminists have been co-opted into the still male-dominated state system. Some Norwegian observers have argued that women in the state apparatus have been disarmed by men in power (see, e.g., Holter, 1981); that as a group they essentially are powerless to affect any substantive change in the system. Research focusing on the extent to which women politicians have been able to influence policies and legislation lends some support to this view. It seems that women politicians tend to follow their party ideologies in respect to specific issues, only seldom achieving group consensus and voting as a bloc (Bystydzienski, 1995; Skjeie, 1992, pp. 111-129).

Another argument in support of this view has been that women are entering "shrinking institutions," that is, state structures that are losing influence, while power shifts to other areas, particularly economic institutions in the private sector, multinational corporations, and the European Union (Skjeie, 1992, p. 70). Moreover, there is overwhelming evidence that government and politics in Norway still remain male-controlled; in order to participate, women have to play by men's rules. Despite the large numbers of women and the rhetoric of gender equality, the state in Norway continues to be dominated by masculine values and structural arrangements that favor men (Bystydzienski, 1995).

At the same time, there is evidence that feminists within the Norwegian state have managed to retain a significant degree of independence and to affect change in favor of women. Co-optation indicates an exchange of ideological commitment for institutionalized power (Skjeie, 1992, p. 134), yet many of the women who have become insiders have not given up their commitment to improving the situation of women and have consistently promoted the inclusion of equality issues in legislative and policy agendas (Halsaa, 1989). Studies indicate that at least one third of all women politicians have held onto their feminist ideologies after entering public office (Hellevik & Skard, 1985; Skjeie, 1992, p. 103). Despite party fragmentation, women in the state have formed occasional coalitions across party and ideological lines and have reached broad agreement on certain issues, such as child care and a shorter work week (Bystydzienski, 1995). Many continue to have strong ties with women's organizations and groups outside the system that help to sustain feminist consciousness (Halsaa, 1989).

For Norwegian feminists in the state, being part of the system poses a dilemma of how to remain committed to the promotion of women's interests and at the same time to participate fully in male-dominated institutions. Hege Skjeie (1992) calls this the problem of "remain[ing] different among peers" (p. 135). Ideally, the state should change to accommodate women as women, as well as the diversity among them (Phillips, 1993). In the meantime, despite the gains Norwegian women have made in representation and in recognition by the state of the importance of gender equality, feminists struggle with the ambiguities entailed by attempts to change the system from within.

Conclusion

The development and record of the women's equality network of equal status offices sprinkled throughout the Norwegian state strongly suggests that the formal charge of these women's policy structures has been translated into real influence in the policymaking process. The ESC, as a prime example of such mechanisms, has played a pivotal role in

coordinating local, regional, and national equality offices,

integrating gender issues into all areas of public policy,

formulating and implementing equality legislation and programs, and

increasing the number of women in the elected, bureaucratic, and corporate sectors of the Norwegian state.

Not only have the women's equality agencies remained intact in times of economic retrenchment and privatization, albeit at reduced levels of funding, but these offices have translated certain demands emanating from established women's groups and the new women's movements into state action. Indeed, as this chapter has maintained, the role of these policy structures was not just a by-product of policymakers pulling women into the state as passive subjects of policy. These

202 COMPARATIVE STATE FEMINISM

offices were shaped by women activists from established women's groups, political parties, and the new feminist movement who saw the presence of effective offices for women's equality as a part of the struggle to improve Norwegian women's position in all spheres of social, economic, and political life. In the final analysis, the ESC and other state agencies involved with women's equality policy are representative of the particular way in which the Norwegian state responds to demands for social justice through the creation of flexible structures that provide an arena to debate, discuss, and eventually address inequities.

Notes

1. Norway is a parliamentary democracy with a multiparty system based on proportional representation. In 1994, eight parties were represented in parliament, ranging from the far-left Red Electoral Alliance to the far-right Progress party. The Labor party (social democrats) had been in control of the Government for 20 years following World War II, after which power shifted several times between the socialist and nonsocialist blocks (Halsaa, 1989, p. 8). In the 1993 election, the Labor party once again obtained a clear majority of seats, followed by the Center (agrarian) and Conservative parties.

2. *Ombud*, rather than *ombudsman*, is the English-language term used in Norway. It has the advantage of being gender-neutral.

3. There are problems associated with the enforcement of the Act. Presentation of evidence is central to the enforcement of a ban on discrimination in connection with job appointments. But in many cases, even if the Ombud is certain that unequal treatment has occurred, it may be impossible to produce evidence that is acceptable to the legal system. And even if the right kind of proof is available, there is often no mechanism for enforcing the resolution (Halsaa, 1989, p. 28).

4. The Labor party was out of power between 1985 and 1986, and then again between 1989 and 1991. Both times a conservative coalition was elected only to be ousted by parliamentary votes of no confidence.

5. For a discussion of radical and moderate interpretations of the 40%-60% quota in Norway see, for instance, Skjeie (1993, p. 246).

12

Women, the State, and the Need for Civil Society

The Liga Kobiet in Poland

Jean Robinson

The *Liga Kobiet Polskich* (Polish Women's League) was housed in a multistory building on Elektoralna Street near Warsaw University. When I first noticed the building in 1979, I asked friends in the Sociology Department across the street whether it would be useful to talk with officials in the *Liga Kobiet* (LK) about women's condition and status in Poland. They laughed at the idea. Even then, before Solidarity, my Polish colleagues did not take seriously an organization that had claimed, at least early in its history, to be working to improve women's rights (LK, 1959, p. 405).[1] In fact, for 44 years, the quasi-governmental organization was the sole state structure responsible for promoting women's social, economic, and political status. It published newspapers and magazines, sponsored research workshops, promoted psychological, legal, and social consultations, founded self-help circles, and articulated the norms for women's public and private behavior. The LK self-consciously claimed that it promoted policies that served the diversity of "women's needs" (LK, 1964, p. 143).

And yet, mention the *Liga Kobiet* to a Polish woman in the late 1980s and, like my colleagues at the university, she would react with contempt.[2] Indeed, the organization whose self-proclaimed purpose was to "defend and further extend the rights of women working in the city and countryside, as wives, mothers, and citizens" (LK, 1959, p. 405) seems to receive little approbation for its work. Did the Liga fail to gain acceptance from the public because it had not been successful in defending and promoting women's rights? because it represented an unpopular image of women's roles? or because of its close association with the communist Polish United Workers Party (PUWP)? Or can it be that the LK's (and by implication the state's) construction of *woman* and *women's interests* was merely the articulation of a particular standpoint that was acceptable to certain groups, like the PUWP, but not to women outside this political party?

If state feminism is understood as "activities of government structures that are formally charged with furthering women's status and rights. . . . [to the extent that] these agencies are effective in helping women as a group and undermining patterns of gender-based inequities in society" (Chapter 1, this volume, p. 1-2), then quasi-government organizations in communist systems, such as the Liga, the All-China Women's Federation, and the *zhensoviety* (Soviet Women's Councils) in the former Soviet Union should be considered in a study of women's policy machinery.[3] After all, these organizations express the desire to help women overcome societal and economic barriers and proclaim the necessity to struggle for equality between men and women. At the same time, women in Poland under Communist party rule, like women in the Soviet Union, did not believe that these structures could promote their interests.[4] Rather, except for Communist activists, women in these countries have seen these satellite organizations as tools for the state's manipulation of women as producers and reproducers.

A broader theoretical question, however, is how to conceptualize state feminism in a state socialist system. Is the presence of an active but not autonomous state-affiliated organization dedicated to promoting the fulfillment of women's needs a positive agent of state feminism? How do we define feminism in diverse ideological systems? Does the literature on state feminism presume a particular relation between state and society, one that is seated on the assertion that the state has been created out of the "collection of practices and discourses" (Pringle & Watson, 1992, p. 63) embedded in liberal democratic histories and the existence of a civil society that enables various groups to articulate their interests and compete over power? If these prerequisites for state-society relations are absent, can we still compare, advanced industrial states with stable democratic systems to states with a different collection of practices?

The Polish case indicates that it is important to look at who defines *woman* and *women's interests*, as well as the content of those definitions, in explaining women's policy machineries in any national context. An examination of the Liga as a product of state socialism, therefore, forces the scholar to better define the state and to clarify the contextual basis of feminism. This chapter will argue that the state's usurpation of a parafeminist agenda and its construction of a neocorporatist women's movement shaped discourse about gender in a particular way. The single-party state dominated all public discussions of what women needed, generating definitions of women's issues that served the interest of the regime. The consequences of this top-down control of women's organizations can be seen in Poland today in the inability of women to organize effectively around issues, a tenacious distrust of feminism in any form, and a noticeably misogynist transitional democratic state.

If Poland teaches us anything, it is that neither the state, nor traditionally constructed political parties, nor established social institutions, such as the Polish Catholic Church, provide sufficient breadth to interrogate the gendering of society. Feminists in the bureaucracy are also not enough, for a state is only as democratic as its citizens. I will suggest that a civil society in which women are a vital part is a necessary ingredient for a state feminism that takes into account not only the needs of the state, but also the variety of needs of women living in society. The following analysis will address these issues by examining the establishment, organization, and activities of the Liga, the meaning of the state, state-society relations, and the ideological and discursive understandings of *women* in these contexts. In the conclusion, I will suggest ways in which state feminism as a theoretical construct is challenged by the Polish case.

Establishment:
Polish Socialism and Parafeminism

The *Liga Kobiet* (LK) was founded in 1945 to act as an arm of the Polish United Workers Party (PUWP) in organizing and mobilizing women to help in the reconstruction of postwar Poland and the construction of a socialist society. Rather than being a product of feminist activism, the LK was defined by the ideological and institutional parameters set by a Stalinist ruling party. The circumstances of its creation have had significant consequences, both for the organization itself and for the perception of it by Polish women. Although women were active in the socialist movement, the anti-Nazi struggles, and other important 20th-century social movements, there has been little evidence of a significant feminist movement or of autonomous women's groups in Poland.

During the interwar period, 80 small women's organizations resembling what Cott (1987) calls the "woman movement" (pp. 3-4) did appear, but there were no significant feminist groups or movement. One of these organizations, the Polish National Organization of Women (PNOW), supported by the right-wing National Democracy Party, published a list of goals in 1928 that were similar to those espoused by the LK in the post-World War II period (Reading, 1992, p. 168). Like the Liga, PNOW worked with orphans, promoted child care, and encouraged self-help for women at home. Also like the LK, the earlier Polish women's organization was not an autonomous organization. As a subsidiary of a conservative political party, it promoted Catholic and patriotic values: Women were encouraged to advance themselves for the good of the "Polish Catholic Nation" (Reading, 1992, p. 168).

In terms of its structure and activities, the LK followed the model established by women's organizations like the PNOW, but in terms of its definition of women's needs, the Liga was based on the Marxist tradition of the PUWP, which defined women's needs in class terms. Women's oppression, in this perspective, was caused by the capitalist and patriarchal system embedded in bourgeois family life. Although the PUWP was not a classically ideological communist party and did not promote itself as the answer to women's problems, it saw the need for a women's organization that could organize, mobilize, and energize women to participate in politics and production. The PUWP leadership created the LK to help ensure that women's "position in the collective economy was strengthened"; that women would get their "share of the continuing development of the economy, culture, and society"; and that "women would be promoted in all professions and all areas of life" (LK, 1959, p. 405).

Since its creation, the general policy goals of the Liga have been neither feminist nor antifeminist. Instead, the LK's action has been driven by a parafeminist approach linked to its Marxist roots. Applying a minimal definition of feminism to the goals of the LK, it becomes clear that at least one of the major defining principles of feminism is missing. Cott (1987, pp. 4-5) argues that late 20th-century feminism requires three core components: an opposition to sex hierarchy, the understanding of gender and sex as socially constructed and thus mutable, and the conscious perception by women that they constitute a social grouping. As Eisenstein (1983, pp. 136-145) and Gordon (1979, p. 107) point out, when feminists talk about the recognition that women constitute a social group, they imply both a personal and political search for understanding oppression and sex hierarchy and, arising from that understanding, a recognition of the need to change the system and structures of oppression.

The first component was no problem for any Marxist party or organization. Marx and, in much more detail, Engels recognized that sex hierarchies were probably the first oppression and called for new socialist societies to eradicate the conditions leading to these divisions. Commonly, this meant removing women from the household and giving them some economic freedom to escape from reliance on men. Bringing women into production would then erase the divisions between the sexes and put working women in the same plight as working men: Under socialism, they would then both be free. The last component of Cott's definition, consciousness, was also critical for Marxists. Indeed, most of the ruling Communist parties have interpreted consciousness as meaning that the identification of one's self as part of a class demands action.[5]

Comprising well-taught daughters of Engels, Lenin, Bebel, Kollontai, and others, the Liga was opposed to sex hierarchy in principle and often in practice and understood that women did constitute a distinct social group. What they did not accept was that the system of oppression operated within the private as well as the public sphere. The social construction of gender, one of the core foundations of (late 20th-century Euro-American) feminist thinking, therefore, remained unrecognized by the LK. And yet, the Liga sought to change women's position in the workplace and understood that this required helping women in their domestic lives. As such, LK members pursued many strategies similar to Western women's movements, always denying that they were bourgeois feminists. It was precisely in their formulation of the solution that one sees their parafeminist character: Helping women to cope with the pressures and difficulties of consumption and reproduction is not the same as understanding the need to change the structure of consumption and reproduction. The parafeminist position of the LK remained mostly unchanged throughout its long history.

Organization

Until the demise of the Communist-led government in 1989, the organization of the LK was determined by its symbiotic relations with the PUWP. The PUWP directly provided all of the LK's funding. High-ranking members of the LK served on the Central Committee of the PUWP, a signal that the organization was closely tied to party positions (Siemienska, 1991, p. 111). Both its presence on the party's Central Committee and reliance on the party for funding meant that while the LK received support for its activities, those activities had to remain within the legitimate boundaries of social action as defined by the PUWP. Thus, at the same time the LK benefited organizationally from its close association with the ruling party, that alliance precluded certain kinds of discourse and action.

Membership within the LK varied over time; in fact, various accounts report different numbers for the same time period. Siemienska (1991, p. 114) says that the height of membership was 2 million in the late 1960s, whereas the LK itself reported a membership approaching 4 million in 1963, and over 4 million in 1964 (LK, 1964, 1965). All sources agree that membership declined in the 1970s because of a change in recruitment. In the 1950s and 1960s, recruitment and retention were based on occupational affiliation with LK circles established in such places as factories, state agricultural enterprises, and workers' production cooperatives. The LK also sought to increase membership by establishing circles of military families, as well as local circles for unemployed homemakers and self-employed domestic workers. After 1968, LK leadership decided to base membership on personal affiliation, which led to a drastic decline in overall membership but an increase in the number of active members dedicated to women's issues.

Nationally the organization was structured along the same lines as the PUWP. The *Zarzad Glowny* (Central Administration) was headed by a chairperson, appointed by the PUWP leadership and assisted by several vice chairpersons, by first secretaries of the Secretariat, as well as by Administrative Members of the Presidium. The Liga had annual meetings of delegates, presumably chosen by leaders at the local level. In addition to the central headquarters in Warsaw, there were departments of the LK at provincial and district levels. Local offices were responsible for creating circles in enterprises, agricultural collectives, and neighborhoods.

Later, active members worked on behalf of the LK to recruit new members and establish circles. Through the provincial and district offices, the LK established self-help circles at the local level, called the *Komitet do Spraw Gospodarstwa Domowego* (Committees for Home Economics Affairs). In addition, the Central Administration established ad hoc committees, including Committees for the Care and Protection of Orphans (1958), legal aid offices (beginning in 1960), and committees for social assistance (1964). During the decade of martial law in the 1980s, the Liga established two autonomous sections, an Organization for Military Families and a Militia Circle.

The LK published a weekly newspaper, *Zwierciadlo* (The Mirror), an occasional monthly paper, *Ty i Ja*, and regular bulletins on relevant issues for women. The Liga also had its own research division, called the Research Service Workshop, which conducted surveys and studies of the socioeconomic situation of women and their families. Reports on this research were passed to PUWP leadership and relevant administrative agencies. The Central Administration of the LK used this research as a basis for policy recommendations to the government. Although it is difficult to determine the extent of its advisory role, Liga reports suggest that government officials consulted the organization on consumption needs and patterns and used the organization to promote certain values about women's roles (LK, 1964, p. 153).

In the 1950s, the Liga promoted an image of Polish women primarily as producers in society. Implicit in its articulation of women's needs was that there were barriers to women's effective work in production. Although the work of the LK in the 1950s and 1960s makes passing reference to inequalities in hiring and promotion, it continued to focus primarily on helping women solve the problems of the double burden. In 1957, the organization identified "raising children, managing domestic housekeeping, and raising the level of culture" (LK, 1959, p. 406) as the most serious problem affecting women. The Liga's response was to organize self-help circles (*samopomocowe zespoly*) so that women could resolve some of their housekeeping problems among themselves. There is no evidence that the LK engaged in any effort to rethink the gendered division of labor within the family, to mobilize men to help in household labor, or to convince the PUWP to take into account the multiple demands on women's time and energies. As such, the LK was not a pioneering feminist organization. To be one would have required that the organization self-consciously charge itself with an activist agenda designed to alter sexual or gender relationships, either at home or in the workplace.

An examination of annual reports on the LK in the *Rocznik Polityczyny i Gospodarczy* reveals its evolution and development as an agency in support of women. It is first important to note that in the period 1958-1986, there were a number of years when the LK's work was not reported: 1959, 1962, 1966, 1969, 1971-1977, and 1979-1985. Although the absence of reports in the 1980s can be explained by the upheavals around the period of martial law, there is no obvious explanation for the lack of reports in the 1970s, unless there was a PUWP or state policy that sought to downplay the role of women in those years. As Siemienska (1990; 1994, p. 615) argues, the 1970s were a period of steady improvement in living standards, coupled with fears of overemployment and a severe drop in the birthrate. The period was also marked by pro-natalist policies and a clear emphasis on the return of women in paid labor to the home. Indeed, many officials asked frequently whether both husband and wife should be employed when the children were small (Koski, 1977).

The rhetoric in the 1958 report, as well as reports of the early 1960s, differs substantially from the discourse in later years. The former concentrates on trying to find methods to open more opportunities for women in employment by training women, fighting discrimination, and promoting solutions designed to help women to cope with housework and child care (LK, 1959, p. 406; 1961, p. 213; 1962, p. 246; 1964, pp. 184-185). The latter is concerned foremost with civic education for women and secondarily with addressing women's domestic difficulties. Attention to advancing women as "co-directors of the state" (LK, 1964, p. 182), a phrase used in 1963 and obviously a perceived problem in the system, disappeared by the late 1960s. Instead, after a Party Plenum in 1964, the LK claimed that most of women's problems had been solved, when they clearly had not.

> In People's Poland, women have realized their fundamental aspirations; they have fully mastered work in politics, the economy, and society. People's socialist politics ensures protective health care, care of mothers and children, a free system of social security, development of cultural and creative outposts, and making possible the full development of active professional and social women. (LK, 1965, p. 152)

A similar claim in 1964—that the state, on the counsel of the LK, would solve women's remaining domestic problems—further contributed to cynical attitudes toward the LK in the late 1970s. By the end of the 1960s, when Polish society was beset by civil unrest over the lack of economic progress, the LK was clearly being used as an organ of the state to encourage obedience to state policies. Thus, the Liga aimed to

> improve ideological and political consciousness of women, to extend cultural, ethical, and professional qualifications of women, . . . and above all to work closely with the state administration and political organizations, as well as with institutions who work on [women's] issues. (LK, 1969, p. 241)

By 1986, after the emergence of *Solidarnosc*, the subsequent practice of martial law, and the decreasing legitimacy of the Communist-dominated state, the LK tried to distance itself slightly from the Communist government by claiming that it brought "together women regardless of their worldview and membership in other political parties" (LK, 1987, p. 241). At the same time, as a dependent organization, the LK could not, and would not, question the hegemony of the party in setting policy and implementing programs. It was subject always to the demands of the PUWP and their reflection in the Polish state.

Even within these parameters, LK leaders claim to have exercised bursts of independence: The 1986 statement that welcomes all women, regardless of political affiliation, was a clear signal to women who had been involved in Solidarity before martial law and in the underground after December 1981 that they could be included in the circle of women. So too, the claim by LK leaders in the late 1980s, albeit unsubstantiated, that they "gave guarantees and bail for women interned during Martial Law . . . and secured their release"[6] suggests that the LK understood it had slightly different interests to protect. That it also presented a challenge to the state and to the church in its opposition to pro-natalist policies and in its attempts to introduce sex education into the schools does suggest that the LK was more than merely a propaganda tool for the party.

Although the LK was the primary vehicle for recruitment of women into the PUWP and leadership positions in government (Siemienska, 1991, p. 114), there were other offices, particularly in the final decade of Communist rule, that had responsibility for addressing the political recruitment of women, as well as their health and welfare. The Ministry of Labor included a Bureau of Women, which had administered policies on employment restrictions based on sex and maternity leaves (Hauser, Heyns, & Mansbridge, 1993, p. 260). In 1982, a Council for Family Matters and a Council for the Elderly and Disabled were established. In 1986, Jaruzelski's government created a deputy secretary of state with responsibility as government representative for women's affairs, within the Ministry of Labor, Wages, and Social Affairs. This Office of Women's Affairs had responsibility for political recruitment and dissemination of contraceptive information, developing child care options, protecting working women, promoting healthy pregnancies, and encouraging fathers to take a more active role in parenting. The deputy secretary of state worked with the LK in all these activities, as well as in research programs on women's occupations, employment, and salaries.

During the transition to democracy in 1989, the new government had considerable difficulty finding a woman who would take over the directorship of the Office of Women's Affairs. Since the Communist period, that office has been moved to the Council of Ministers (a higher-level state executive body) and renamed the Office of the Undersecretary of State for Women and Family (USWF). The new office's tasks have been diminished to cover policy issues related to children, youth, and families, excluding past areas such as father's participation in family life and contraceptive education. Since 1990, the USWF has attempted to organize a women's lobby and has encouraged the recruitment of women into political and administrative offices. The LK structure still exists, but its name has changed to the Democratic Union of Women. It seeks to become an umbrella organization for all Polish women's groups, although its efforts are hampered by its prior association with the PUWP. Neither the Office for Women and the Family nor the Democratic Union of Women has been noticeably successful in recruiting women into political positions nor in advocating for women since 1989.

Policy Influence and Activities

The constant recognition by the LK that women faced "problems with domestic life" (LK, 1969, p. 241) led to the LK's development of research agendas, adult education programs, and self-help organizations that primarily focused on how to facilitate "women's reconciliation of family obligations with work" (LK, 1969, p. 241). One enduring focus was to provide instruction and aid for women in cities and countryside. Social-legal aid circles were established in firms and neighborhoods to counsel women in their multiple roles as family caretakers and workers, including family conflicts, educational issues, prevention and management of alcoholism within families, and discrimination in employment. The LK also set up clinics to provide training for mothers with young children and to coordinate child care, orphanages, and children's camps. In 1965, the LK claimed that its primary task was to strengthen "women's civic education" and to "help women to conduct a more rational domestic life within their families" (LK, 1966, pp. 186-187). Policies in the pre-1989 period concerning half-time work, abortion, and maternity leave indicate the influence of the LK in women's policies. Yet, the impetus for these policies came from economic conditions and not a desire on the part of state actors to reconstruct gender relations in society.

Perhaps the most feminist of the LK's proposals was to introduce the notion of half-time work in 1963 and in 1964, to "promote efforts to provide employment for women in traditionally 'male' occupations" (LK, 1965, p. 153). Although the availability of half-time work addressed the excessive workload of women, it did nothing to change the demands of domestic labor or to provide a more financially secure position. Women's employment in "male" occupations was a short-lived propaganda campaign. Clearly, the LK understood its mission as providing assistance to women so that they could do their assigned tasks at work and at home more efficiently. The LK neither questioned who was doing the assigning nor what the tasks falling to women were. Rather, the LK acted as a mobilizational arm of the PUWP, and thus of the Polish state, when there was a need to encourage women's participation in politics and the workforce.

Until 1989, abortion was the primary form of contraception in Poland. The government reversed a 1932 ban on abortion in 1956, and by 1959 executive provisions allowed for abortion on demand in the first trimester for any woman who gave a statement about her difficult economic or social situation. Although in later decades the state promoted pro-natalist policies, it never rescinded legal abortion. At the same time, the state did not develop contraceptives because of the leadership's unwillingness to invest in consumer goods. The LK attempted to promote sex education and education about contraceptives, but its efforts were stymied by the close relation between the state and the Catholic Church in Poland. The Church, the only organization allowed to have any kind of autonomous voice during the Communist years, aside from the short period of Solidarity's activism, consistently opposed the abortion decrees, state provision of contraceptives, sex education, and the funding of family planning societies.

In 1989, the Church organized a parliamentary movement to pass a new law that would have outlawed all abortions and imposed criminal penalties on the woman as well as the doctors assisting her. A slightly more moderate version of the proposal became law in 1993; under it only doctors can be imprisoned for violations, and abortion is allowed in cases of rape or danger to a woman's health (Jankowska, 1991). In 1990, the Church convinced the Polish Medical Association to approve a resolution declaring that performing abortions was a violation of the Hippocratic oath. The Church also convinced the new government to remove sex education texts and materials, developed in part by the LK, from all schools. In 1990 religious instruction was introduced into public schools, providing another way for the church to affect popular opinion, if not behavior. The Church also insisted that the Office for Women's Affairs be renamed the Office for Family Affairs and be headed by a married woman "believer" with at least one child (Hauser et al., 1993, p. 271). Although they finally compromised on the name, Church leaders insisted that the state represent Catholic views on matters of contraception, abortion, sex roles, and, of course, sex itself.

In 1989, I spoke with several feminists in Warsaw and in Poznan who tried to explain to me the difficulties they were encountering organizing marches and rallies against the proposed antiabortion bill. Most women identified with Catholicism (although not with the Church's teaching) and were afraid to come out in public in favor of abortion. Leftists and LK activists who wanted to join the feminists in their marches also sullied the reputation of feminists and made them the enemy. As Janowska, Martini-Fiwek, and Goral (1991) remark, "the emancipation of women is associated with the overthrown regime; many people consider it a relic of the Communist system" (p. 174). As is obvious after the passage of the abortion bill, after parliamentary efforts to withdraw legalization of contraceptives, and after church-sponsored legislation to define men as the only permissible heads of household, Polish feminists have not figured out how to frame a claim for changes in women's options without treading on very dangerous ground. There is no language yet, nor a place where the new words and ideas can be spoken.

The story of maternity leave in Poland is also one of the state recognizing that it had interests in common with those of the Church, despite the rhetorical positions of the LK. During discussions in summer 1980, Solidarity insisted that one of its "Twenty-One Demands" be 3-year maternity leave for women workers. Even after the advent of martial law, when most of the roundtable agreements were broken, maternity leave remained. The post-1981 legislation allowed for 16 weeks (18 weeks for subsequent children) paid leave, followed by a "child rearing leave" of up to 3 years, or 6 years for a consecutive birth, accompanied by cash payments based on need, prohibitions against firing, and protection of seniority or retirement benefits. Although the policy permitted women to retain their jobs in principle, the cash payments were not sufficient to compensate for lost wages, nor were they tied to inflation. Simultaneously the government cut back on funding for preschool, day care, and kindergartens. Thus, although in theory women's jobs were protected, the practical consequence was that women were eased out of the market, faced with drastic cuts in income, and made more dependent on the men in their homes. Meanwhile, both Solidarity and the church argued that the natural place for women was in the home caring for their children; as the economy faltered in the late 1980s, and as the transition to a market economy made its impact, it is no surprise that women's unemployment reached record numbers.

The limited policy influence of the LK must be placed within the context of women's status. In 1989, on the eve of the peaceful transition to a non-Communist government, the conditions for women's work at home and in the paid labor force had not significantly improved for 20 years. Women were still 46% of the workforce, primarily engaged in female-dominant occupations (sales, service, textiles, teaching, child care, health care), which tended to offer lower salaries, less advancement, fewer educational opportunities, and fewer benefits. Women working in these occupations earned 30% less than men in the same fields. Furthermore, while working an average 40-hour workweek, working mothers faced full-time parenting obligations at home, with 60% of men giving them occasional help. The majority of the unemployed in Poland were women as of 1991; 60% were women between the ages of 20 and 34.[7] Women have been the first fired and the last hired, while most of the social supports once provided by the socialist government, such as child care and maternal support, have been reversed.

In cities, apartments were cramped and hard to clean; shopping was a daily routine, involving hours of standing on line at the butcher, the baker, and the vegetable stand. Refrigerators were expensive, automatic washing machines (that is electric agitators, with or without a wringer) were hard to find, and ropes hung inside apartments and outside on balconies often served as clothes dryers. Time studies showed that if men assisted at all in domestic chores, it was for occasional shopping and child care: On the average, men worked 2.05 hours on domestic chores each day, mostly standing in lines, compared with women's 5.6 hours of domestic work.[8] The provision of child care was inadequate to cope with the need of employed mothers. The hours of schooling did not fit well with full-time work in offices or factories, so in the end, both children's care and women's employment opportunities were jeopardized.

Conclusion:
The Liga Kobiet, the State, and Society

The state was not always the omnipotent structure of totalitarianism so often represented; in fact it was permeable to certain interests, such as the Church. The state's definition of the ideal woman varied according to economic or political interests, at times combined with the interests of the Church. Thus, woman was pictured as the heroic socialist tractor driver in the 1950s or Matka Polka, representing Poland's future procreation and reproduction in the 1980s.[9] The LK only had legitimacy to act within the parameters set by the state. As a dependent organization, it could not support alternative definitions of women that questioned the economic or social order, especially given the underdeveloped nature of civil society in Poland.

Janina Frentzel-Zagorska (1990) argues that the "soviet-type one-party system excludes any independent civil society" (p. 760). The Polish state, until the 1970s, did not allow potential existence for a civil society with an "independently structured population with different mechanisms of mediation" (Frentzel-Zagorska, 1990, p. 759). As Lena Kolarska-Bobinska (1990) indicates, "not all grass-roots initiatives during the past years were based on contestation and self-defence, . . . yet all of them emerged in a landscape dominated by the state in every respect" (p. 277; see also Arrato, 1993, pp. 198-200). Thus, none of the women's organizations and offices described could escape from the domination of state interests. Those interests, this chapter has argued, did change over time, sometimes in response to demands from organizations like the church, sometimes in recognition of ideological imperatives, but never in response to the autonomously articulated interests of women.

In terms of the issues addressed by the *Liga Kobiet*, it is important to recognize the paternal nature of state socialism,[10] as well as its hegemonic character. It has been argued that Poland saw the glimmerings of a civil society in the 1970s, with the emergence of the independent trade union and self-organization of workers, *Solidarnosc*; with the social activism of the Church;[11] with the formal institutionalization of Solidarity in 1981; and with the increasing activism of the Church throughout the 1980s. Yet, the expanding influence of the Church over public affairs, as well as its close ties with Solidarity, in the end doomed the birth of a democratic civil society in Poland.

Kolarska-Bobinska (1990, pp. 279-281) suggests that the current political culture in Poland, where people refuse to participate or even care about politics, is a consequence of being forced to participate in the Communist years, of being unwilling to judge or accept personal culpability for the past, and of being in a transition period where changes are still superficial. But more is going on as well: The opportunities for engaging in associative behavior in a civil society have been shaped by the remaining dominant forces in Polish society: the Church, the remnants of the Solidarity leadership, and the reformed members of the defunct PUWP. Because the major players are still the same in many instances, the terms of the discourse affecting women have not changed. The notion of the social construction of gender is still not speakable.

Research to date has shown that femocrats and state feminist policies appear to be products of political systems with open competition among political parties for government control, relatively open systems of recruitment into public state administration, and certain established rights and liberties for citizens (e.g., Eisenstein, 1991; Hernes, 1987). These countries also have a multiplicity of autonomous associational groups, which aggregate and articulate a variety of political and social interests. Thus, feminists in these postindustrial countries have numerous options for joining groups that seek to influence policy and to organize and facilitate change in neighborhoods and communities. Women's policy offices in these countries operate within environments in which feminism is an acceptable (if not always widely accepted) political ideology. They thrive where the state is relatively permeable to influence from within and without. It is not just that these are democratic states; it is that the democratic states are both energized and restrained by a civil society that itself is based on principles that are often in a process of becoming more democratized (Arrato, 1993, pp. 198-200).

This study of the *Liga* and Polish politics suggests that we have to do more than just add the modifier *democratic* to the concept *state feminism*. It is the existence of a civil society with "new structures of public discussion and political influence" (Arrato, 1993, p. 297) that enables the voicing of alternative visions of gender relations and that enables state feminism to act to accomplish feminist goals. Such a civil society would not allow a state without women to exist, especially in the context of an organized women's movement. As Pringle and Watson (1992) argue, "what intentionality there is [in the state] comes from the success with which various groupings are able to articulate their interests and hegemonize their claims" (p. 63). State feminism implies this kind of articulation and hegemonizing, even if it is only temporary and partial. In Poland, it was (and is) not only the word *feminism* that had bad connotations, it was also the hegemonic state that is problematic. That hegemony is best countered by the existence of a civil society in which women, in their multiplicity, can express and act on their needs and interests.

Notes

1. Each year the LK published reports on its work and research in annual government publications called *Rocznik Polityczyny i Gospodarczy* [Political and Economic Yearbooks]. These reports are entitled *Liga Kobiet*. The text will refer to them with LK and the date of publication. They are listed in the bibliography under Liga Kobiet. All translations from the *Rocznik* are mine, with the help of Jack Bielasiak.

2. This attitude, found through my own research in Poland, has been confirmed by other studies (e.g., Bystydzienski, 1989; Titkow, 1984, 1993).

3. For research on the Chinese and Soviet organizations, see, for example, Davin (1976), Honig and Hershatter (1988), and Lapidus (1978).

4. It appears that there is more support for the work of the All-China Women's Federation than for comparable women's organizations in other Communist countries. Also, the ACWF seems to play a more active role in promoting state policies for women.

5. Marxists disagree about the meaning of consciousness. See Giddens (1971) for an early discussion. For an applied analysis, see Noonan (1994).

6. Reading (1992, p. 172), from her interview with Elzbieta Gasiorowska, secretary of the Lodz branch, Liga Kobiet.

7. For a complete study, see Janowska et al. (1991). An alternative interpretation is presented by Leven (1991).

8. Data on the conditions of work and the structure of employment have been gathered by the State Statistical Office. The overview presented here is a composite from the following sources: *Kobieta w Polsce* [Woman in Poland]. Warsaw: G.U.S., (1986); *Kobieta w Polsce*. Warsaw: G.U.S., (1990); Morgan (1984); United Nations (1991).

9. The cultural icon of Matka Polka iterates the fusion of church, virginity, maternity, and Polish nation. It is a commonly used symbol of the integrity and longevity of Polish culture in the face of external domination; it can also symbolize concretely the rejection of feminism in Polish culture.

10. Watson (1993) makes a compelling argument for the transition from a paternal to a fraternal patriarchy in the transition from communism to democracy.

11. In addition to the literature cited elsewhere in this chapter, see Yuval-Davis (1992), Ely (1991), Connell (1990), Keane (1988), and Soper (1991).

13

The Power of Persuasion

The Instituto de la Mujer *in Spain*

Celia Valiente

Government offices involved with the promotion of women's status arrived later in Spain than in other Western countries. This late start was due to the fact that from the second half of the 1930s until 1975 Spain was governed by a right-wing authoritarian regime that actively opposed the advancement of women's rights and status. Furthermore, during the 19th and most of the 20th centuries, the feminist movement was weaker and its influence less noticeable in Spain than in other Western democracies. Nevertheless, in 1994 the *Instituto de la Mujer* (IM) or the Woman's Institute, the main women's policy office at the national level, is comparable to agencies in other advanced industrial democracies in terms of goals, budget, and personnel.

The Institute was founded in October 1983, six years after the first democratic elections were held in Spain and one year after the *Partido*

AUTHOR'S NOTE: I would like to thank Justin Byrne, Elisa Chuliá, Robert Fishman, and Josu Mezo for their comments on earlier drafts of this chapter. These drafts were prepared for the European Consortium for Political Research Joint Sessions of Workshops, Madrid, Spain, April 17-22, 1994; and the Conference "Crossing Borders: International Dialogues on Gender, Social Politics, and Citizenship," Stockholm, Sweden, May 27-29, 1994.

Socialista Obrero Español (PSOE, Socialist party) first came to power. It remains an important site for women's policymaking within the Spanish state. The IM differs from women's policy machinery in countries with stable democracies in three notable areas. First, the Institute is closely linked to one political party, the PSOE. This means that IM's top posts are filled mainly by Socialist party members or individuals who do not belong to any party. The Institute has not employed people who are active members of other political parties. This connection to the PSOE means that in the event that the Socialists lose control of parliament, the future of the IM is uncertain. Second, like most bureaucratic agencies in the Spanish government, the IM is primarily staffed by civil servants; few are former feminist activists. Third, there are no cooperative links, either formal or informal, between IM femocrats and feminist activists.[1]

This chapter will examine these three areas of contrast by discussing the establishment, organization and policy influence of the IM, as well as its relations with women's groups and movements.

Establishment

Surveys suggest that Spanish citizens are more favorable to the state playing a major role in society than citizens of other postindustrial countries (Beltrán, 1990, pp. 318-319). For example, in 1988, 75% of those interviewed in Spain agreed with the statement "the state is responsible for all citizens and has to take care of all people who have problems,"[2] compared with 44% in France (in 1985) and 26% in the United States (in 1985). In Spain, only 23% of those interviewed agreed with the statement "citizens are responsible for their own welfare, and have to take care of themselves when they have problems," compared to figures of 49% in France, and 74% in the United States. This apparent characteristic of Spanish political culture may encourage the establishment of state institutions to help social groups, such as women, with a set of common pressing problems.

This strong support for state intervention in Spain underscores the extent to which Spanish citizens have displayed a high level of support for the idea of women's policy offices, such as the IM. For instance, in July 1985, less than 2 years after the foundation of the Institute, 68% of Spanish women thought that the existence of a women's policy agency was very necessary or quite necessary, whereas 7.9% thought it was scarcely or not necessary. About 5% of women chose the answer "it depends on what the institution does," and 18.8% chose the option "I do not know/I do not answer." Public opinion polls of women in December 1987 and of men and women in December 1988 and December 1991 show that these views on the necessity of a women's policy office have not varied (*Instituto de la Mujer,* Metra Seis).

Spanish feminists did not make a strong unified call for the creation of women's equality institutions in the 1970s and early 1980s. Indeed, feminist attitudes about state institutions involving women's policy have varied widely. Some groups supported the establishment of the IM, arguing that the objective of a higher degree of formal and real gender-based equality could be attained through legal reforms and equality policies. According to this view, the state could be used to the advantage of women citizens if a significant number of committed feminists were well-established in key decision-making positions.

Other feminists were very skeptical about the usefulness of such structures, believing that their effectiveness depended on many factors, such as the feminist commitment of the employees who would staff the new agency. These feminists neither completely supported nor opposed the creation of the IM, choosing instead to wait until they could evaluate the Institute's performance after some years. A third group of feminists maintained that women should neither try to be equal to men nor attempt to achieve the same rights and status that male citizens already enjoyed. Rather, they argued that women should reorganize all aspects of public and private life in a new, nonhierarchical form. Because these feminists saw the state as an institution that contributed to the perpetuation of the unequal relationship between women and men, they felt that the best strategy to follow was to stay as far away from the state as possible.[3]

At least two contradicting factors have influenced these feminist evaluations of the usefulness of state institutions for women. On one hand, feminist groups that formed in the late 1960s and early 1970s were illegal and participated in the opposition to the authoritarian regime (Scanlon, 1990, p. 94). To varying degrees, this experience left many feminists suspicious of political power. On the other hand, the PSOE was in power when the IM was founded. Thus, for the first time since the 1930s, the government was in the hands of a party that overtly promoted the advancement of women's rights. Based on its governing record under the Second Republic in the 1930s and its electoral platform in the 1980s, Spanish feminists were ready to give credence to the PSOE's commitment to women's rights.[4] Besides, the feminism associated with the center in the 1920s and 1930s, liberal feminism, had disappeared during the dictatorship, so that most Spanish feminists came from the Left (Threlfall, 1985, p. 47).

A crucial ingredient in the establishment of the IM was the PSOE's growing commitment to gender equality. This was not an easy process, because the PSOE was a social democratic party. Like similar parties in other countries, the PSOE tended to be more concerned with class inequalities than with gender differences, and feminist activists were often contemptuously labeled bourgeois. Nonetheless, in 1976 a women's caucus, *Mujer y Socialismo*, was formed and in 1981, a member of the caucus was elected to the PSOE's Executive Committee, with others following her in successive years. In December 1984, party leaders decided to raise the women's caucus to the federal executive level, where it became the women's secretariat. The feminists in the secretariat successfully added clauses involving women's issues to PSOE congress resolutions, electoral programs, and other documents. These Socialist feminists also pushed for the inclusion of a women's policy office in the Socialist cabinet.

In their attempts to commit the PSOE to state institutions for women's policy, these feminist Socialists sought to create an office that would emulate the Socialist Ministry of Woman's Rights in France, which they perceived to be highly successful. They also used examples of similar offices in other West European countries to reinforce their arguments for a women's policy agency with PSOE activists, elected officials, and bureaucrats, who were reticent about establishing such a bureau. As one director of the Institute said, this line of argument was particularly compelling in the context of the strong political support for integrating Spain into the group of economically developed and politically democratic countries. The nations Spain rushed to emulate had, for the most part, some form of government office for women's equality (personal communication, Carlota Bustelo,

IM director from October 1983 to July 1988). Feminist socialists managed to include a pledge "to create an equality commission guaranteeing nondiscrimination against one gender" in the PSOE's 1982 electoral program. Right after the Socialist's electoral victory in 1982, Javier Solana, Minister of Culture, gave Carlota Bustelo, a well-known former PSOE deputy and feminist activist, the task of establishing the IM. The Act of October 24 (no. 16/83), 1983, formally set up the IM.

Organization

The *Instituto de la Mujer* is not a ministry but an *organismo autónomo* (autonomous body) within the Ministry of Culture. Autonomy here does not mean independence from the political party in office, but autonomy from ministerial hierarchy. Unlike other departments, where there is an intermediate administrative layer between agency director and minister, the Institute's director is directly responsible to the minister. The IM's budget increased from $5 million to nearly $17 million, or 325%, between 1984 and 1992.[5] In the early 1990s, the Institute had a staff of more than 150 people; 182 in 1990, and 166 in 1991 (Instituto de la Mujer, 1991, pp. 11-13; 1992, pp. 18-20). The internal organization of the IM is as hierarchical as any other Spanish government office. Most of the staff are *funcionarios* (civil servants), differentiated by salaries and administrative grade. They have been recruited from within the bureaucracy. As with most closed systems of administration, entry into the civil service is determined by *oposición* (examination). Very few of the IM's staff were recruited because of their record in the feminist movement.

The Spanish state is composed of offices (mainly ministries), each of which tries hard to preserve and augment its own powers. In this context, it is extremely difficult to create a new independent state organ to formulate and implement women's policies, which usually overlap with the competencies of several other state bodies. As a result, the IM has neither the power nor the budget to formulate and implement most gender equality policies. Instead, it has to convince more powerful state offices, which usually have more resources, to elaborate women's equality policies. Aware of this dynamic, the first femocrats in the IM structured the Institute to devote most of its resources, time, and energy to forging and nurturing bonds with other state offices.

Since 1985, the IM's director has been aided by the *Consejo Rector* (CR) or advisory council, which is primarily composed of representatives from the major ministries. Until the late 1980s, a complete *Consejo Rector* met at least once every 6 months, and a reduced committee met at least once every quarter. The advisory council has the role of directly involving ministerial representatives in the formulation, implementation, and evaluation of equality policies. Since this initial period of CR action, *Convenios* (cooperation agreements) between the IM and the ministries have been signed, and the *Consejo Rector* has met only sporadically (personal communication, Purificación Gutiérrez, IM director from April 1991 to September 1993).

The IM originally was divided into three departments, which were expanded to four after 1989. A large part of one department, the *Subdirección General de Cooperación y Difusión* (Subdivision of Cooperation and Publicity), is devoted to building and developing relationships with *Comunidades Autónomas* (regional governments) and *Ayuntamientos* (local councils).[6] In general, the IM has collaborated with some regional governments in the creation of regional equality institutions and in the establishment and functioning of programs concerning women, for instance, refuges for battered women. The Institute has also helped local councils set up women's policy structures as well, but to a much lesser extent.[7]

The IM was first attached to the Ministry of Culture and then moved to the Ministry of Social Affairs created in 1988. In comparison to other ministries, such as those of the Economy or the Presidency, both have a peripheral status in the state structure, a factor that helps to explain the marginalization of women's issues on the government's agenda. Since 1988, however, the Ministry of Social Affairs has been actively involved with advancing women's rights and status. Matilde Fernández, minister of social affairs from 1988 to 1993, and Christina Alberdi, minister since 1993, dedicated much of their political activity prior to their appointments to feminist causes. As a result, they have been important in lending intergovernmental legitimacy to the IM. Both women have defended the issues and demands raised in the IM and within feminist circles to the cabinet. Before 1988, in contrast, the

Institute depended on the minister of culture, Javier Solana, a man who displayed sympathy toward women's issues and respect for the IM's autonomy but who had not been active in feminist groups or movements (personal communication, Carlota Bustelo, IM director).

Policy Influence

The evaluation of the IM's influence in Spanish society is difficult because, in the context of its relatively recent creation, much of its political and social impact may not yet be detectable. Nonetheless, an examination of the extent to which the Institute has met the five major goals announced by its act of foundation and its regulations can shed some light on the IM's policy influence.[8]

The first major objective was to promote policy initiatives for women through formal enactment of policy statements, such as legislation or decrees. In order to assess how far this goal has been achieved, it is important to bear in mind the legal status of Spanish women and the state of equality policies in 1983. In some respects, formal equality was already a reality in 1983 (Threlfall, 1985, pp. 60-61). For example, family law provided for joint administration of matrimonial property. In other areas, legal reforms had already been enacted and policies formulated, but their implementation was still incomplete in 1983. In 1978, for instance, the advertising and selling of contraceptives was permitted, but their distribution through the National Health System was not organized. Still, in other areas of women's rights, there was still a great deal of progress to be made. Until 1985, abortion was a crime punishable under the penal code.

Before 1987, IM staff tried to promote and coordinate women's equality measures in different ministries through the meetings of the *Consejo Rector*. By 1987 it was clear to Carlota Bustelo, then Institute director, and other femocrats that different policy instruments were necessary to avoid the dilution of their efforts and to circumvent the unequal commitment of different ministries to gender-based equality. To address these problems the IM designed a new instrument, the equality plan, which presented a list of goals for ministries to achieve within a specific time period. The IM staff prepared the first equality plan in 1982, the *Primer Plan para la Igualdad de Oportunidades de las Mujeres 1988-1990*. It consisted of a comprehensive set of measures and reforms to be taken by 13 ministries, beginning in January 1988 and ending in December 1990. Before presenting the plan to the cabinet, the Institute negotiated its contents with most ministries, in order to sensitize the cabinet to the equality measures and to prevent the inclusion of specific items that would not be implemented by the ministries involved.

Although it is difficult to summarize the contents of the 120 legal reforms and equality actions proposed by the *Primer Plan*, six different types of measures can be identified (IM, 1990, pp. 15-101):

1. Legal reforms aimed at attaining equality between men and women before the law
2. Initiatives for nonsexist education
3. Equal employment measures
4. Women-specific health programs
5. The development of international cooperation projects related to women in other countries
6. The promotion of feminist associations in Spain

One of the main shortcomings of the plan was that, with the exception of legislative reforms, it was characterized by a high level of abstraction. For instance, Action 3.1.8 was "to carry out studies of female employers." Yet nothing was said about who was going to conduct such studies, how many were to be made, which institution was to pay for them, what their characteristics would be, and who should receive the results.

When IM staff carried out an evaluation of the implementation of the plan, they concluded that it was highly successful; out of the 120 measures planned, 116 were taken (IM, 1990, p. 106). The IM's conclusion, however, must be considered with extreme caution. The vague nature of the original objectives makes it difficult to evaluate whether or not they have been achieved. Also, the data and information that constitute the basis of this evaluation were provided by the responsible ministries themselves. This evaluation, therefore, may have overemphasized the positive aspects of their equality actions. A second equality plan was drawn up for the period of 1993-1995 (IM, 1993). Like the first plan, it contains equality policies that are general and unclear.

Despite the mixed review of the equality plans, femocrats in the IM have been persistent and successful in engaging ministries in the formulation of some of these policies. Ultimately, of course, each ministry has the final word in deciding what those policies are. Even after a ministry has publicly committed itself to following a particular policy, the IM has no power to penalize it for failure to fulfill its commitment. Femocrats, in fact, have often succeeded in persuading other government agencies to act, but only to the extent that the decision makers have been willing to be persuaded. Still, if the IM had not existed, it is unlikely that many ministries would have implemented the equality measures they have put into practice in the last decade.

The second aim forwarded by the founding documents of the Institute was to study all aspects of women's situation in Spain. This is an important task, because when the IM was founded in 1983, little research of this type existed, particularly compared to the level of research on women's status in other advanced industrialized democracies. One of the four main departments of the IM, the *Subdirección General de Estudios y Documentación*, is devoted to the promotion of women's studies. The IM has published books, given grants to researchers, established awards and prizes for the best books and articles, commissioned pieces of research, and established a documentation center in Madrid to provide information to researchers and feminists. These activities have also contributed to promoting the IM's public image. Given that the IM can organize these research activities independently without the approval of other ministries, this part of the Institute's mission is perhaps the most effective.

The IM's third founding goal was to oversee the implementation of women's policies. It has been mainly through the Institute's legal department, *Servicio de Informes Jurídicos,* and the meetings of the Consejo Rector that this objective has been carried out. In the CR, ministry representatives have to report on the implementation of equality policies within their area of responsibility. The IM, however, does not have any power to sanction a state body that fails to implement equality measures or that implements policies in an unsatisfactory manner. Possibly because of these limits, IM staff have concentrated their efforts on other objectives they consider easier to achieve.

Fourth, the IM is responsible for receiving and handling *denuncias,* women's discrimination complaints. It can only provide legal information to victims and initiate a legal complaint with the appropriate authorities when women victims come forward on their own. It can neither represent women in court nor lodge complaints without the victim's permission. The number of these complaints has been low: 48 in 1986, 86 in 1987, 84 in 1988, 86 in 1989, 60 in 1990, 21 in 1991, 24 in 1992, and 38 in 1993 (personal communication, Charo Padilla, head of the IM legal department). According to the IM staff, this low rate is a result of many women's fear of taking legal action and a low level of awareness about women's rights (personal communication, Charo Padilla and Cristina Blanca, head of the IM information centers).

The fifth major goal of the IM was to increase women's knowledge of their rights. Middle-aged and elderly women were socialized at a time when qualities such as self-abnegation and sacrifice were considered the greatest female virtues. The principal agents of this socialization were the Catholic church, official women's organizations of the authoritarian political regime, and traditional families. Many women of this generation, therefore, see themselves as bearers of obligations rather than citizens with rights. To achieve the goal of education, the IM has set up *centros de información de los derechos de la mujer* (information centers) in a number of cities, where women can freely obtain information about their rights by inquiring in person, by phone, or by mail. In 1984 there were 3 centers created, 4 in 1985, 10 in 1986 and since 1987, 1. In 1991, the Institute established a toll-free rights information phone number.[9] Although the task is not impossible, it will take time to change well-established attitudes, especially among older generations.

The IM has only an indirect influence on policymaking; thus investing its resources in areas, such as research and dissemination of information, over which it can exert the most influence. The Institute has won public support for these activities. In 1991, about 50% of the population knew about the IM, and a high proportion of those polled have consistently held favorable opinions of its performance. In 1985, 57% of women saw the work of the Institute in a positive light, and in 1991, when the survey was administered to both men and women, 78% of those surveyed gave the IM a positive rating (IM, Metra Seis, 1985-1991).

Relations With Feminist
and Women's Organizations

The Spanish feminist movement has always been fragmented. According to IM data, approximately 100 women's associations (not all of them feminist) exist at the national level, and best estimates put their number throughout the country at around 3,000.[10] For most feminists, this fragmentation is a rather positive feature of the movement, because it reflects the diversity of women's interests. In contrast, most femocrats see it as a problem that may hinder their collaboration with feminists, because the movement has not one, or a few, spokespeople, but many.

The Spanish feminist movement has been historically weak, with its activities only involving a minority of women. Durán and Gallego (1986, p. 205) estimate that by the mid 1980s the number of feminist activists accounted for less than 0.1% of adult women. Recently, others have questioned the alleged weakness of the movement in Spain. Kaplan (1992, pp. 208-209) suggests that organizations with headquarters in Madrid and Barcelona show signs of strength and gives the example of national feminist conferences being regularly attended by between 3,000 and 5,000 women. Nonetheless, in comparison with other Western countries, the movement in Spain has not achieved high visibility in the mass media or initiated many public debates.

Generally speaking, informal relationships between IM personnel and members of feminist organizations are weak. There are two reasons for this absence of stronger links. First, for the most part, Institute femocrats were not feminist activists before they entered the institutions. Second, many feminists, especially in the early 1980s, deeply mistrusted people who worked in state institutions, an attitude that has since changed somewhat. Consequently, feminist access to IM decision making was almost nonexistent before 1988 and is still extremely limited. For instance, although the Consejo Rector is supposed to include six people who demonstrate a long commitment to gender equality, called *vocales*, they often have little contact with feminist groups. The Institute's director submits nominations to the parent minister, who officially approves them. These suggestions are based on individual career paths and not on any requisite amount of time spent in women's groups and/or feminist organization.

In 1988, the government formed a commission to monitor the implementation of the first equality plan. The *Comisión consultiva para el seguimiento del Primer Plan para la Igualdad* (CCPP) was exclusively composed of feminists and was supposed to provide femocrats with observations and recommendations for future plans. The CCPP could have been the beginning of a long-lasting collaboration between femocrats and feminists, but the opportunity was apparently lost. Feminists bitterly complained that they were being asked to evaluate a plan they had had no role in preparing. The government did not ask the CCPP to participate in drawing up the second equality plan. Feminists also suspected that the IM staff was not interested in their findings. Numerous disagreements arose among the feminists involved, and some of them dropped out of the Commission before its works had been completed.

After the Commission had finished its tasks in the early 1990s, the government invited three representatives of feminist organizations and representatives of the two major Spanish unions, *Unión General de Trabajadores* and *Comisiones Obreras* to serve on the Consejo Rector (IM, 1991, p. 143). These representatives are now the only formal channel Spanish feminists have to the IM's decision-making process. Paradoxically, they obtained this access at a time when the CR had virtually ceased to meet. This irony helps to explain why some feminists question the desirability and usefulness of their participation in this body.

Close informal relationships between IM personnel and feminist organizations, combined with access to the Institute's decision-making process, might have reduced feminists' distrust of femocrats and encouraged at least some activists to focus their efforts on collaboration with state institutions. Without these two conditions, many feminists have opted to focus on protest-oriented activities and continue to maintain their distance from the women's policy offices, which appear to have no place for them.

For their part, Institute femocrats explain that because the feminist movement is weak and the Spanish population rarely forms associations, the state should therefore promote the emergence of associations by providing them with subsidies and other types of support, such as space in its buildings, materials, information, and advice on organizing activities.[11] Approximately 10% to 15% of the IM's budget has been devoted to subsidizing women's (not necessarily feminist) organizations.[12] It should be noted that subsidies of this type also exist in other countries, for instance France (Mazur, 1994, p. 30), the Netherlands (Outshoorn, 1994a, pp. 12-14), and Germany (Ferree, 1991-1992). In the early years of the Institute, subsidies were given to associations without any criteria for the sort of activities to be organized. This changed in the late 1980s, when the IM started subsidizing only programs strictly defined in accordance with the IM's priorities.

Members of women's groups hold different opinions about the IM's subsidies policy. Although some appreciate it, most feminists are deeply critical of the amount of support they receive from the Institute. Some argue that they do more for the improvement of the situation of women than do IM femocrats, with their high salaries and prestigious and interesting posts. These feminists complain about the fact that most of the IM budget is devoted to maintaining the institution (paying for salaries, office material, and ongoing expenses), rather than to promoting the activities of women's associations. Other activists think that many of these subsidies are given to organizations ideologically close to the PSOE, and not to those who work hardest for feminist causes. Still others think that the Institute is attacking feminist autonomy by imposing its own criteria about the type of projects feminist groups have to run in order to receive subsidies. Indeed, like the creation of the CCPP and the late feminist appointments to the CR, many critics see these subsidies as another "poisoned gift" from the IM. Feminists also argue that because the bureaucratization of the process has increased greatly in the last few years, feminist groups are now required to spend a great deal of time on the formal procedures of applying for funds.

Finally, some feminists suspect that subsidies might have served to coopt the movement by rewarding those organizations that support IM activities: It appears to them that the less an organization protests against IM policies, the more subsidies it receives. In fact, the feminist movement is now less protest-oriented in Spain than it was in the 1970s. This trend might have been reinforced by the IM's policy of subsidies, but other factors also influenced this tendency: the absence of unifying and mobilizing causes (with the main exceptions of abortion and violence against women) and the recognition of the diversity of women's interests.

Conclusion

This chapter has argued that one of the main achievements of the IM has been to involve other state bodies in making equality policies. Generally, acceptance of these policies among politicians, civil servants, and society is on the rise. And today Spanish femocrats face what Boneparth (1980) has called "the luxury of diffuse opposition" (p. 4), in that there has been no widespread conservative reaction to their initiatives. Indeed, there are few organized groups in state or society whose principal objective is to limit or eradicate equality policies and to return women to their traditional roles. In part this could be due to the way in which the IM has initiated women's equality policies, by always seeking the cooperation of other political governmental structures. As Rockman notes (1990, p. 37), this type of policymaking is certainly time and energy consuming. But once several actors have agreed on a particular policy, the support thus obtained makes the probability for success and acceptance much greater.

The IM is linked to the PSOE in the sense that the Institute's staff generally accepts the official party position on women's issues. At the same time, the IM does not favor the mobilization of the feminist movement (or of public opinion) as a way of advancing demands that go beyond PSOE gender equality compromises. For example, the IM has avoided the controversial abortion issue. The July 5, 1985, Act (no. 9/1985) allows abortion only in three situations: when the woman has been raped, when pregnancy seriously endangers the life of the mother, and when the fetus is malformed. As such, it is one of the most restrictive laws in Europe. Although the majority of IM femocrats favor a more permissive abortion law, as of June 1994, femocrats have neither made public statements nor mobilized against the 1985 law.

The IM has not been able or perhaps, willing, to break the traditional Spanish pattern of policy formulation and implementation, which affords social groups limited influence in the policy process (Valiente, 1994). Indeed, the IM has appeared to cast its lot with the PSOE. In the event of a conservative party electoral victory, IM femocrats' close ties to the ruling Socialist party and their distance from potential feminist support threaten the long-term future of the *Instituto de la Mujer*.

Notes

1. The sources for this chapter include published and unpublished IM documents, legislation, political party documents, press articles, and 31 in-depth personal interviews, conducted in 1993, with IM personnel, members of feminist organizations, and women's sections within trade unions, as well as with the Minister of Social Affairs.

2. All translations are by the author.

3. Information on the feminist movement came from personal interviews with Cristina Garaizábal (Women Against Physical Abuse Group); Lourdes Hernández (Alliance of Women's Groups from Neighborhoods and Villages in Madrid); Lucía Mazarrasa (Forum of Feminist Politics); Justa Montero (Pro-Abortion Commission); Ana M. Pérez del Campo (Separated and Divorced Women's Association); Empar Pineda (Lesbian Feminist Group); Isabel García-Pascual, M. Angeles de Lope, and Pilar Sauces (Free Women); María Jesús Vilches (*Comisiones Obreras*, a trade union); and Lucía Villegas and Carmen Muriana (*Unión General de Trabajadores*, a trade union). Those interviewed are not representative of the feminist movement as a whole but of some important currents within it.

4. The first truly democratic regime was established in Spain during the Second Republic (1931-1936). Between 1931 and 1933, a coalition of Republican (liberal) parties and the PSOE governed the country. Many legal reforms and policies for women were instituted then, including voting rights, the prohibition of discrimination, the establishment of divorce, the abolition of prostitution, and the organization of a maternity insurance scheme (Valiente, 1994, pp. 244-295).

5. The IM budget, in Spanish pesetas (U.S. dollars in parentheses) increased from 707.06 (5.2) million in 1984 to 2,297.4 (16.7) in 1992 (IM, 1992, pp. 36-40). The exchange rate on March 26, 1994, was 137 pesetas for one dollar.

6. Spain is a strongly decentralized state with 7 autonomous regions.

7. This is a preliminary evaluation of the relations between the Institute and other women's agencies at the regional and local level, which needs to be complemented by closer analyses of these territorial units.

8. October 24, 1983 (no. 16/83) Act and Royal Decree August 1, 1984 (no. 1456/84).

9. Women's rights information centers have responded to the following number of inquiries (personal communication, Cristina Blanca):

Number	Year
18,891	1984
31,685	1985
50,164	1986
45,730	1987
57,633	1988
60,701	1989
65,583	1990
55,366	1991
58,469	1992
52,812	1993

By the end of 1993, 160,435 calls had been answered.

10. Information provided by Mar García and María Antonia Carretero, from the IM's *Subdirección General de Cooperación*.

11. This is not a point of view particular to the IM's staff. It was also expressed by bureaucrats in the Ministry of Social Affairs.

12. The amount of money spent in this way was as follows:

Spanish Pesetas (in millions)	U.S. Dollars (in millions)	Percent of IM Budget	Year
53.3	0.39	7.3	1985
78.3	0.57	10.5	1986
110	8.46	9.4	1987
282.9	2.06	21.7	1988
201.7	1.47	14.3	1989
333	2.43	16.5	1990
265	1.93	12.1	1991

NOTE: Figures are from Instituto de la Mujer, 1992, p. 65, and percentages have been calculated from data contained on pp. 36-40 and 68.

14

The State's Equality for Women

Sweden's Equality Ombudsman

R. Amy Elman

Feminists have long argued that women are deterred from organizing effectively against their oppression because they have historically had inadequate redress through existing political institutions. In Sweden, efforts to include women in politics began in the early part of this century, with the extension of suffrage and the creation of women's sections in established political parties. In 1980, the state joined the effort by establishing an Equality Ombudsman, which was supposed to interdict sexual inequality at work. Many greeted these and similar initiatives with enthusiasm; they equated increased participation in the wage labor market and political inclusion with greater power for women. Despite these efforts, however, sexual inequality persists in Sweden. Its causes may lie beyond the reach of the state,[1] perhaps because, as Catharine MacKinnon (1989) argues, male dominance existed "prior to the operation of law, without express state acts, often in intimate contexts, as everyday life" (p. 161). Yet, in turning to the present, as this chapter will suggest, state intervention itself may impede the development of more innovative policies and programs that could radically counter male privilege.

Feminists are beginning to consider, on their own terms, the issue of whether male hegemony is distilled, compromised, or solidified when states are solicitous of women's needs and interests. More specifically, the question arises: Who benefits most from the state's incorporation and/or institutionalization of women's concerns? This chapter explores the answer to this query by reflecting on the state agency in Sweden most often associated with, and in formal charge of, promoting equality between men and women—the Equality Ombudsman. An overview of the structure of the Swedish state and the organization of feminists within it reveals the ways in which the Ombudsman's approach to gender-based inequities regulated women's labor without effectively mitigating sexual harassment and violence against women.

Establishment and Organization

THE CORPORATE STATE
AND SWEDISH POLITICAL CULTURE

Sweden is a corporatist state insofar as public policy results from a highly institutionalized form of group access. Until recently, the division of resources, services, and benefits was largely the product of tripartite agreements (among government officials, employers, and organized labor). The Conservative Government, in office between 1991 and Fall 1994, together with a recalcitrant employer's confederation and weakened labor, have obviated the tripartite character of this state. This does not, however, mean that Sweden is no longer a corporate state. After all, states retain their character long after governments wish to alter them.

Swedish policymaking power remains concentrated in the prime minister's cabinet, where ministers hold great power and responsibility for policy formulation. The cabinet represents the party (or coalition) that controls a majority of the seats within the Riksdag and reflects its policies. Yet Swedish policy also reflects the preferences of opposition parties and interest groups. The relative strength of the contemporary Swedish state is reflected in the preparation and implementation of legislation. Legislation is adopted at the national level, and the state's bureaucracy is the channel through which reforms are abandoned or pursued.

The preparation of laws is essentially the task of state-appointed investigatory commissions and bureaucrats who work under the direction of a minister. Indeed, commissions and bureaucrats are often given directives by the appropriate ministry, "which outline the problems to be considered, the goals to be achieved, and sometimes even the approaches to take to reach these conditions" (Peterson, 1977, p. 48). By the time legislation is presented to the Riksdag, parliamentary majorities are relatively easy to obtain, as Governments emerge from disciplined party majorities that can ensure their legislation is usually passed. This tightly orchestrated legislative process has underlined the imposing authority and centralization of the Swedish state.

Despite an increasing number of disillusioned youth and some occasional complaints, Swedes generally possess an almost implicit faith in their regulatory structures. Such faith is rooted in the emergence of the Swedish state, which in the late 17th century dramatically reduced the privileges of male aristocrats through land confiscations. In return, nearly 80% of Swedish nobles earned their living as public officials. The state similarly incorporated the Lutheran church; clergymen became state employees. The development of a large bureaucratic state capable of providing attractive employment was, in part, "facilitated by a fairly widespread positive public attitude to state intervention" that resulted from the transfer of lands to peasant ownership (Allardt, 1986, p. 203). Thus, many of the antagonisms that came to characterize other European states were avoided early in Sweden. The integration of opposition through state employment enhanced the commitment of otherwise inimical factions and permitted the state's expansion.

Sweden's unique history is a crucial factor in explaining why its state has "not traditionally been conceived as an oppressive monolith." In fact, "the state has in many respects carried the image of being the benefactor of the common people" (Allardt, 1986, pp. 202-203). Intent on maintaining this image, Sweden's political elite emphasize consensus over conflict and generally do not exploit advantages. As Anton (1980) states,

> Swedish officials prefer to pull rather than push, avoid confrontations, are generous when ahead and accommodating when behind less be-

cause they are humane individuals . . . than because they perceive the potential consequences for *themselves* that can arise from different styles of action. (p. 296)

The pressure to conform is great. The penalty for those who either refuse or prove too socially inept is ostracism and alienation from political life.

Sweden is ethnically and culturally homogeneous. Alternative points of view are not easily tolerated. This does not necessarily mean that dissenters meet with overt oppression. As Erik Allardt (1986) explains, they "are not hindered in expressing or practicing their views, but they are often disregarded by the political organizations and the media" (p. 211). Hugh Heclo and Henrik Madsen (1987) also assert that the Swedish system necessitates social consanguinity as a prerequisite for political recognition.

Any individual not playing by the rules of group interaction is essentially alone and vulnerable, with no place to go. There is simply no alternative mechanism to commission work, no alternative structures of corporate representation, no alternative process for getting along in public life. (pp. 21-22)

Sweden's feminists also play by the rules. Birgitta Wistrand (1981), former chair of Sweden's oldest women's association (Fredrika-Bremer) explains, "Demonstrations, clashes, and defiance have not in general been our weapons, nor aggressive feminism our style. We have reached an accommodation with the establishment" (p. 6). This culture of accommodation simultaneously inhibited the development of an autonomous feminist movement oriented toward antisystem activities and set the foundation for the Equality Ombudsman. Indeed, women and organized women's interests were absent from the definition of women's equality as a political problem. Understanding the emergence of this issue will shed further light on the Ombudsman's approach to sex equality policy.

DEFINING WOMEN'S INEQUALITY

Sexual inequality became a political problem in the 1960s when Sweden began to experience a labor shortage and the state needed a cheap source of labor to maintain economic growth. Unions viewed Swedish women as a preferable alternative to the continued reliance on immigrant labor (Jonung & Thordarsson, 1980). Therefore they provided a growing chorus of support for women's entrance into the wage labor market. By 1967, union officials and the Director General of the National Labour Market Board declared that women "be regarded as every bit as valuable a part of the labour market as men" (Leijon, 1968, p. 32). The increasing attention extended to working women did not result from an overwhelming constituency demand from women themselves (Adams & Winston, 1980, p. 250). Without an autonomous movement within which women could discuss and challenge the conditions that affected their lives, official policy discussions about women often continued among men only (Hirdman, 1994, p. 11).

In the 1970s, a new generation of Social Democrats set out to change Sweden; among them was the new prime minister, Olof Palme. Assuming office in 1968, Palme was anxious to distinguish himself. In 1972, he reiterated labor leaders' assertions that women had an irrefutable right to work and established an executive council, the Advisory Council to the Prime Minister on Equality Between Men and Women. Palme instructed the Council to initiate state plans for sexual equality and expected it to stimulate support for and interest in sexual equality within public agencies.

During its 4 years in existence (1972-1976), the Advisory Council created 100 new positions in public employment offices to devote special attention to women's employment problems. The underlying assumption was that such difficulties resulted from the poor educational and occupational choices women made and that they could be "helped to make the right ones" (Sundin, 1992, p. 107). The focus was on the need for women, not men, to change their behavior. Newly appointed officials would provide women with the necessary occupational guidance. In addition, the Council helped establish nontraditional job-training programs and subsidies to industries that introduced quotas for new hires. These quotas stipulated that neither sex should fill more than 60% of the positions with any employer.

Apprehensive employers and union officials obtained exemptions to hire new male recruits with special skills. They argued that the absence of such riders would result in poorly trained employees who would then compromise Sweden's competitiveness. As a result, although more women achieved access to a segment of the labor market that had previously been inaccessible, only 35% of the new recruits were women (Rollén, 1980, p. 194). Nontraditional training programs also fell short of their intended effect because gender segregation emerged within the very firms that were given the equality grants (Sundin, 1992, p. 110).

The most significant effect of the Council's activities did not result from the specific initiatives it pursued but rather from the ideological foundation it helped establish. In 1972, a Swedish delegation traveled to the United States to examine the newly adopted 1972 Amendments to the 1964 Civil Rights Act. They returned, declaring that such legislative intervention did not suit Sweden. Gender-based inequities were thus dismissed through the corporatist assumption that equality for women workers is best achieved through collective bargaining. This was not the first time that organized labor and the Social Democrats emphasized collective bargaining and dismissed legislative initiatives specifically designed to counter sex discrimination. Sweden's largest trade union confederation (LO) had rejected the ratification of a 1951 International Labor Organization Article (100) that promoted the principle of pay equity and legislative intervention against wage differentials between women and men. Nine years passed until it was adopted. Then, in 1970 the Social Democrats rebuffed a legislative proposal from the Liberal party to counter sex discrimination at work. A decade elapsed before they changed their position, and then only after they ensured the primacy of collective agreements.

Organized labor's resistance to equality policy initiatives outside of collective bargaining was consistent with the union's insistence that "women's problems stem from their being workers and not from being women" (M. Wadstein, assistant ombudsman, personal communication, August 1988, Stockholm). The Council consequently promoted the concept of gender-neutrality as a solution to sexual inequality. "There is," they warned, "always the danger that taking special measures on behalf of one sex will entrench traditional modes of segregated treatment and work against equality between men and women in the long run." Their solution: an "all-embracing view . . . to underpin reforms that will distribute work more evenly between the two sexes" (cited in Ruggie, 1984, p. 175).

From within this gender-neutral context, all gender-specific measures were implicitly characterized as equally suspect and potentially threatening to sexual equality. "Indeed, it became nearly immoral to talk about the needs and demands of women when the push was for equal opportunities for everyone" (Wistrand, 1981, p. 13). Under the guise of promoting sexual equality, the Council obscured the existence of inequality; it simply placed women and men on the same level, as if one sex held no power over the other. Reflecting this stance, Sweden's reports to the United Nations on efforts to promote sexual equality were entitled *Side by Side*. The historical conditions that first prompted the need for state redress were thus ignored. Gender neutrality set the stage for the bureaucratization of issues identified with sexual equality. As a consequence, official language used to describe women's policy issues and institutions was explicitly made gender neutral. For example, women's councils became family councils, which focused on worker's rights and parental responsibilities (see, e.g., Hirdman, 1994).

THE BUREAUCRATIZATION OF EQUALITY

In 1976, after 44 years of uninterrupted governance, the Social Democrats lost control of the Government. The victorious center right, or bourgeois coalition (composed of the Moderate, Liberal and Center parties), proceeded with the gender-neutral agenda of its predecessors. In an attempt to curry favor with women voters, the efforts of the new Government were more assertive than the leftist coalition they replaced (Elman, 1993). The Government immediately issued an ordinance enjoining the promotion of equality in the civil service. In addition, it transformed and changed the name of the Advisory Council to the Prime Minister on Equality Between Men and Women to the Equal Opportunities Commission. No longer an executive council, this body was to be appointed by parliament. All parties were determined to have influence on a burgeoning area of state policy.

In 1979, the Riksdag passed the Swedish Act on Equality Between Women and Men at Work (Equal Opportunities Act or EOA). Like Title VII of the U.S. Civil Rights Act of 1964, it is restricted to the workplace and forbids employers to discriminate against an employee or job applicant on the basis of sex. In contrast to American law, the Act does not recognize the possibility of sex discrimination among coworkers nor does the Act apply unless sex discrimination results in a disadvantageous distribution of duties or dismissal. The limited reach of the legislation was largely due to the strength of the predominantly male unions and their historical reticence in acknowledging gender conflict as politically significant. To date, Sweden has no anti-sex discrimination policies that extend beyond the labor market.

The EOA established an independent state agency, the *Jämställdhetsombudsmannen* (Equality Ombudsman; *JÄMO*), to oversee enforcement. The cabinet appoints each director for a period of, at most, 6 years. There are nine on staff within the agency, the structure of which has remained essentially unchanged since it was founded (L. Sillén, public relations officer, Equality Ombudsman, personal communication, February 1994, Stockholm). In addition, the legislation authorized the Equal Opportunities Commission to fine recalcitrant employers at the Ombudsman's request. The EOA provided additional opportunities for the state's expansion in the area of women's equality policy.

By 1982, the issues concerning sexual equality were so varied and complex that an Equality Affairs Division was established in the Ministry of Labour to coordinate the Government's policies. More recently, the division moved to the Ministry of Health and Social Affairs, also known as the Ministry of Equality Affairs. Such transfers typically correspond to the needs and abilities of each cabinet (C. Von Redlich, Principal Administrative Officer, personal communication, Stockholm, February 1994). Ministers with the greatest interest in and experience concerning equality are usually responsible for the division and the policies that emanate from it. The minister also oversees less formal advisory bodies, such as the Council on Equality Issues. The Council consists of representatives from 28 different groups (including women's organizations, political parties, and employer and employee organizations) and meets four times a year to discuss equality issues and exchange information.

Role and Effect of the Ombudsman

Despite their original opposition to the passage of equality legislation, the Social Democrats now support the EOA and maintain the bureaucracies that resulted from it.[2] Nonetheless, their reservations and those of organized labor had important consequences for the Ombudsman's office. Fearful of losing its influence within the corporate bargaining structure, labor allowed the EOA's passage only after the parties permitted its collective agreements (with employers) to take precedence over the legal provisions of the act. Consequently, during the first 14 years of its establishment, JÄMO's role in advocacy and supervision of the Act was limited to the 10% of the labor market where collective agreements do not exist.

This agency was expected to promote sexual equality, but had no recourse when its expectation was not met: "equality was recommended, not mandated" (Eduards, 1991, p. 173). In other words, gender inequality was not effectively interdicted. More recently, before losing power, the right-wing government expanded the agency's authority by revising the EOA. As of July 1994, the Ombudsman oversees all areas of the labor market. Although it is presently impossible to determine the effects this new reform will have, one can understand the limits of JÄMO's power to date by examining its attempts to counter sexual harassment at work.[3]

In 1983, JÄMO brought its first sexual harassment case before the Labor Court. The case concerned the promotion of a man who had sexually harassed 17 of the women he was appointed to supervise as office manager. The Ombudsman maintained that a better qualified woman was overlooked for the same position and insisted that the man's sexually abusive behavior rendered him unfit for the appointment. JÄMO lost the case. "The male-dominated Labour Court did not look seriously upon the man's behavior. He was excused with the argument that 'he had not managed to control himself' " (Hagman, 1992, p. 1).

In its efforts to counter sex discrimination, the Ombudsman noted a persistent pattern of sexual harassment at work and was determined to examine its prevalence. In 1987, JÄMO launched the first and only Swedish survey on the scope and distinctiveness of sexual harassment at work. The study, called the "FRID-A" Projekt, found that nearly 20% of respondents had been sexually harassed at work.[4] The public's attention was drawn to sexual harassment only after JÄMO issued its findings. Prior to this study, this abusive behavior had not acquired a name in Sweden. The notion of sexual harassment was principally derived from the United States where the chief investigator of the FRID-A project, Ninni Hagman, spent time studying American harassment policies. In addition, JÄMO was inspired by legal developments in Australia and New Zealand. As Birgitta Wistrand (1981) wrote, "The ideas behind the movement for women's rights" in Sweden "have their sources abroad" (p. 10).

After releasing its study, JÄMO insisted that sexual harassment in Sweden was a significant problem. The Ombudsman claimed that the survey's findings were similar to several American studies. Of those subjected to harassment, few requested any help from their unions or personnel departments, in spite of the fact that many claimed that they had suffered physically and/or mentally. Women disclosed that they kept silent for fear of reprisal. Many who did complain said that they had suffered retaliation at work. One third of all those sexually harassed stated that they had to leave their place of employment.

The FRID-A project made explicit the connection between sexual harassment and occupational segregation by sex: "Sexual harassment is an assertion of power that men use to keep women out of male-dominated jobs and to keep women in female-dominated working places down" (JÄMO, 1987, p. 6). The Ombudsman thus explained why large state investments in nontraditional occupational training programs and child care are necessary but insufficient in mitigating sex segregation.[5] The Ombudsman concluded her report to the government by stating that "the United States is 10 years ahead of Sweden when it comes to measures against sexual harassment" (p. 3). The Ombudsman estimated that hundreds of thousands of the 2 million women in the labor market experience sexual harassment and claimed that it constitutes a threat to "women's economy, health, and pleasure in work" (p. 6). In response, the Ombudsman suggested that the Equal Opportunities Act be amended to expressly prohibit sexual harassment in the workplace.

The Government responded to JÄMO's request by launching an investigation of the implementation of the entire EOA, publishing its results in 1990 (SOU, 1990:41). It noted that the Act provided little substantive change for working women and that much needed to be done to obtain sexual equality in the Swedish wage labor market. The report also acknowledged that Sweden's definition of discrimination was "narrower than the definitions which exist elsewhere in Europe" and that entry into the European Union (EU) would require that the law be revised to include relief for those harmed by indirect discrimination (SOU, 1990:41, p. 38). In anticipation of EU membership, the government later amended the EOA in 1992 to comply with EU regulations.

Despite revisions to the EOA, cautious restraint continues to best characterize the state's approach to sexual equality. For instance, although many requested that the reach of the Act be extended to include areas such as education, the government insisted that the EOA "is a judicial labour law . . . that should not be extended to community life on the whole" (SOU, 1990:41, p. 34). Consequently, women remain without legal protection in areas like education. In its cursory discussion of sexual harassment, the Government emphasized existing avenues of remedy for complainants. It stated that "serious" instances of sexual harassment "must be approached under the provisions of the Criminal Code" (SOU, 1990:41, p. 38). The investigation failed to note, however, that with the exception of rape or assault, serious cases of sexual harassment have never been successfully pursued by these means.

For less serious cases, the Government insists that sexual harassment be considered a work environment problem and that it be addressed through an existing Occupational Safety and Health Act. Thus far, no harassment cases have been successfully pursued through this channel. The Occupational Safety and Health Act was essentially established to promote a positive, healthy work atmosphere for employees. The Act neither provides a definition of sexual harassment nor mentions sex discrimination in any way.

The Government did state that there are situations where sexually harassed women have little remedy. "There are forms of sexual harassment where a demand for, or suggestion of, sexual compliance is tied to threats of disadvantages at work, or to a promise of certain privileges" (SOU, 1990:41, p. 38). To counteract these particular instances, the government amended the Equal Opportunities Act. The Act now reads: "An employer may not subject an employee to harassment because the latter has rejected the employer's sexual advances or lodged a complaint about the employer for sex discrimination." Ninni Hagman (1992) notes that this amendment does not specifically prohibit sexual harassment: "Not until he [the employer] . . . punishes her for rejecting his sexual advances with some *other* kind of harassment, such as failing to raise her wages . . . is he considered to be subjecting her to sex discrimination" (p. 12).

The shortcomings of the reform gave rise to a series of criticisms (Dahlberg, 1992; Hagman, 1992). Critics noted, for example, that the law fails to provide relief to women harassed by coworkers. Moreover, unless harassment results in a disadvantageous distribution of duties or dismissal, no harm is considered to have occurred under the law. Consequently, sexual harassment per se is legally unrecognizable as a distinct abuse that is intrinsically prejudicial. The specific injuries that stem from such abuse are essentially concealed. It is, therefore, unlikely that the revised EOA will dramatically advance the position of Swedish women.

Despite JÄMO's role in drawing attention to sexual harassment and convincing the government to review the EOA, its ability to influence the content and enforcement of the new equality policy has been minimal. Even the Equality Ombudsman openly acknowledged the relative powerlessness of this office (SOU, 1990:41). Former Deputy Ombudsman Margareta Wadstein (personal communication, 1988) also commented on the inability of JÄMO to intervene in sex discrimination cases.

> We can only ask a court to fine employers . . . if they have no equality agreements. . . . Most complaints we receive come from women who work in places bound by collective agreements—so we have to refer them back to their union for help.

From 1980-1990, the Ombudsman brought 36 cases before the Labour Court and lost approximately two thirds of them. The Equal Opportunities Commission, originally established by the EOA to render decisions concerning infringements by employers outside of collective agreements, has not ruled on any cases in 10 years (SOU, 1990:41).[6] This situation clearly underlines the symbolic nature of both the EOA and the Commission. Moreover, Wadstein (1989) declared that the Act "became an offensive instrument for strengthening men's position in the labor market" (pp. 29-30). As the terms of men's employment improved, women's socioeconomic position deteriorated in the 1980s.

Without any real enforcement authority, the Ombudsman's most influential function is to provide employers, unions, and the public at large with information pertaining to sexual equality in general and the equal opportunity law in particular (JÄMO, 1992, p. 1). This charge is more important than it might appear—the dissemination of information is of tremendous symbolic and practical value. The stellar reputation that Sweden enjoys in the field of women's rights is largely the result of state-sponsored public information campaigns. In turn, the state's authority in this area is bolstered by this reputation.

The Ombudsman's Relations
to Women's Advocacy Organizations

Eduards (1989) writes that most Swedish women's organizations "have sought to avoid conflict in favor of adoption and 'respectability' in a resistant and male-dominated political structure. . . . The majority of women political activists work within established political institutions" (pp. 15-16). Many feminists work for reforms within governmental bureaucracies and/or women's sections of parties, as opposed to autonomous women's projects and organizations. Political parties, in particular, have been "remarkably efficient in co-opting both women and women's demands." Eduards (1989, p. 16) attributes this to the attitude, held by political parties, that "the gender issue is too important" to be left to women. Although four of the five main political parties have special women's sections, which act as (women's) interest groups within the party,[7] women must defer to the "larger" party agenda (Haavio-Mannila et al., 1985). Helga Hernes (1988) suggests that the loyalty women traditionally have extended to the parties has compromised the effectiveness with which they could otherwise collaborate and mobilize to achieve common objectives.

Whereas individual feminists have been active in Swedish politics, no extensive autonomous feminist movement has emerged. Many have noted this, but few have grasped the contempt to which feminists are subjected. As Hilda Scott (1982) writes, "There is probably no Western country where hostility to 'feminism' as opposed to 'women's liberation' is so out of proportion to the strength and militancy of the avowed feminists in the women's movement" (p. 158). Indeed, the culture places a premium on conflict avoidance and the maintenance of borders between public and private life. Much of Swedish society has therefore shunned newer forms of feminism, which politicize the most private aspects of life, especially sexuality. They refuse to acknowledge that women's insubordination stems from male domination. As a consequence, the major political players in Sweden, including women's organizations both inside and outside of the political parties, have refused to consider explanations of women's disadvantaged position in Swedish society in terms of male-dominated institutions.

As Skard and Haavio-Mannila (1986) note,

> At a time when the women's liberation movement was sending shock waves throughout the . . . rest of the industrialized world, social scientists in the Nordic countries began a gender-role debate . . . [centered] on the two roles of women—in the family and in the labor force—and how they should be combined. (p. 183)

Instead of an autonomous feminist movement based on the notion of overturning the patriarchal system, the mechanisms of the double burden have been the focus of political parties, trade unions, and reform-oriented groups interested in improving women's lives. This approach to women's subordination, as well as the ensuing proliferation of expert opinions concerning women's double burden, was institutionalized into the feminism of the Equality Ombudsman.

The absence of a significant autonomous feminist movement has meant that the Equality Ombudsman has set its own agenda. In conjunction with political parties and organized labor, the Ombudsman pursues work-related inequities, often neglecting the demands of individual feminists who seek remedies for discrimination against women in other areas. Following the logic that "Swedish equality policy is fundamentally concerned with the ability of each individual to achieve economic independence through gainful employment" (Swedish Institute, 1993, p. 1), JÄMO contends that "if work for equality is to be effective, it must be taken at places of work" (JÄMO, 1992, p. 4).

Acceptance of this plan implies that women should focus on obtaining sexual equality through increasing their presence in the wage labor market. Thus, in claiming to combat inequities associated with work, the state has been able to avoid taking action against sexual inequality elsewhere (Elman, 1993; Elman & Eduards, 1991). More specifically, it has been reticent to address gender inequality or welfare in terms of violence against women, even when women's sections and feminists in various organizations have demanded government action in this area. That demands for legislation to stop violence against women emerged largely from outside of the Equality Ombudsman underscores the distance between feminists and the state that claims to mobilize on their behalf.

Since 1864, when Swedish men were first denied the right to batter their wives, only two legal reforms have been specifically adopted for battered women. The first was initiated by women in the Center and Liberal parties in 1980 and was passed by the Riksdag 2 years later. Although the Ombudsman generally maintains an informal relationship to the women's sections of the political parties, it was not involved in this reform effort. The first reform acknowledged the fear and reluctance of battered women to report their assailants and, therefore, enabled a third party to file a formal complaint against a batterer. In this manner, it provided police and prosecutors with greater flexibility in pursuing criminal action. There has not, however, been an increase in the numbers of men arrested and/or successfully prosecuted under this reform.

More recently, Sweden's National Association of Battered Women's Shelters (ROKS), arguably Sweden's largest and most significant feminist organization, worked with the Communists and all the women's sections of political parties (although not with the Ombudsman) to obtain the right of battered women to gain orders of protection. Prior to the adoption of this proposal in 1988, police officers were unable to take any action against a batterer unless he had already harmed the woman. Under this second reform, the batterer's mere contact with or presence near the woman he abused constitutes a punishable offense. Unlike similar reforms adopted in the United States, Great Britain, and other countries, arrest was never mandated. The powers of the police, like those of the prosecutors, remain discretionary. In fact, the government found that "the possibilities of police intervention in situations [the woman] experiences as threatening or frightening are very small" (BRÅ, 1989, p. 39).

These reforms are unenthusiastically enforced (BRÅ, 1989; Elman & Eduards, 1991). Nonetheless, state agencies insist that "efforts to prevent various forms of violence against women have high priority in Sweden" (Swedish Institute, 1993). It was precisely the adoption of these reforms that provided the state with ammunition for its assertion. Violence against women is largely conceived as separate from efforts to obtain work-related equality, which the state has chosen to permanently institutionalize. On those few occasions that the government has appointed temporary commissions to examine the physical/ sexual abuse of women, the Equality Ombudsman has not been consulted.[8]

Conclusion

That the state should be interested in promoting "women's interests" at all is politically paradoxical. Although access to the labor market may prove beneficial to women, the state's access to women's relatively inexpensive and well-disciplined labor clearly advances the interests of the capitalist state and, more specifically, the men living within it. For them, women's equality meant "a more efficient use of human capital, more incomes to tax, more skilled labor to fill their labor shortage, and greater support for their party" (Leghorn & Parker, 1981, pp. 78-79).

As this chapter has argued, Swedish women were only peripherally involved in the determination of what equality is and how best to achieve it (Hirdman, 1994). The Equality Ombudsman, whose responsibilities, in part, entailed the authoritative enunciation of women's interests, had little power to intervene effectively on their behalf in the work place. In equal employment legislation, JÄMO's role was restricted to drawing attention to problems of sex discrimination and advising the government to take action; significant input in formulation and implementation of women's equality policy was not an intended part of the Ombudsman's original mission.

JÄMO has also been conspicuously absent from the struggle for better policies to redress violence against women. Indeed, the absence of a powerful autonomous feminist movement and the Swedish tendency to define sex discrimination in terms of economic inequality have combined to disengage the principal state equality office from feminist-inspired efforts to force the government to protect women against sexual violence. In the final analysis, Sweden's Equality Ombudsman represents the state's version of a feminist agenda and not a feminist state.

Notes

1. Throughout this chapter, the term *state* will refer to numerous systems of coercion that structure the relationships between civil society and public authority (Stephan, 1978; Weber, 1981, p. 82). *Government*, by contrast, refers primarily to the party or coalition in power.

2. The Social Democrats returned to power from 1982 until 1991, when the bourgeois coalition again resumed power.

3. Sexual harassment is commonly understood as "the imposition of unwelcome sexual demands or the creation of sexually offensive environments" (Rhode, 1989, p. 231). Although sexual harassment occurs in a variety of contexts, it is most often associated with the labor market. The focus here will be on harassment at work.

4. The survey was sent to 4,000 working women and slightly more than half responded ($n = 2,108$).

5. Sweden's wage labor market remains highly segregated. Recent government surveys of 52 occupational fields showed that only 5 had an equal distribution of men and women in 1990. Moreover, in 13 fields, at least 90% of the employees were of the same sex (Swedish Institute, 1993, p. 3).

6. Five cases had, however, been withdrawn and almost 50 disputes were resolved through arbitration (SOU, 1990).

7. The one exception is the Communist party, which has tried to incorporate women by insisting that women's concerns are inextricable from other issues.

8. Two commissions have recently been established. One is charged with investigating violence against women, the other with investigating prostitution. In both instances, the Ombudsman was not consulted (Sillén, personal communication, 1994). For a more recent analysis of battery as well as rape and sexual harassment, read Elman, 1993. See Elman, 1995, concerning the issue of pornography in Sweden.

15

The Oldest Women's Policy Agency

The Women's Bureau in the United States

Dorothy McBride Stetson

When the United Nations Commission on the Status of Women recommended in the 1970s that member states establish policy machinery to eliminate discrimination against women, it seemed appropriate that one of the oldest agencies charged with advancing women's interests, the Women's Bureau in the U.S. Department of Labor, provided advice. To this end, the Bureau published a guide in 1975, recommending the creation of two types of institutions (U.S. Department of Labor, Women's Bureau, 1975, 1978).

First, this machinery should include an independent permanent bureau with adequate full-time staff and a "principal officer" who would serve "as a member of the policymaking team of government, whose viewpoints and recommendations are sought in the determination of policies and decisions related to economic and social planning" (p. 8). Activities of such a bureau would be coordinated with other government agencies through formal and informal arrangements. Second, governments should establish commissions on the status of women made up of "prestigious individuals" who serve voluntarily but with adequate staff assistance.

To what extent has the United States itself followed these recommendations? This chapter will argue that the Women's Bureau has only partially complied with its own proposals. Indeed, few would argue that the Bureau, a permanent agency for women's policy issues, has either adequate resources for its charge or a director who is part of any top policymaking team.[1] Commissions on the status of women have come and gone, some playing important roles, but there has not been a national Commission on the Status of Women since 1980.[2] There have been a variety of advisory committees, task forces, and interagency committees, but most of these have been temporary and ad hoc.[3]

Despite its limitations, the Women's Bureau (WB) remains the primary manifestation of women's policy machinery found in the United States. This chapter will summarize the creation and development of the Bureau and describe its organization and activities. Then, it will explore the Bureau's role in policymaking and its relations with interest groups. Finally, the conclusion will examine the pattern of gender policymaking in the American political system.

Establishment

The establishment and development of the WB must first be placed within the context of state-society relations in the United States. In general, Americans have a strong aversion to an active role for government in society and the economy. Based on what has been called "absolute liberalism," the American "state" operates in a stateless political culture (Wilsford, 1991, Chapter 3) As a consequence, in domestic affairs, government institutions are fragmented and tend to be dominated by powerful interest groups. Federalism layers the powers of the state along vertical lines, and presidential separation of powers divides leadership along horizontal lines. The distribution of policymaking power in the United States, therefore, makes it easier for interest groups to capture state agencies (e.g., Lowi, 1969; McConnell, 1966). This generally dilutes the political executive—the president, cabinet, and layers of political appointments within governmental departments or the Administration.

Given the relative weakness of the administration, compared with cabinets in parliamentary systems, and the autonomy of social groups, government agencies in the United States must forge relationships with supportive interest groups to advance a new policy agenda that might contradict the status quo. Otherwise, the power of department-level agencies, such as the WB, is determined by presidential pro-grams and the personal resources of the political appointees that head them.

Congress established the Women's Bureau by statute in 1920, the result of the political clout developed by women's organizations through the 70-year struggle for the vote. The politics surrounding these origins reflect the concern of progressives and social feminists about the abysmal treatment of women in factories during World War I (Sealander, 1983; Zelman, 1980). The Bureau predates the contempo-rary women's movement and, in fact, played an active role in shaping the movement's organizational and ideological framework in the mid-1960s.[4]

Following World War II, progress on women's policy was frustrated by the unresolved conflict between demands for equality defined in terms of nondiscrimination, favored by proponents of the Equal Rights Amendment to the constitution, and demands to preserve and extend special protections for women in the workforce, endorsed by advocates in labor unions and the Democratic party. In 1963, the President's Commission on the Status of Women found common ground, and Congress passed the Equal Pay Act. In 1964, the Civil Rights Act (Title VII) prohibited discrimination based on sex in em-ployment. Frustrated over the unwillingness of the government to enforce the new antidiscrimination legislation in the area of gender, some representatives to a national conference of state commissions on the status of women in 1966 formed the first leadership group for the National Organization for Women (NOW). NOW became the center of the nationally organized women's movement in the United States.

The Women's Bureau of the U.S. Department of Labor, under the directorship of Esther Peterson, was at the center of all these activities. It was the catalyst that forged the compromises on the 1963 Equal Pay Act, it provided the resources to state commissions, and it created the space for the nucleus of the organized women's rights movement. No doubt the United States would have had a movement without the contribution of the Women's Bureau:

However, without the active application of governmental resources to the needs of the movement's infrastructure, the movement's resources, pattern of national mobilization, and issue construction undoubtedly would have been quite different. . . . In short, governmental activity promoted nationalization of the women's movement—the root of any movement—and hastened its development. (Duerst-Lahti, 1989, pp. 267-268)

Although the events of the early 1960s were momentous, they did not transform the WB. The statute (19 USC 11-16) creating the Bureau remained unchanged, still providing for the president to appoint "a director, a woman . . . with the advice and consent of the Senate," and an assistant director, appointed by the secretary of labor. Congressional appropriations would provide salaries for "a chief clerk, special agents, assistants, clerks, and other employees." The Bureau's statutory duties also remained unchanged: "to formulate standards and policies which shall promote the welfare of wage-earning women, improve their working conditions, increase their efficiency, and advance their opportunities for profitable employment" and to investigate "all matters pertaining to the welfare of women in industry."

The year 1966 is an appropriate starting point for studying the Bureau's place as a representative of women's interests inside the state. After that year, the Bureau operated in a new political and social environment, which included both the dramatic increase in women's participation in the labor force at all levels and the growth and maturation of a national women's movement.

Organization

The Act establishing the Women's Bureau placed it in the Department of Labor. A tiny agency within that department, the Bureau employs around 80 people, with a budget of less than $8 million. The director has the prestige and clout that comes from a presidential appointment confirmed by the Senate. The assistant director and immediate staff are also politically appointed. Most other employees are career civil servants and serve as specialists in various areas of Bureau activities. A limited clerical staff completes the Washington office of the Bureau. Each of the 10 regional offices of the Department of Labor houses a WB administrator and one or two staff members.

Each director has reorganized the Bureau's structure, usually grouping the staff into several hierarchically organized sections based on type of policy activity. In 1993, Director Karen Nussbaum introduced organizational innovations based on her experience in clerical unions and in accord with President Bill Clinton's initiatives on the "high tech" workplace of the future. Instead of hierarchical divisions based on function, Nussbaum used more egalitarian groups, working on common substantive projects in subject areas especially pertinent to ongoing policy debates; namely, new jobs, better jobs, creating a family-friendly workplace, public outreach, and women in the global economy. She also eliminated the formal separation between professional and clerical staff.

The Bureau's influence depends on its administrative position within the Department of Labor, the status and talents of the director, and the attitude of the Administration she represents. After decades of near invisibility, the Bureau's standing rose in the 1960s with the successes of Director Esther Peterson, who also held the position of Assistant Secretary of Labor. When she became head of the Wage and Labor Standards Division, a major agency within the Department of Labor, the Bureau moved with her to that division. Soon Peterson took a position on the White House staff, but the Bureau remained in the division, a location that limited its flexibility and access to other agencies.

Nevertheless, Elizabeth Koontz, another activist director, made the most of her position, and in 1972 the Secretary of Labor issued an order designating the director as special counselor on women's programs and establishing an interdepartmental coordinating committee on women's concerns within the Department of Labor.

In 1978, the Bureau returned to the Office of the Secretary, where it continues to reside. This action was followed in 1980 by the secretary's order formally establishing the functions of the Women's Bureau within the Department of Labor and charging its national and regional offices with the coordination of "activities and programs that relate to or may affect the participation of women in the Nation's work force or in the economic or social development of the nation." Heads of all Department of Labor agencies "are responsible for coordinating with the WB on policies and programs which impact upon women," including information sharing, consultation, and staff expertise. This coordinating role was reaffirmed in 1989 and again in 1992. These formal orders served as a resource for the Bureau, supplementing its limited staff and funds to help it influence the policies and programs of much larger and wealthier agencies. The effectiveness of this new resource, like the Bureau's influence in general, largely depends on the director and the priorities of the president.

Since Esther Peterson, nine women have been confirmed by the Senate as directors of the Women's Bureau. Only three came to the job with experience in women's work issues or feminist and women's advocacy organizations: Elizabeth Koontz (1969-1973), Alexis Herman (1977-1981), and Karen Nussbaum (1993-present). Each director's strength derived from different sources. Koontz had a long career as an educator and head of the National Education Association; Herman was a trusted adviser of Labor Secretary Ray Marshall; and Nussbaum had close ties with the women's labor movement and the feminist community.

The type of person the president names as director depends on his political power and the perspective of the White House staff toward labor issues and women's rights. Thus, during the Administrations of Ronald Reagan and George Bush (1981-1992) when labor-related issues and women's equality were given a low priority, directors were characterized as "less than attentive, let-them-eat-cake" administrators (Noble, 1993b). The Clinton Administration has placed labor law reform and job training high on its agenda, appointing a WB director with labor union experience who was "determined to keep the question 'What does this mean for women?' on the minds of policymakers and power brokers" (Noble, 1993a).

Activities and Policy Influence

The 1920 statute creating the Women's Bureau gave it responsibility to "formulate standards and policies" and to "investigate and report" on all matters pertaining to the welfare of women in industry. These duties form the core of the activities of the Bureau today. The Director of the Women's Bureau is the adviser on women's issues for the secretary of labor. She also works with other agencies of the federal government, serving on interagency task forces and commissions. The federal Office of Management and Budget has a clearance process and a list of agencies that must comment on all bills from Congress and the Administration as well as on proposed regulations. The WB is a regular part of the clearance process on legislation and regulations that affect women in the workplace. Thus, the staff is aware of initiatives and has the opportunity to try to influence the Labor Department's response to proposals.

The Bureau gathers data on a variety of matters relating to women and work. These form the basis for a regular series of publications, ranging from the monthly newsletter, *Women and Work*, to periodic reports in the series *Facts on Working Women*. The *Handbook of Women Workers*, published in 1969, 1973, 1983, and 1994, remains an unequaled source of information on all aspects of women's employment in the United States. The Bureau also publishes pamphlets and monographs on special topics, such as job training, child care, and maternity and family leave laws. A popular publication is the *Working Woman's Guide to Her Job Rights*, which contains information on the major federal laws protecting women from discrimination and guaranteeing rights in the workplace.

The Bureau has no authority to administer antidiscrimination laws directly. One important enforcement agency in this area, the Office of Federal Contract Compliance (OFCC), is in the Department of Labor. It has responsibility for monitoring compliance with the executive order that prohibited sex discrimination in employment practices of government contractors. The Bureau has been able to work closely with the OFCC in developing and applying regulations in the enforcement of this order. With respect to the other major enforcement agency, the Equal Employment Opportunity Commission, which implements Title VII of the Civil Rights Act, the Bureau can only provide information to working women on how to file complaints on their own.

In 1978, for the first time, the Bureau was granted authority and a budget to fund special projects; these subsidies are now a permanent part of its activities. Grants are to be used to seek "innovative and effective solutions to barriers that prevent the full utilization of working women" (U.S. House of Representatives, 1993, p. 635). They have been continually used to fund displaced-homemaker training and counseling projects, child care, corporate linkages, initiatives for minority women, employment training, and counseling for nontraditional occupations.

The Bureau also tries to serve as a catalyst for developing networks and coalitions of women's advocacy organizations. In the 1960s and 1970s, it worked with the Citizens' Advisory Council on the Status of Women to form coalitions on equal rights policy issues, and it continues today to provide a place for groups to get in touch with each other to work on specific legislative initiatives. The Bureau has funded and convened national and regional conferences that bring together employers, women's advocacy organizations, government agencies, and community groups to discuss topics such as child care and job training.

The WB has a growing role in the international arena. The State Department turns to the Women's Bureau to provide information and representation in carrying out U.S. responsibilities in the area of women's issues in international organizations. The director is also the U.S. representative to the Organization for Economic Cooperation and Development (OECD) working party on the role of women. She attends meetings of the United Nations Commission on the Status of Women and the Commission on Women of the Organization of American States. The Bureau organized regional meetings on behalf of the State Department to gain input from nongovernmental organizations in preparation for the 1995 Conference on Women in Beijing. The following three case studies of women's policy formation will further illustrate the extent and nature of the WB's policy influence.

EQUAL RIGHTS FOR WOMEN: 1966-1972

The dominant women's policy issue in the 1960s and early 1970s at the national level was the controversy over equal rights. The debate was greatly influenced by the civil rights movement for African Americans and Hispanic Americans. Support for the idea that sex, like race, is a characteristic with little effect on individual abilities grew among women active in organizations such as the American Civil Liberties Union (ACLU), Business and Professional Women's Clubs, and American Association of University Women (AAUW). Initiatives to prohibit race discrimination in education and private employment (Titles VI and VII of the Civil Rights Act of 1964) and among government contractors (Executive Order 11246) provided the rationale, means, and language for similar laws prohibiting sex discrimination. In addition, the Equal Rights Amendment (ERA), which had been stalled in Congress for over 40 years, became the top priority of the growing liberal feminist wing of the women's movement.[5]

Until the 1960s, this equal rights feminism had confronted staunch opposition from women on the Left. Advocates for working women had wanted to hold on to special protective laws. Many activists argued that race and sex discrimination were not the same; whereas race may not affect a person's situation, sex did matter because women had different roles in family and society. Policymakers also clung to the belief that because most women preferred to remain at home as wives and mothers, they had little interest in or need for equal opportunity in employment or education.

Between 1966 and 1972, the advocates for equality and nondiscrimination attracted supporters and won many battles. These victories include the following:

Strengthened enforcement of antidiscrimination provisions of Title VII
A ban on sex discrimination among government contractors (Executive Order 11375, in 1968)
Passage of Title IX in 1972, banning discrimination in education programs receiving federal funds
Congressional acceptance of the ERA, also in 1972

The network driving these policy successes grew from the foundation Esther Peterson established around the WB to push through the Equal Pay Act in 1963. Under Mary Keyserling (1964-1969), the WB coordinated and sustained the growing number of state commissions on the status of women that followed in the wake of the report of the President's Commission on the Status of Women (PCSW) (Mead & Kaplan, 1965). Well into the 1970s, the Bureau provided staff support and leadership for the Citizens' Advisory Council on the Status of Women (cacsw).[6] Successor to the PCSW, the cacsw was housed in the WB and took up a wide variety of policy issues ranging from family law to abortion to sex discrimination in employment. As Wandersee (1988) states, "Because it [the cacsw] was located in the Women's Bureau, it [the WB] was able to distribute cacsw recommendations and position papers to state commissions, women's organizations, and individuals, thereby strengthening the emerging national network" (pp. 18-19).

Through its role with the cacsw and the sponsor of the state commissions on the status of women, the Bureau became the administrative core of a policy network on sex equity, defined in terms of nondiscrimination and the removal of sex as a legal basis for classifying people. This institutional role was enhanced by the personal leadership of Director Elizabeth Koontz, who led the Bureau to campaign for enforcement of equal employment opportunity laws and to ratify the Equal Rights Amendment. Thus, in 1970, when Koontz formally announced Bureau and Department of Labor support for the Equal Rights Amendment, the announcement served to bring government agencies and congressional advocates into the winning national coalition.

Although the WB remained central to women's rights activities inside the state during the 1970s, the energy and resources of nongovernmental organizations grew to outpace the resources of the femocrats. The emerging national "women's lobby" cut a permanent niche in the Washington policy scene through successive struggles on such issues as abortion rights, International Women's Year, and enforcement of equal education policy (Ferree & Hess, 1985). Drawing on the resources of the growing women's movement, the Bureau in turn was able to play a central role within the Department of Labor.

PREGNANCY DISCRIMINATION: 1970-1978

An illustration of the workings of this new policy community on equal rights is found in the case of the Pregnancy Discrimination Act (PDA) of 1978. The early policy successes of liberal feminism did not resolve a problem that had long confronted working women in the United States: the absence of job and income protection for pregnancy and childbirth (Stetson, 1991). Employers routinely used pregnancy or potential pregnancy as a reason to fire or not to hire women; most refused to reserve seniority and pay for those who returned to work after giving birth. By the 1970s, as more and more women joined the workforce in full-time jobs, complaints of pregnancy discrimination grew, reinforcing beliefs that until this issue was resolved, women would have little hope of equal employment opportunity. Maternity leave policy, slow to arrive on the national policy agenda, appeared to many to be a form of protective labor law. Liberal feminists argued that such special protections for women reinforced the idea that women were a separate, expendable workforce and increased the costs to employers of hiring women. The policy problem was how to provide women workers with the very real need for job-protected maternity leave within the liberal feminist framework of gender neutrality and antidiscrimination.

The cacsw took up the issue and produced a policy recommendation in 1970. Their solution was to define pregnancy as a temporary job-related disability—a gender-neutral concept—rather than as maternity leave—a special policy for women. Conventional labor policy treats disability leave as a right; unions bargain for disability leave and benefits so that workers who are injured or too ill to work will not be summarily fired or lose their seniority and pay status. Four states require employers to provide disability insurance for employees. In the 1960s, nearly all such plans excluded pregnancy from coverage. Women's Bureau Director Koontz argued that employers who fail to include pregnancy as a temporary disability were discriminating against women. Thus, she urged the EEOC to issue regulations to employers, indicating that pregnancy discrimination was illegal sex discrimination under Title VII (Koontz, 1971). The EEOC, which had previously told employers that excluding pregnancy benefits was not sex discrimination, reversed itself in 1972 and issued a new regulation along the lines of the cacsw proposal.

The battle, however, was not yet over, and employers sought relief in court. Two Supreme Court rulings in the mid-1970s agreed with employers that excluding pregnancy from a list of covered disabilities affected only a subclass of women, not all women, and thus it did not constitute sex discrimination (*Geduldig v. Aiello*, 1974; *General Electric v. Gilbert*, 1976). Advocates of pregnancy disability leave fought back in Congress, securing the Pregnancy Discrimination Act (PDA) of 1978, an amendment to Title VII of the Civil Rights Act. The PDA prohibits discrimination against pregnancy in all aspects of employment and requires those employers who have disability policies to include pregnancy.

Although femocrats in the WB and the cacsw provided a policy definition that allowed reconciliation of maternity leave with liberal feminist beliefs, leadership of the struggle against pregnancy discrimination shifted from the state to the growing coalition of nongovernment women's advocacy groups, including NOW, the Women's Equity Action League, AAUW, and women in labor unions. Thus, in their analysis of the process leading to the PDA, Gelb and Palley (1982) gave much of the credit to the Campaign to End Discrimination Against Pregnant Workers, a coalition of 300 groups, and made no mention of the Women's Bureau (pp. 154-166). In fact, by 1978, the Bureau had shifted its attention to other issues.

JOB TRAINING: 1975-1992

Equal rights laws prohibiting sex discrimination in employment and education have only slightly reduced the gender gap in pay and status because they have not significantly affected the system of education and job training that recruits women into female-dominated, lower-paying jobs. Job training itself is segregated, with programs directed to two distinct workforces: men in skilled, unionized, industrial jobs and welfare mothers who need jobs to get off welfare. This dualism blocks welfare reform, because segregated tracks in job training and vocational education sustain sex separation and female poverty (Radin, 1991). Furthermore, well-insulated policy networks that distribute federal funds for job training and vocational education to the male-dominated segment of the workforce appear to be impervious to efforts to link policy goals to economic equality policy in a way that would overcome this occupational segregation (Harlan & Steinberg, 1989, p. 7).

Major federal policies in this area authorize federal agencies, through grants and regulations, to entice states to establish educational and training programs for target populations in their jurisdictions. Aside from demonstration and pilot projects, agencies do not conduct the training or education directly. Although there are no formal barriers, job training and vocational education programs tend to perpetuate job segregation by enrolling women for female-dominated occupations such as hair dressers, secretaries, and hospital attendants. These programs work within existing norms and practices that sustain segregated practices through a combination of tradition, inertia, and market demand for cheap service workers.

To remedy this, advocates have sought legislation to target the special needs of women workers. However, the ensuing statutes providing aid to displaced homemakers and training for women in nontraditional occupations are add-ons and afterthoughts to the main business of job training and vocational education. They provide very little money and demonstrate the marginal place of gender concerns and the status of women in these policy networks. Advocates for women workers have been able to attract the attention of some members of Congress. They have not, however, been able to infiltrate the dominant policy community of unions, state governments, and agencies in the Department of Labor and Education, which retain control over federal resources.

The WB also works on the periphery of these policy networks. With its limited resources, the Bureau can aid what might be called mini policy communities of advocates for displaced homemakers and women seeking jobs in construction and trades. The Bureau has funded demonstration projects and convened conferences for displaced homemakers. It provides data to advocacy groups and Congress on the status of women in nontraditional jobs. Once funds are allocated to the Department of Labor, as with the Non-traditional Employment for Women Act (1991), the Bureau works with the Employment and Training Administration in managing the awarding of grants.

Through its access to the OFCC, the Bureau has been able to exert a certain degree of influence over job training. In 1978, under the leadership of Alexis Herman and against union opposition, the WB waged a successful campaign within the Department of Labor to require government contractors to set affirmative action goals and timetables for placing women in male-dominated apprenticeship programs. These actions, however, were not followed up by an aggressive outreach program to bring enough women with ability and interest into candidate pools and make a dent in continued occupational segregation (Glover, 1989). Presidential Administrations between 1980 and 1992 discouraged any such direct action on behalf of women or minorities. Indeed, for the most part, Bureau activities have not attracted the attention of feminist groups nor provided a means of access for them to male-dominated policy networks in this policy area.

Relations With
Women's Advocacy Organizations

In the American political system, close relations often develop between state agencies and organized groups of their constituents. Until the 1950s, the WB was the domain of the social feminists of the Women's Trade Union League, who had been instrumental in its creation. By the time Esther Peterson took over as director in 1961, however, the agency had no close bonds with any outside group. Then, it was able to play its pivotal role in the formation of the moderate wing of the contemporary feminist movement. Since the 1960s, however, although communication continues between feminist organizations and the Bureau, as the policy case studies suggest, each has become peripheral to the main activities of the other.

For Bureau staff, the primary constituency is the 60 million U.S. women workers. However, this constituency remains largely unorganized. In 1992, only 7.4 million women were members of labor unions (IWPR, 1994). National and regional offices of the Bureau have tried to help women form advocacy organizations, to support organizational activities, and to facilitate the formation of networks among organizations at the national and regional levels. Most of the direct action in this area occurred during the 1970s. The Women's Bureau allocated funds to the trade union studies center at Cornell University, which, in turn, helped form the Coalition of Labor Union Women (CLUW). According to Foner (1980), CLUW was

> the first inter-union organization formed by trade union women on their own initiative to push for their special needs within the labor movement and in society as a whole. It brought the women's movement into the trade unions, emphasizing in its "Statement of Purpose" that women, as women, shared a need to organize and fight for their collective interests. (p. 521)

The Bureau played an even more active role in the founding of Washington Union Women (WUW) in 1972. WUW regularly held meetings of trade union women in the Washington area, and the Bureau served as the secretariat for its activities during the 1970s.

These activities stopped during the Reagan Administration. No longer did the Bureau aid union organizations; instead it sponsored workshops for women in management. Congressional critics of the shift away from women in labor unions convened hearings in 1984 (U.S. House of Representatives, 1984). They heard evidence that Reagan's director, Leonora Cole Alexander, actively discouraged regional administrators from aiding working women's groups. The president of CLUW regretted that channels between activists and the Bureau had been severed in favor of attention to a tiny number of corporate-level women and entrepreneurs.

After the Reagan-Bush era, Bureau outreach activities once again shifted. President Clinton's director, Karen Nussbaum, redirected the staff to help the organizational efforts of working women in lower-paid occupations. Staff sought direct input from women through the distribution of questionnaires to millions of workers. Responses also identify a visible constituency to top Administration officials.[7] Within its very limited resources, the WB has the potential to assist its constituency in building the organizations essential to their efforts to change employer and state policies and practices. How such resources are used depends on the priorities of the director and the ideology of the administration that appoints her.

For their part, feminist organizations appreciate the Bureau's historic place in women's history but do not rely on it to advance a women's policy agenda. Once characterized as the home of "woodwork feminists" (a term coined by Freeman, 1975) who were essential to the success of initial campaigns for equality, the Bureau now seems to many politically active feminists to be merely part of the governmental woodwork. The feminist policy agenda is the domain of the women's lobby, a complex network of advocacy organizations employing policy experts and able to mobilize effective nationwide campaigns on such issues as abortion rights, health care, and family leave. Leaders meet in Washington through the Civil Rights Clearing House, the Clearing House on Women's Issues, and the Council of Presidents of women's organizations. WB staff have informal contacts with these organizations but are unlikely to have much impact on their effectiveness.

Self-defined feminist organizations, such as NOW, Older Women's League, Wider Opportunities for Women, and the Campaign for a

Feminist Majority, do not look to the WB as a channel of access to policymaking or as a reliable ally on issues promoting a feminist policy agenda. And, despite its proximity to the OFCC, the Bureau is not considered to have any role in the enforcement of antidiscrimination and affirmative action laws. When the Department of Labor is headed by a sympathetic secretary, feminist organizations will work with Bureau staff. Nevertheless, leaders remain doubtful that state bureaucratic agencies can do much to ease the way toward achieving feminist policy goals. This skepticism does not arise from any theoretical analysis of the patriarchal state (such as found in Pateman, 1988, or Ferguson, 1984). They remember instead how a change in political party in the White House in 1981 sharply curtailed support from the Bureau for most feminist issues. This doubt is reinforced by a clear-eyed assessment of the Bureau's limited resources, narrow statutory authority, and remote location within the Department of Labor.

The WB continues to provide an important resource to both its constituency of women workers and the women's policy lobby: information. The Bureau collects and publishes all kinds of data about women workers and makes it accessible to the general public. It runs a clearinghouse of its own to provide information to groups and individuals about the earnings gap, job segregation in many types of jobs, and all the laws that affect women workers, including family and medical leave, pregnancy discrimination, and sexual harassment. Such information has long been used by individuals and groups of women workers to fight for their own rights.

The Bureau staff seems comfortable not to be a policy initiator or advocate and to remain apart from controversy by providing resources that enable women workers and their advocates to advance their interests within other organizations. As a service agency, it can respond to the needs of diverse groups of women workers. By focusing on specific problems, such as displaced homemakers, child care, job training, or union organizing, the Bureau can accommodate potentially contradictory goals of equal opportunity and nondiscrimination, affirmative action for women, and support for the special problems women have in juggling work and family responsibilities.

Conclusion

Ideology, like its organization and activities, has been flexible at the WB. A major shift in the ideology of women, work, and government occurred during the 1960s, when the long-standing concepts of special protections for women workers gave way to support for an equal rights ideology and set of laws. Since then, the Bureau has not been associated with a particular type of feminism, instead favoring services to special groups of women workers:

> Training for displaced homemakers and women offenders
> Child care services
> Special problems of minority and Native American women
> Initiatives for bringing women into nontraditional jobs

Although the Bureau's resources seem puny in comparison to other governmental structures, they do permit flexibility for directors, if interested, to respond to feminist ideas about process and structure. Few directors have had feminist agendas. Those who did, such as Elizabeth Koontz and Karen Nussbaum, have been able to mobilize the Bureau toward those ends. Without a permanent organized constituency, however, few gains in the direction of feminist goals are permanent.

Feminists and other women's advocates outside government may find a tiny opening to decision making in the Administration through the Bureau if conditions are right. Conditions depend on the skills and priorities of the director, the support of the secretary of labor, and compatibility with the president's policy agenda. Even if the door is open, advocates soon learn that their bureaucratic ally gains them only a marginal position with respect to unyielding labor policy networks. Nevertheless, the WB has some resources: a statute guaranteeing permanence and a role in policymaking, a small staff, a director appointed by the president, and some grant funds. It speaks for women's issues to one of the major cabinet secretaries, but it does not have a role in the cabinet or White House. It cannot advocate policy beyond what the president desires. Rather, it works within the bureaucracy and among various commissions, task forces, and interagency committees. Conflicts about gender policy issues are not the business of any established policy community in Washington. The organized women's lobby must continue to seek access on its own to a variety of more or less permeable policy networks in education, welfare, crime, military, and labor.

Notes

1. In 1994, two other government offices were staffed by civil servants working on special women's issues: the Office of Women's Business Ownership in the Small Business Administration of the Department of Commerce and the Office of Research on Women's Health in the National Institute of Health.

2. Previous CSWs were the President's Commission on the Status of Women, 1961-1963; Citizen's Advisory Council on the Status of Women, 1963-1975; President's Task Force on Women's Rights and Responsibilities, 1969-1970; National Commission on the Observance of International Women's Year, 1975; National Advisory Committee for Women, 1978; President's Advisory Committee for Women, 1979-1980.

3. For example, the Interagency Committee on Women in Federal Law Enforcement, established in 1977; National Advisory Committee on Women's Educational Programs, established in 1974; Defense Advisory Committee on Women in the Service, established in 1951; Interdepartmental Task Force on the UN Conference in Nairobi, 1985; Task Force on Women, Minorities, and the Handicapped in Science and Technology, 1987-1990. In 1991, Congress established the Glass Ceiling Commission, with a special assignment to make recommendations for removing barriers to employment advancement of women and minorities. President Reagan also appointed a Task Force on Legal Equity, which reviewed laws and regulations for gender bias.

4. For excellent accounts of the Women's Bureau during the 1960s see Duerst-Lahti (1989); Zelman (1980); or Harrison (1988).

5. Other parts of the U.S. women's movement included the Women's Liberation Movement and radical feminist activists. These tended to be diverse and generally shunned national organizations and conventional Washington-based lobbying activities (Wandersee, 1988).

6. Small letters are used in this abbreviation to differentiate the U.S. Citizen's Advisory Council on the Status of Women (cacsw) from the Canadian Advisory Council on the Status of Women (CACSW).

7. The results of this survey were recently published in a U.S. Department of Labor report (1994).

16

Conclusion

The Case for State Feminism

Amy G. Mazur
Dorothy McBride Stetson

The cases presented in this book provide the material for answering the major analytical questions posed by the comparative study of state feminism (see Introduction). A central goal of this study is to determine whether any agency in the sample of advanced industrial societies shows evidence of state feminism: Do state structures assigned by political leaders to improve the status of women contribute to the formation of feminist policy and increase the access of women's movement activists to the political process?

The women's policy machineries in all countries in this book, with the exception of Poland, are feminist: These states advance feminist political goals. In contrast to the structures of the welfare state or of the liberal state, which have excluded feminist policy from political debate, those established with a mandate to focus directly on women's status have the capacity to turn leaders' attention, in some cases for the first time, to laws and regulations that can change the status of women in relation to men. Agencies in 13 countries have had some influence in the development and implementation of policies that advance women's status and challenge gender hierarchies.

Likewise, all but the Polish *Liga Kobiet* have taken steps to empower organizations and activists dedicated to raising women's social and economic positions in the policy process. Whereas the welfare state has tended to lock women into roles as clients of services rather than as participants in determining outcomes, women's policy machineries have used resources to help nongovernmental feminist and women's advocacy organizations fight for their own policy agendas. And, in many cases, the femocrats themselves are closely linked with these organizations. Like the liberal state, however, some state feminist agencies have tried to control such groups and shape their definitions of what is feminist. In many countries, the femocrats face tensions between the demands of their political or bureaucratic roles and their ties with nongovernmental feminist activists.

The discovery that state feminism exists in advanced industrial societies has been possible due to the assumptions and definitions that frame this study. In contrast to studies of the welfare state and the liberal state, we have not looked at the state as a single monolithic entity, but rather as a site of a variety of internally differentiated structures and processes. This assumption has enabled us to look for those sites where specialized agencies focusing on the status of women are located. The findings have also depended on distinguishing between two uses of *feminism*: one that enabled contributing authors to provide information on distinctive patterns of feminist policies within each country and a working definition for the cross-national comparative analysis (see Chapter 1). As will be seen in the comparative analysis in this chapter, contributing authors' definitions were useful in identifying which nongovernmental organizations were feminist. The comparative definition identifies the feminist policy areas used to compare the capacity of state agencies.

Having discovered the existence of state feminism, the next task is to measure the variation among states' policy machinery in the achievement of feminist goals and to suggest explanations for the patterns found. The next section of this chapter will present the analytical typology that structures the comparative analysis of the women's policy machineries examined in this book. This typology is first constructed using the 12 "most similar" cases. Then the "contrasting" cases of Spain and Poland will be treated in relation to the typology. Finally, the analysis will discuss why women's policy offices in certain countries gained higher levels of state feminism than in other countries in terms of the four major contextual variables outlined in the beginning of the book: politics of establishment, organizational features, conceptions of the state, and the form of the women's movement.

Typology of State Feminism

The typology of state feminism in Figure 16.1 classifies women's policy machinery described in the country case studies according to two criteria:

1. *Policy influence*, that is the participation of each women's policy office in the formation of feminist policies that promote the status of women and/or undermine patterns of gender hierarchy
2. *Policy access*, that is the degree to which women's policy machineries develop opportunities for society-based actors—feminist and women's advocacy organizations—to exert influence on feminist policies

The comparative typology classifies cases according to dichotomous measures (high/low) of policy influence and policy access. Four types of state feminism result:

Type 1—High Influence/High Access
Type 2—High Influence/Low Access
Type 3—Low Influence/High Access
Type 4—Low Influence/Low Access

Although Type 1 is the most state feminist and Type 4 the least, Types 2 and 3 at this point must be considered to be equally effective state feminist actors, in the absence of criteria for ranking either direct policy influence or provision of policy access for feminist interests as being of greater value.

Each of the case studies in this book describes women's policy machinery from its origins through a variety of activities and in the context of a country's political and social currents in the past 30 years. This typology captures only part of the story behind each case. To

LEVEL OF POLICY ACCESS

		High	Low
		Type 1 High Influence High Access	Type 2 High Influence Low Access
LEVEL OF POLICY INFLUENCE	High		
	Low	Type 3 Low Influence High Access	Type 4 Low Influence Low Access

Figure 16.1. Typology for Cross-National Comparison of Levels of State Feminism

classify a case according to policy influence and policy access, we examine the machinery during the period when it was the most active in each country (this may be different time periods in different cases). For most cases, one agency—a bureau, council, or ministry—was the center of women's policy activities. In Canada, Germany, Ireland, and Italy, however, two or more agencies are treated.

Policy influence is measured by determining to what extent women's policy offices had an impact on equal employment policy (EEP) for women, that is, any state action seeking to eliminate direct and/or indirect discrimination based on gender in hiring, firing, professional training, and promotion (Ratner, 1980). In advanced industrial societies with stable democratic governments, EEP is feminist in that it advances the status of women and attacks a major aspect of gender-based inequities. Women's policy machineries are classified as having high policy influence if they have had a clear role in determining the content of EEP at any stage of policy formation, including preformulation, formulation, implementation, and evaluation. Low policy influence occurs when women's policy structures have no clear effect on EEP development and/or implementation. The influence of a given country's women's policy structure(s) is classified in comparison with similar offices in other countries, rather than in comparison with other agencies in that national setting.[1]

The policy access dimension of state feminism focuses on a second way women's policy offices might advance the feminist political agenda, that is, through helping women's advocacy organizations find access to policymaking arenas inside the state. Offices can do this directly by recruiting organization leaders into policy networks or by forging alliances with relatively powerful and well-organized society-wide actors. Indeed, many have argued that it is only through the joint action of well-placed insiders and outsiders with certain levels of organizational capabilities that women's equality policies will rise on the political agenda, to become formalized and to be authoritatively implemented (Freeman, 1975; Gelb, 1989; Lovenduski & Randall, 1992; Mazur, 1995; Meehan, 1985; Outshoorn, 1991; Steinberg, 1988).

Femocrats can also aid feminist access indirectly by providing opportunities and resources to groups and individuals outside of the state to allow them to participate autonomously in policy formulation and implementation. This support can be achieved by providing state funds to organizations involved with policies that advance women's status or by inviting women's policy experts, activists, and/or representatives from feminist associations into state arenas of policymaking. It is important that state feminist inclusion of societal actors empower those interests without co-opting or dominating them. If interests become overly dependent on the state, not only is their autonomy threatened, but their own fortunes become intertwined with those of the policy offices, and these are often linked to the fate of a governing party coalition.

Policy machineries that score high on the policy access dimension are those that have provided access directly or indirectly to feminist groups, interests, and activists in such a way that they became more powerful actors in the policy process. Those machineries that fail to reach out to feminist interests, or that tend to make interests subservient to the goals and fortunes of official versions of feminism, will be classified as low on the dimension of policy access.

Classifying the Countries

TYPE 1: HIGH INFLUENCE/HIGH ACCESS

As the comparative typology in Figure 16.2 shows, women's policy machineries in Australia, the Netherlands, Norway, and

LEVEL OF POLICY ACCESS

		High	Low

	High	Type 1
		High Influence
		High Access
		   Australia, OSW
		   the Netherlands, DCE
		   Norway, NESC
		   Denmark, DESC
			Type 2
			High Influence
			Low Access
			   Sweden, JÄMO
			   Great Britain, EOC
			   France, MDF
			
			   [Spain, IM]

	Low	Type 3
		Low Influence
		High Access
		   Germany, FB
		   United States, WB
		   Canada, several
			Type 4
			Low Influence
			Low Access
			   Ireland, MSWA,
			   JOCWR
			   Italy, ESC, ESONC

LEVEL OF POLICY INFLUENCE

Figure 16.2. Comparative Typology of State Feminist Offices

Denmark meet the criteria for this highest category of state feminism. All are centralized offices that have been successful in integrating gender equity principles into many policy areas, especially equal employment policy, and all have empowered women's groups to similar degrees.

Australia's Office of the Status of Women (OSW) in the department of the federal Prime Minister and Cabinet (PM&C) acts as a hub to coordinate the efforts of other women's policy units in specific ministries. This hub system, along with the OSW's powerful location in the PM&C and its ministerial position from 1982 to 1988, has allowed OSW femocrats to coordinate a gender audit of government policy, injecting women's equality issues into a cross-section of policy areas. The Women's Budget statement, for instance, forced all federal agencies and departments to take account of gender. The OSW also played a central role in formulating the 1984 Sex Discrimination Act and the Affirmative Action Act, through cabinet and parliamentary decision-making arenas (Sawer, Chapter 2).

The OSW has tended to empower women's groups without making them dependent. Up until 1993, it provided secretariat services for national women's advisory boards and councils. Its extensive grant allocations have contributed to "enabling new sections of women to become organized and [to] assisting more established groups to fulfill their representation and advocacy roles in more professional ways" (Sawer, Chapter 2, p. 31). Recent increases in program grants and the shift away from the OSW's secretariat services suggests the OSW's policies in this area may go even further in strengthening the women's groups' own resources outside state arenas.

Like the OSW, the *Directie Coordinatie Emancipatiebeleid* (Department for the Coordination of Equality Policy, or DCE) in the Netherlands is situated in a powerful location—the Ministry of Social Affairs (after 1981). It has a large staff, a junior minister, and since 1986 its own cabinet committee to coordinate a cross-sectoral approach to women's equality policymaking. The DCE's 1985 policy document, the *Beleidsplan*, set the goals for women's equality policy for all ministries, giving it a strong emphasis on labor market policy. Although, as Outshoorn (Chapter 10) asserts, the DCE was unable to get its authoritative version of antidiscrimination legislation into law, DCE femocrats successfully convinced parliamentarians hostile to a gender-specific bill to retain references to sex discrimination in the 1994 EEP law. Thus, like other state feminist offices with high levels of policy influence, the DCE can directly affect the content of EEP legislation, albeit not to the extent that femocrats and feminists on the outside would wish.

The DCE has been most successful in distributive policies, devoting much of its budget to setting up women's bureaus in provinces and towns and subsidizing local women's projects. Rather than co-opting or weakening feminist groups, DCE funding has "provided the Dutch women's movement with a strong state-subsidized backbone, allowing for both continuity in organization and institutionalization of new initiatives" (Outshoorn, Chapter 10, p. 177). In the past, Dutch femocrats have been criticized by more radical members of the women's movements for being "bread feminists," but these critiques have subsided in recent years as DCE funding has clearly helped feminist groups. Many DCE femocrats were active in the new feminist movements, and one deputy minister of the DCE had been a founding member of the moderate feminist group, *Man-Vrouw-Maatschappij* (Man-Woman-Society).

The Equal Status Council in Norway (ESC), which reached its zenith of activity in the late 1970s, is a tripartite council with the resources and staff to set government priorities on women's equality initiatives in all areas of public policy. The ESC initiatives led to Norway's most ambitious plan of action. In 1981, the Labor-led parliament adopted the Council's proposal as its own 5-year Action Plan to Promote Equal Status Between the Sexes. The reports of the ESC have also been important in drawing the attention of policymakers in the cabinet and parliament to gender-based inequities in employment. The ESC, therefore, has an important role in getting EEP on the policy agenda and generating proposals for prospective EEP initiatives and measures.

As Bystydzienski (Chapter 11) asserts, the ESC has contributed to the emergence of an equality policy network, an "equal status segment," throughout Norway that has gone far in pushing the state to improve women's position in society. The ESC served as an effective forum for all feminist interests to contribute to equality policy goals. Most important, the ESC has empowered women's interests through coordinating and supporting equal status committees in counties and municipalities, which, with the support of the ESC in the 1980s, served as important avenues of women's recruitment into elected office and corporate bodies.

Like its Norwegian counterpart, the Danish Equal Status Council (DESC) is a corporate body that directly represents women's interests within the state policymaking arena. Since its creation in 1975, with members from labor, management, moderate feminist groups, and more recently from women's studies programs, the DESC has played "a decisive role in the preparatory phases of amendments and new legislation and . . . is heavily involved in the implementation of existing equal opportunities legislation" (Borchorst, Chapter 4, p. 59). Although the Council's membership was originally closed to second-wave feminist representation and, as Borchorst argues, the DESC's action has been restrained to the "political niche" of an equal opportunities policy based on gender-neutral approaches to women's equality, the DESC has remained a constant influence within this expanding niche.

The DESC has also been an important channel for women's groups to gain direct access to policymaking through representation on the Council. As Borchorst states, "statements and strategies of the DESC are largely influenced by women's organizations" (Chapter 4, p. 71). The DESC also has contributed to increasing women's representation in all political offices. Indeed, more than empowering feminist groups through direct grants, the ESCs in Denmark and Norway have empowered women's interests by bringing them into corporate and electoral segments of the state.

TYPE 2: HIGH INFLUENCE/LOW ACCESS

France, Sweden, and Great Britain have offices with high levels of policy authority, but they offer lower access to feminist groups than machineries in Australia, Netherlands, Norway, and Denmark. France's *Ministère des Droits de la Femme* (MDF), a central ministry with an extensive territorial administration, proposed the 1983 equal employment law in conjunction with the Socialist party's legislative agenda. The wide powers of the Ministry also permitted Yvette Roudy and her staff to oversee implementation of the new law. Opposition from a Socialist prime minister and trade unions, however, prevented the MDF from getting a more authoritative version of the bill through the legislative process. As a consequence, the law created a powerless equal employment commission rather than effective enforcement structures.

Although the MDF pursued an extensive policy of funding women's groups and associations, these efforts did not go far in empowering women's interests in the policy process. The tendency to fund groups sympathetic to the Socialist Ministry's mission, the poor administration of these funds, and the allocation of a good portion of the subsidies to the quasi-state Women's Rights Information Centers circumscribed the extent to which these subsidies helped independent women's interests. Also, although in the beginning some feminist activists worked in the Ministry, these feminists left the administration to be replaced by career civil servants and Socialist party loyalists.

Despite inauspicious beginnings, the Equal Opportunities Commission (EOC) in Great Britain has been instrumental in EEP in the 1980s. Under the feminist leadership of Joanna Foster and Valerie Amos, the EOC harnessed the extensive power given to the QUANGO under the 1975 Sexual Discrimination Act to become an "active legal protagonist" (Lovenduski, Chapter 7, p. 123) and to contribute to developing more authoritative EEP through the 1986 Sex Discrimination Act and the 1983 Equal Value Amendment.

The EOC has been reluctant to get close to organized women's communities, and its initial arm's-length approach to new feminist groups discouraged most equal opportunities-oriented women's groups from close collaboration with the Commission. As Lovenduski (Chapter 7) asserts, local authority women's committees developed their own equal opportunity networks outside of the EOC because of its early inaction. A part of the new feminist strategy of the EOC in the 1980s was to work closely with the EEP networks that had emerged independently of the EOC. With its feminist-oriented staff, the EOC began to work more actively with a wider range of feminist groups, but these nascent efforts to give better access to equal opportunity groups are being put into question by a shift to a more conservative equal opportunity policy under Prime Minister John Major.

The 1979 Equal Opportunities Act established the Swedish Equality Ombudsman or JÄMO to enforce new equal employment policy. Originally limited by the narrow scope of the act, JÄMO was responsible for enforcing employment equity in the 10% of the labor market in which collective agreements did not exist; there it was authorized to identify problem areas for women and take discrimination cases to the labor courts. At the same time, the Ombudsman played a key role in bringing sexual harassment in the workplace to the public's attention and contributed to the treatment of sexual harassment in the workplace in the 1992 Equal Opportunity Act, albeit, as Elman (Chapter 14, this volume) points out, in a highly indirect manner.

Alternatively, JÄMO has done little to empower feminist activists or organizations. In addition to failing to bring in feminists as staff members or advisers, it has resisted calls from autonomous feminist groups to expand its purview to sex inequality outside the workplace. Instead, it has worked with feminist activists in the political parties and through parliamentary groups in trade unions, embracing, according to Elman (Chapter 14), a state-inspired definition of what would advance women's status by focusing on gender-neutral notions of equality.

TYPE 3: LOW INFLUENCE/HIGH ACCESS

Policy offices in Canada, Germany, and the United States have gone further in mobilizing feminist groups than have offices in Sweden, France, or Great Britain. Yet offices in these three countries have significantly less policy influence. The array of policy machinery in Canada has empowered women's groups in the policy process. Indeed, the femocrats, although marginalized from central policy processes, have aided groups on the outside, like the National Action Committee (NAC). With most of its funds coming from state feminist offices, specifically the Women's Program, the NAC had a symbiotic relationship with the state feminist offices until the mid-1980s (Geller-Schwartz, Chapter 3).

Still, Canada's "eclectic array" of machinery for the most part has been "muddling through" women's employment policy issues, with no single controlling purpose (Geller-Schwartz, Chapter 3, p. 48). Unlike other countries in this volume, Canada created women's policy offices sprinkled through the government with no central coordinating body. As a result, if femocrat agendas did not match the government agenda, they were "ignored, silenced, or used to subvert the very goals they seek" (p. 53). The lack of real policymaking influence meant, for instance, that in the campaign for equal pay for work of equal value, femocrats in the Women's Bureau who wanted to see the new legislation enacted found their only option was through giving anonymous "tips" to members of the NAC who were spearheading the campaign.

In the United States, the Women's Bureau reached its apex in the 1960s and 1970s under feminist-oriented directors, contributing indirectly to the formulation and implementation of specific policies related to women's employment equality, including the 1963 Equal Pay Act, affirmative action training programs, and the definition of pregnancy leave as a disability. During its activist years, the Bureau was more important in providing resources and infrastructure at the federal and state levels by serving as "the administrative core of a policy network on sex equity" (Stetson, Chapter 15, p. 263). The network included moderate feminist pressure groups, energized through grants and regional and national conferences sponsored by the Bureau. At the same time, the Bureau's lack of formal policymaking powers and marginal position in the mainstream decision-making process has meant that when the WB provided access to outside groups, it did not guarantee its own influence over policy. Further, the hostile approach of the Reagan and Bush administrations to equal opportunity policy stymied these networking efforts in the 1980s. To many politically active feminists, the Bureau now seems to be just "part" of the governmental woodwork (Stetson, Chapter 15, p. 268).

Germany, a federal system like Canada and the United States, differs in that the viable policy machinery is at the state and local level, not the federal level. As Ferree (Chapter 6) states, it is "impossible to provide a single assessment of the impact" (pp. 105-106) of the 1,100 women's affairs offices, or *Frauenbeauftragte* (FB) in former West Germany and the 400 in the former German Democratic Republic. Their roles in policy vary widely, and in the absence of strong national EEP, they are relegated to "sensitizing other government departments to the women's dimension of their mission" (p. 103). They are affected, in this, by the deep divisions in the political culture over the role of women in family and at work.

FBs have had significantly more effect on directly and indirectly aiding a wide range of groups to develop policy skills. Many of the women who work as FBs come from autonomous feminist groups that emerged in the 1970s, and as a consequence, they work closely with such groups in the community. At their most active, Ferree (Chapter 6) observes, the FBs have made major contributions in forging a "women's public" (p. 107) to support women's policy issues and keep them in a visible place on the political agenda. And to some extent, they have had a positive effect on overcoming the split between the moderate women's lobby and the more radical autonomous feminists that arose in the 1970s.

TYPE 4: LOW INFLUENCE/LOW ACCESS

Of the 12 "most similar" cases presented in this book, Ireland and Italy place in this lowest state feminist category. Ireland's two institutions, the Ministry of State for Women's Affairs (MSWA) and the Joint Oireachtas Committee on Women's Rights (JOCWR), are limited by articles 41 and 42 of the Catholic church-informed constitution to policy areas that would not clash with protecting the family and with women's role as caretaker within the family. Not only were abortion and divorce policy off limits for both offices, but neither office was able to take an official position on equal employment policy. Beyond their highly limited jurisdictions, the two offices had little formal policymaking power.

The MSWA, with no staff or budget, became nothing more than the minister acting as a spokesperson. But even in that role she was prohibited from taking a feminist position. During its short life, the Ministry introduced programs for women at the local level, published reports discussing women's inferior status, and publicized government measures that addressed "constitutionally safe" problems. The MSWA gave small grants to women's groups, but most groups avoided it because of its powerlessness and restricted jurisdiction.

The recommendations of the JOCWR on selected women's policy issues were based on its own research and submissions from interest groups. A parliamentary committee, its reports were not ever formally debated in parliament or intended for mass distribution. Like other parliamentary committees in Ireland, the JOCWR was not meant to have a strong hand in dictating the content of legislation. The reports did serve as a source of information and proposals for parliamentarians and cabinet members on various pieces of women's rights legislation. By inviting women's groups to present their views, the Committee has provided only the merest hint of policy access. As they had spurned the MSWA, many feminist groups refused to participate in the JOCWR proceedings because of its connection to what they perceived as the patriarchal state.

Italy's Equal Status Committee was established to overcome the appearance of a weak EEP and has an official responsibility to promote the policy, strengthened by the provisions of the 1991 Affirmative Action Act. However, its role in the policy process remains marginal. According to Guadagnini (Chapter 9, this volume), the "ESC has not developed into the robust defender of equal rights that many expected" (p. 162). The site of effective equal employment policy and practice is not the state agencies at all, but rather the collective bargaining process. And, although the ESC counted representatives of the unions and employers among its members, it plays no role in these negotiations.

Both the ESC and Equal Status and Equal Opportunity Nation Commission (ESONC) have participated in promoting equality statutes in the parliament. The ESC developed proposals for legislation and drafted the Affirmative Action Act of 1991. Tina Anselmi, activist Christian Democrat chairwoman of the ESONC, was prominent in support of the Affirmative Action Act, equality for women entrepreneurs, and maternity leave. However, her role owed more to her own personal resources as a party leader than to any clear policy-initiating activity of the 29-member ESONC.

With respect to policy access, Italy's national equality agencies have both direct and indirect links with women's organizations but remain remote, almost estranged, from feminist groups. Representatives of women's associations serve on both national commissions: 7 of 29 on ESONC, and 11 of 23 on ESC. Indirectly, ESONC has focused its energies on increasing women's participation generally in politics. According to Guadagnini (Chapter 9), ESONC's greatest achievements are its activities in raising women's political culture by distributing information to women about their rights and supporting research on the status of women "in a country where women's studies are not acknowledged by universities" (p. 156).

The relations between the national policy machinery and the fractious feminist movement have been distant. Among many reasons for this situation are the partisan divisions that stymie development of effective gender consciousness. As in Germany, the most promising links between feminists and the state in Italy are likely to occur at the local level, where "cooperation among feminists, women's organizations, and equal opportunity commissions has indeed been more effective" (Guadagnini, Chapter 9, p. 165). Even there, however, the cooperation has focused on service projects, such as the center for women immigrants in Turin, rather than on facilitating the access of society-based actors in the women's movement into the arenas of decision making.

The Contrasting Cases:
Spain and Poland

In Chapter 1, we pointed out that 12 of the cases were drawn as "most similar" from the population of advanced industrial societies with stable democratic systems. In addition we selected two contrasting cases: Spain and Poland. Spain moved to democratic government in the 1970s, in the midst of the second-wave feminist movement in the rest of Europe. It presents an opportunity to see if a newly democratizing country can use women's policy machinery as effectively as countries with more long-term democratic histories. Poland represents the more recent trend of democratization—the transition from communism. Looking at the women's policy machinery under communism allows us to see if the communist egalitarian tradition offers a possible model for state feminism.

Spain's *Instituto de la Mujer* (IM) presents a case that can be incorporated into the typology classifying the "most similar" cases, especially with respect to policy influence. Like the Swedish Ombudsman office, it has taken a relative important role in EEP formation but a less active role in helping society-based groups get involved with the policy process. Since 1985, the *Consejo Rector*, the IM's advisory council, has provided the Institute with a formal channel to influence women's policy initiatives in other ministries. Also, through its two equality plans, the IM conducts an open discussion with ministries about equality policies and sets goals for future policies.

The record of the agency in providing access and mobilization opportunities to nonstate groups is low to nonexistent, and this is one aspect that reflects the recent authoritarian power structure. There has been near total exclusion of feminist activists on the staff of the Socialist-linked IM. The IM's advisory council did not include women's group representatives until 1990, nor did the IM ask individual feminists or members of feminist organizations to participate in drawing up its equality plans. However, with 10% to 15% of the budget earmarked for group subsidies, the IM has a potential to empower women's groups on a more local level. Strict qualifying stipulations and claims that subsidies are given according to political affiliation have led many feminist observers in Spain to question the effectiveness of the IM's subsidization policy (Valiente, Chapter 13, this volume). Thus, although Spain is a newly democratized country, it could be situated with the Type 2 countries.

Lingering doubts about whether any of the cases discussed so far operate as state feminist actors can be laid to rest by looking at the highly contrasting Polish Women's League, the *Liga Kobiet Polskich*. As a satellite organization of the Communist Polish United Workers Party (PUWP) in a state socialist system, the LK was used by the leadership of the party to maintain its authoritarian control over society. Rather than taking an independent role in suggesting women's policy initiatives that challenged the status quo in gender relations, the mass-oriented LK promoted the dominant Marxist definition of women as producers in the economy and in the family, a definition that, as Robinson (Chapter 12) argues, "served the interest of the regime" (p. 204). Thus, whereas the LK claimed to "defend and further extend the rights of women working in the city and countryside, as wives, mothers, and citizens" (LK, 1959, p. 405), it did not challenge Marxist notions of gender that contributed to sex-based hierarchies in Polish society.

The LK also mobilized women on a mass level to support the PUWP and recruited women at the elite level to serve in the leadership of the party and in the Communist party-controlled government. The LK was not allowed to give women's groups the means to act independently within the system, either to affect public policy or to help women. As Robinson (Chapter 12) shows, the legacy of the LK continues to impede feminist unity and policy influence, even after the authoritarian regime of which it was a part has collapsed.

Explaining Variations
in State Feminism

This section will look for similarities among the high state feminist cases and differences between them and the lower state feminist cases in terms of the four independent variables expressed in the analytical questions raised in Chapter 1 (this volume): politics of establishment, organizational forms, conceptions of the state, and politics of the women's movement. It is our conclusion that the absence of any of the four conditions in countries lowers the ability of state feminist offices to influence equality policy and give access to women's groups.

   ◆ Does the politics surrounding the establishment of policy machinery explain its effectiveness in promoting feminist goals?

The highest state feminist offices, Australia's OSW, The Netherlands DCE, the ESCs in Norway and Denmark, were all created under the initiatives of Social Democratic Governments that placed gender equity on their policy agendas, amid relatively strong pressure from moderate feminist groups—*Man-Vrouw-Maatschappij* in the Netherlands, the Women's Electoral Lobby in Australia, the National Council of Women in Norway and the Danish Women's Society in Denmark. Although most other countries' offices tended to be created under left-wing Governments, with the exception of JÄMO, active feminist pressure groups were usually less prevalent, particularly in Ireland, France, and Spain. In Italy, neither factor was present. Agencies were created by a center-right Government, albeit with Socialist participation, and in the absence of feminist pressure.

◆ Do certain organizational forms increase the likelihood that policy machinery will further feminist goals?

All of the agencies in the highest category had centralized cross-sectoral approaches to promoting gender equality into mainstream policy. The two tripartite commissions in Denmark and Norway were part of a wider strategy to integrate gender equity in all policy areas and provided the policy frameworks for this enterprise in their official reports. Similarly, the DCE in the Netherlands and the OSW in Australia both served as administrative nerve centers for interministerial women's policy correspondents and territorial relays. In the other countries with centralized agencies—France, Spain, Ireland, and Sweden—none were set up to coordinate women's equality policy in an authoritative manner. For instance, in France the powerful women's rights ministry was unable to penetrate the structure of other administrative bastions. In Canada the dispersed state feminist policy machinery lacked a respected and influential central coordinating office. Although Italy opted for a cross-sectoral approach, as in Canada, there was little coordination.

◆ To what extent does the conception of the state affect the likelihood that policy machinery will further feminist political goals?

The concept of the state in the political culture in all high state feminist countries defined the state as the major actor for dealing with social inequality, with societal interests being brought into the state to cooperate in developing social justice policy, albeit in different ways. For example, the Dutch tradition of state-society relations and Norway's and Denmark's neocorporatist relations set the stage to give women's interests effective access to policymaking. In Australia, the "political tradition to look to the state for a response to social issues" and the "concept of the state as a vehicle for social justice" (Sawer, Chapter 2, pp. 23-24) were embraced by the Liberal and Labor parties.

In the countries with state feminist offices in lower categories, the concept of a strong equality state with high levels of vertical interest-group cooperation was not as prevalent. Despite its strong state historical tradition, the Federal Republic of Germany has emphasized decentralization, creating the space for some *Länder* governments to be activist but for others to restrain interest in women's policy machinery. In the United States, strong antigovernment sentiments and the tendency toward pluralist interest-group action contributes to the idea of statelessness. Italy combines a centralized, sclerotic state with widespread practice of avoidance of state solutions to problems. Policy is effectively implemented outside the state.

The French state is seen as very powerful and impenetrable to emerging social interests. A recent legacy of authoritarianism may impede effective inclusion of women's interests into the state arena in Spain. A pro-state approach is prevalent in Canadian political culture, but the civil service tradition of neutrality has made top bureaucrats suspicious of femocrats promoting an equality agenda. In Ireland, the constitution made it the state's role to carry out Catholic doctrine, which places a premium on women's role in the home, a major impediment to the action of Irish state feminist offices.

◆ Is a particular form of women's movement more compatible with the development of strong state feminism?

In the high state feminist countries, women participated actively in outside feminist groups as well as in established trade unions and political parties. Furthermore, women were equally attracted to newer autonomous women's liberal movements and to the mainstream political and moderate reform-oriented groups they eschewed. While the radical feminist groups concentrated on consciousness-raising among women at the grass-roots level and thrust gender-based discrimination on to the public agenda, the moderate feminist groups directly pressured political party elites and politicians to establish and operate feminist women's policy machinery. Thus, even though the two groups were often in conflict, their combined influence set the stage for more effective state feminist offices. State feminism is weaker in countries where other patterns prevail. Feminist organization does not reach these high levels in Spain, Ireland, and France. In France, for instance, where antisystem groups have been more prevalent than reform-oriented groups, state feminism seems to be weaker. Autonomous radical feminist movements are weaker than moderate reform groups in the United States, Canada, and Sweden. In Italy, women's associations are strong and growing, and the autonomous feminist groups sustain vibrant cultural activities. Yet the ideological, partisan, and organizational divisions have stymied any meaningful cooperation.

Conclusion

This study suggests that women's policy machinery will reach high levels of state feminism, on the one hand, when the state is defined as a site of social justice and has the structural capacity to institutionalize new demands for equality and, on the other, when society sustains widely supported feminist organizations that challenge sex hierarchies through both radical politics from outside and reform politics in unions and parties. If these conditions exist, politicians and policymakers at the supranational, national, or subnational levels of government are likely to set up structures that introduce gender equity principles to many policy sectors and bring representatives of women's interests into the state to participate in that policy. If these conditions do not exist, then although politicians may establish women's policy offices, these units will have a hard time either influencing women's equality policy or empowering women's interests in society or both. As the contrasting case of Poland shows, when feminist organization is absent and the state is impervious to democratic influence, women's policy machinery may even be used as a tool for authoritarian control.

Given that the chapters in this volume consist of an initial cataloguing of state feminist offices and as such do not represent similar levels of analysis or methods of measurement, the propositions about state feminism under study constitute a first step in the development of a comparative theory of state feminism. Future research in this area will be necessary to explore the validity of these claims and to design studies that work toward a further understanding of the complex relationship between feminism and the state.

Note

1. It is important to note that the ability of state feminist offices to influence policy is generally limited by their often marginal position within the governmental hierarchy and the low priority individual governments may give to gender-specific issues. Indeed, in all countries in this study, more powerful state and society actors blocked the work of women's policy machineries or brought the work to a halt, often when elections brought in conservative Governments less interested in promoting sex equality. The policy influence of these structures also tends to be diluted by their cross-sectoral purview in a bureaucratic world of policy specialization.

References

Adams, C., & Winston, K. (1980). *Mothers at work*. New York: Longman.

Adamson, N., Briskin, L., & McPhail, M. (1988). *Feminist organizing for change*. Toronto: Oxford University Press.

Advies. (1977). *Advies organisatie emancipatiebeleid* [Advice organization of women's public policy]. The Hague: Emancipatiekommissie.

Allardt, E. (1986). Representative government in a bureaucratic age. In S. Graubard (Ed.), *Norden—the passion for equality* (pp. 200-225). Oslo: Norwegian University Press.

Almond, G. A. (1988, September). The return to the state. *American Political Science Review, 82*(3), 853-874.

Almond, G., & Verba, S. (1963). *The civic culture*. Princeton, NJ: Princeton University Press.

Ambler, J. (Ed.). (1985). *The French socialist experiment*. Philadelphia: Institute for the Study of Human Issues.

Andersen, A., & Nielsen, R. (1990). *Ligestillingslovene* [Sex discrimination acts]. Copenhagen: Juristog økonomforbundets Forlag.

Andersen, B. R. (1983). *Two essays on the Nordic welfare states*. Copenhagen: AKF.

Anderson, D. (1991). *The unfinished revolution*. Toronto: Doubleday Canada.

Anderson, J. E. (1990). *Public policymaking: An introduction*. Boston: Houghton Mifflin.

Anon. (1987, September). Feminism in the public service. *Hersay: Newsletter of the NSW Women's Advisory Council*, No. 4.

Anton, T. (1980). *Administered politics: Elite political cultures in Sweden*. Boston: Martinus Nighoff.

Arkins, A. (1988). The committee of the 24th Oireachtas. *Irish Political Studies, 3*, 91-97.

Arpaillange, P. (1992). *Report on the women's rights structures*. Paris: Cour des Comptes.

Arrato, A. (1993). *From neo-marxism to democratic theory: Essays on the critical theory of Soviet-type societies*. New York: M. E. Sharpe.

Australian National Advisory Committee, IWY. (1976). *Report*. Canberra: Australian Government Publishing Service.

Baalsrud, E. S. (1992). *Free and equal? Female voices from central and eastern Europe*. Oslo: Equal Status Council.

Bagihole, B. (1994). *Women, work, and equal opportunity*. Aldershot: Avebury.

Ballestrero, M. V. (1985). *Parità e oltre. Donne, lavoro, e pari opportunità* [Equality and beyond: Women, work, and equal opportunity]. Rome: Ediesse.

Beccali, B. (1985). Le politiche del lavoro femminile in Italia: donne, sindacati e Stato tra il 1974 e il 1984 [Politics of female work in Italy: Women, unions, and the state from 1974 to 1984]. *Stato e mercato, 15*, 423-457.

Bégin, M. (1992). The Royal Commission on the Status of Women in Canada: Twenty years later. In C. Backhouse & D. H. Flaherty (Eds.), *Challenging times* (pp. 21-38). Montreal: McGill-Queens.

Beleidsplan Emancipatie [Policy paper on the improvement of women's status]. (1985). *Handelingen Tweede Kamer, zitting 1984-1984, 19502* (Official proceedings of the Second Chamber of Parliament), nrs. 1-19.

Beltrán, M. (1990). La administración pública y los funcionarios [Public administration and civil servants]. In S. Giner (Ed.), *España: sociedad y política* (pp. 315-352). Madrid: Espasa-Calpe.

Berghahn, S. (1993). Frauen, Recht, und langer Atem: Bilanz nach über 40 Jahren gleichstellungsgebot in Deutschland [Women, the law, and the need for endurance: Evaluating over 40 years of formal equal rights in Germany]. In G. Helwig & H. M. Nickel (Eds.), *Frauen in Deutschland 1945-1992* (pp. 71-138). Bonn: Bundeszentral für politische Bildung.

Bialas, C., & Ettl, W. (1993). Wirtschaftliche Lage, soziale Differenzierung und Probleme der Interessenorganisation in den neuen Bundesländern [Economic situation, social differentiation, and problems of interest representation in the new federal states]. *Soziale Welt, 44*(1), 52-75.

Birnbaum, P. (Ed.). (1985). *Les elites socialistes au pouvoir 1981-1985* [Socialist elites in power]. Paris: PUF.

Black, N. (1992). Ripples in the second wave: Comparing the contemporary women's movement in Canada and the United States. In C. Backhouse & D. H. Flaherty (Eds.), *Challenging times* (pp. 94-109). Montreal: McGill-Queens.

Boneparth, E. (1980). A framework for policy analysis. In E. Boneparth (Ed.), *Women, power, and policy* (pp. 1-14). New York: Pergamon.

Bonnevie, E. S. (1953). *The status of women in Norway today* (Norwegian Social Policy Series). Oslo: Norwegian Joint Committee on International Affairs.

Borchorst, A. (1986). Statsfeminisme eller afledningsmanøvre. Om dansk ligestillingspolitik gennem 20 år [State feminism or diversionary manoeuvres: On 20 years of Danish policies of equal opportunities]. In *Årbog for kvindestudier AUC 1986* (pp. 59-94). Aalborg: Universitetsforlag.

Borchorst, A. (1989). Kvindeinteresser og konflikter [Women's interests and conflicts]. *Forum for kvindeforskning, 3*, 21-34.

Borchorst, A. (1994a). The Scandinavian welfare states—Patriarchal, gender neutral or woman-friendly? *International Journal of Contemporary Sociology, 31*(1), 45-68.

Borchorst, A. (1994b). Welfare state regimes, women's interests, and the EC. In D. Sainsbury (Ed.), *Engendering welfare states: Combining insights of feminist and mainstream research* (pp. 26-44). London: Sage.

Borchorst, A., & Siim, B. (1987). Women and the advanced welfare state—a new kind of patriarchal power? In A. S. Sassoon (Ed.), *Women and the state: The shifting boundaries of public and private* (pp. 128-157). London: Unwin Hyman.

Böttger, B. (1990). *Das Recht auf Gleichheit und Differenz: Elisabeth Selbert und der Kampf der Frauen um Art. 3 II Grundgesetz* [The right to equality and difference: Elisabeth Selbert and women's struggle for Article 3 (II) of the Basic Law]. Munster: Verlag Westfälisches Dampfboot.

BRÅ. (1989). Lagen om besöksförbud: En uppföljning [The law concerning orders of protection: An investigation of their implementation]. Stockholm: Author.

Bussemaker, J. (1991). Equality, autonomy, and feminist politics. In E. Meehan & S. Sevenhuijsen (Eds.), *Equality politics and gender* (pp. 52-71). London: Sage.

Byrne, P., & Lovenduski, J. (1978). Sex equality and the law in Britain. *Women's Studies International Quarterly, 1,* 131-167.

Bystydzienski, J. M. (1988). Women in politics in Norway. *Women & Politics, 8*(3/4), 73-95.

Bystydzienski, J. M. (1989). Women and socialism: A comparative study of women in Poland and the USSR. *Signs, 14*(3), 668-684.

Bystydzienski, J. M. (1995). *Women in electoral politics: Lessons from Norway.* Westport, CT: Praeger.

Canadian Advisory Council on the Status of Women. (1979, October). *10 years later: An assessment of the federal government's implementation of the recommendations made by the Royal Commission on the Status of Women.* Ottawa: Author.

Canadian Department of Labour. (1964, September). *Labour Gazette,* pp. 772-774.

Canadian Department of Labour. (1975, January). *Labour Gazette,* pp. 10-21.

Canadian International Development Agency. (1986, June). *Women in development: CIDA action plan.* Ottowa: Author.

Caporaso, J. A. (Ed.). (1989). *The elusive state: international and comparative perspectives.* Newbury Park: Sage.

Chubb, B. (1992). *The government and politics of Ireland* (3rd ed.). London: Longman.

Cohen, M. G. (1992). The Canadian women's movement and its efforts to influence the Canadian economy. In C. Backhouse & D. H. Flaherty (Eds.), *Challenging times* (pp. 215-224). Montreal: McGill-Queens.

Collier, D. (1991). New perspectives on the comparative method. In D. A. Rustow & K. P. Erickson (Eds.), *Comparative political dynamics: Global research perspectives* (pp. 7-31). New York: Harper Collins.

Collier, D., & Mahon, J. E. (1993, December). Conceptual "stretching" revisited: Adapting categories in comparative analysis. *American Political Science Review, 87*(4), 845-855.

Commissione Nazionale per la Parità e le Pari Opportunità tra uomo e donna. (1994). Relazione al Presidente del Consiglio dei Ministri sull'attività svolta [Report to the President of the Council of Ministers on the activity being carried out]. Rome: Presidenza del Consiglio dei Ministri.

Connell, R. W. (1990). The state, gender, and sexual politics. *Theory and Society, 19,* 507-544.

Cornelißen, W. (1993). Politische Partizipation von Frauen in der alten Bundesrepublik und im vereinten Deutschland [The political participation of women in the "old" Federal Republic and in unified Germany]. In G. Helwig & H. M. Nickel (Eds.), *Frauen in Deutschland 1945-1992* (pp. 321-350). Bonn: Bundeszentral für politische Bildung.

Cott, N. (1987). *The grounding of modern feminism*. New Haven, CT: Yale University Press.

Daalder, H. (1974). *Politisering en lijdelijkheidheid in de Nederlandse politiek* [Politicization and passivity in Dutch politics]. Assen: Van Gorcum.

Dahlberg, A. (1992). Dåligt skydd mot sexuella trakasserier [Bad protection from sexual harassment]. *Morgonbris, 1.*

Dahlerup, D. (Ed). (1986). *The new women's movement.* London\Beverly Hills: Sage.

Dahlerup, D. (1987). Confusing concepts—confusing reality: A theoretical discussion of the patriarchal state. In A. S. Sassoon (Ed.), *Women and the state: The shifting boundaries of public and private* (pp. 93-127). London: Unwin Hyman.

Dahlerup, D. (1990). Da ligestilling kom på dagsordenen [When equality rights were put on the agenda]. In D. Dahlerup & K. Hvidt (Eds.), *Kvinder på tinge* (pp. 158-220). Copenhagen: Rosinante.

Dahlerup, D. (1993). From movement protest to state feminism: The women's movement and unemployment policy in Denmark. *NORA. Nordic Journal of Women's Studies, 1,* 4-21.

Daley, A. (Ed.). (1995). *The Mitterand era: Left Politics and political mobilization in France.* New York: New York University Press.

Darcy, R., Welch, S., & Clark, J. (Eds.). (1994). *Women, elections, and representation* (2nd ed.). Lincoln: University of Nebraska Press.

Davin, D. (1976). *Woman-work.* Oxford: Clarendon Press.

Debates, Canadian House of Commons, 7th Session, 21st. Parliament, V-5420. (1952-1953).

De Cristofaro, M. L. (Ed.). (1993). *La legge italiana per la parità di opportunità delle lavoratrici. Commento alla L. 10 aprile 1991. n. 125* [The Italian law for equal opportunity for women workers]. Naples: Edizioni Scientifiche Italiane.

Delphy, C. (1984). Les femmes et l'état [Women and the state]. *Nouvelles Questions Féministes,* Spring, 5-19.

Diamond, I. (Ed.). (1983). *Families, politics, and public policy.* New York: Longman.

Dijkstra, T., & Swiebel, J. (1982). De overheid en het vrouwenvraagstuk: emancipatie als mode en taboe [Government and the women's question: Policy as fashion and taboo]. In *Socialisties-Feministiese Teksten* (Nr. 7, pp. 42-62). Amsterdam: Feministiese Uitgeverij Sara.

Dobberthien, Marliese. (1988). Ein dorniger weg: Frauenförderung in den gewerkschaften [A thorny path: Affirmative action for women in the unions]. In O. Stein & M. Weg (Eds.), *MACHT macht frauen stark: Frauenpolitik für die 90er Jahre* (pp. 138-144). Hamburg: VSA-Verlag.

Dowse, S. (1975). *Power in institutions—the public service.* Transcript of discussion at the 1975 Women and Politics Conference. Canberra: National Library of Australia.

Ds. (1992). *Act concerning equality between men and women* (92). Stockholm: Allmänna Förlaget.

Duchen, C. (1986). *Feminism in France from May 1968 to Mitterrand.* London: Routledge, Kegan and Paul.

Duerst-Lahti, G. (1989). The government's role in building the women's movement. *Political Science Quarterly, 104*(2), 249-268.

Dumont, M. (1992). The origins of the women's movement in Quebec. In C. Backhouse & D. H. Flaherty (Eds.), *Challenging times* (pp. 94-109). Montreal: McGill-Queens.

Durán, M. A., & Gallego, M. T. (1986). The women's movement in Spain and the new Spanish democracy. In D. Dahlerup (Ed.), *The new women's movement: Feminism and political power in Europe and the USA* (pp. 200-216). London: Sage.

Dyson, K. (1980). *The state tradition in Western Europe.* New York: Oxford University Press.

Edelman, M. (1985). *The symbolic uses of politics.* Urbana and Chicago: University of Illinois Press.

Eduards, M. (1989, November). *The third way: On women's politics and welfare policies in Sweden.* Paper presented to seminar, Women, Power, and Strategies for Change, The Swedish Institute, Stockholm.

Eduards, M. (1991). The Swedish gender model: Productivity, pragmatism, and paternalism. *West European Politics, 14,* 166-181.

Ehrmann, H. W., & Schain, M. (1992). *Politics in France.* New York: HarperCollins.

Einhorn, B. (1993). *Cinderella goes to market: Citizenship, gender, and women's movements in east central Europe.* New York: Verso.

Eisenstein, H. (1983). *Contemporary feminist thought.* Boston: G. K. Hall.

Eisenstein, H. (1990). Femocrats, official feminism, and the uses of power. In S. Watson (Ed.), *Playing the state: Australian feminist interventions* (pp. 87-103). London: Verso.

Eisenstein, H. (1991). *Gender shock: Practicing feminism on two continents.* Boston: Beacon Press.

Eisenstein, H. (1995). *Inside agitators: Australian femocrats and the state.* Philadelphia: Temple University Press.

Elder, C. D., & Cobb, R. W. (1983). *The political use of symbols.* New York and London: Longman.

Elman, R. A. (1993). Debunking the Social Democrats and the myth of equality. *Women's Studies International Forum, 16,* 513-522.

Elman, R. A., & Eduards, M. (1991). Unprotected by the Swedish welfare state: A survey of battered women and the assistance they received. *Women's Studies International Forum, 14,* 413-421.

Elshtain, J. B. (1983). Antigone's daughters: Reflections on female identity and the state. In I. Diamond (Ed.), *Families, politics, and public policy: A feminist dialogue on women and the state* (pp. 300-311). New York: Longman.

Elshtain, J. B. (1990). *Power trips and other journeys: Essays in feminism as civic discourse.* Madison: University of Wisconsin Press.

Ely, J. (1992). The politics of "civil society." *Telos, 93,* 171-191.

Emancipatiekommissie (EK). (1976). *Aanzet tot een vijfjaren plan* [Design for a 5-year plan]. The Hague: Author.

Emancipatie. Proces van verandering en groei (1977). [Women's public policy: Process of change and growth], Handelingen Tweede Kamer (Official proceedings of the Second Chamber of Parliament), zitting 1976-1977, 14496, nr.1-2.

Encel, S. (1994). Politicians. In R. Nile (Ed.), *Australian civilisation* (pp. 141-161). Melbourne: Oxford University Press.

Equal Opportunities Commission. (1988). *From policy to practice: An equal opportunities strategy.* Manchester: Author.

Equal Status Council. (1989). *The Norwegian Equal Status Act with comments*. Otta: Engers Boktrykkeri A/S.

Equal Status Council. (1990). *Women's status in Norway*. Oslo: Author.

Equal Status Council. (1993a). Norway's national report for the 4th United Nation's World Conference on Women, 1995 (draft). Oslo: Author.

Equal Status Council. (1993b, July). *Publikasjonsliste* [List of publications]. Oslo: Author.

Ergas, Y. (1986). *Nelle maglie della politica. Femminismo, istituzioni e politiche sociali nell'Italia degli anni '70* [In the texture of politics: Feminism, institutions, and social policy in Italy in the 1970s]. Milano: Franco Angeli.

Evans, P., Rueschemeyer, D., & Skocpol, T. (Eds.). (1985). *Bringing the state back in*. Cambridge: Cambridge University Press.

Ferguson, K. E. (1984). *The feminist case against bureaucracy*. Philadelphia: Temple University Press.

Ferree, M. M. (1991-1992). Institutionalizing gender equality: Feminist politics and equality offices. *German Politics & Society, 24 & 25*(Winter), 53-66.

Ferree, M. M. (1993). The rise and fall of "mommy politics": Feminism and German unification. *Feminist Studies, 19*(1), 85-119.

Ferree, M. M. (1994a). After the wall: Explaining the status of women in the former GDR. *Sociological Focus, 28*, 597-623.

Ferree, M. M. (1994b). "The time of chaos was the best": The mobilization and demobilization of the women's movement in East Germany. *Gender and Society, 8*(4), 597-623.

Ferree, M. M. (1995). Patriarchs and feminism: The two women's movements of post-unification Germany. *Social Politics 2*(1), 10-24.

Ferree, M. M., & Hess, B. B. (1985). *Controversy and coalition: The new feminist movement*. Boston: Twayne.

Ferree, M. M., & Young, B. (1993). Three steps back for women: German unification, gender, and university "reform." *PS: Political Science and Politics, 26*(2), 199-205.

Findlay, S. (1987). Facing the state: The politics of the women's movement reconsidered. In H. J. Maroney & M. Luxton (Eds.), *Feminism and political economy: Women's work, women's struggles* (pp. 31-50). Toronto: Methuen.

Fineman, M. A., & Thomadsen, N. S. (Eds.). (1991). *At the boundaries of law: Feminism and legal theory*. New York: Routledge.

Fitzgerald, G. (1991). *All in a life: An autobiography*. London: Macmillan.

Folketingstidende [Parliamentary proceedings]. (1974). Copenhagen.

Folketingstidende [Parliamentary proceedings]. (1978). Copenhagen.

Foner, P. S. (1980). *Women and the American labor movement, from World War I to the present*. New York: Free Press.

Franzway, S., Court, D., & Connell, R. W. (1989). *Staking a claim: Feminism, bureaucracy, and the state*. Sydney, Australia: Allen & Unwin.

Freeman, J. (1975). *The politics of women's liberation*. New York: David McKay.

Frentzel-Zagorska, J. (1990). Civil society in Poland and Hungary. *Soviet Studies, 42*(4), 759-777.

Gallagher, M. (1988). Ireland: The increasing role of the centre. In Gallagher and Marsh (Eds.), *Candidate selection in comparative perspective* (pp. 119-144). Sage: London.

Gallagher, M. (1993). Parliament. In J. Coakley & M. Gallagher (Eds.), *Politics in the Republic of Ireland* (2nd ed., pp. 126-149). Dublin: Folens & PSAI Press.

Geduldig v. Aiello, 417 U.S. 484 (1974).

Gelb, J. (1989). *Feminism and politics*. Berkeley: University of California Press.

Gelb, J., & Palley, M. L. (1982). *Women and public policies*. Princeton, NJ: Princeton University Press.

Gelber, S. (1971). A year after the report: Where are we now? In *Women's bureau '71* (pp. 20-28). Ottawa: Canadian Department of Labour.

General Electric v. Gilbert, 429 U.S. 125 (1976).

Gerhard, U. (1990). *Gleichheit ohne Angleichung: Frauen im Recht* [Equality without identity: Women in the law]. Munich: C. H. Beck.

Giddens, A. (1971). *Capitalism and modern social theory*. Cambridge: Cambridge University Press.

Giroud, F. (1976). *Cent mesures pour les femmes* [One hundred measures for women]. Paris: Documentation Française.

Glover, R. W. (1989). Apprenticeship: A route to the high-paying skilled trades for women? In S. L. Harlan & R. J. Steinberg, (Eds.), *Job training for women: The promise and limits of public policies* (pp. 269-289). Philadelphia: Temple University Press.

Goericke, L.-L. (1989). *Kommunale Frauengleichstellungsstellen—der gebremste Fortschritt* [Local-level women's equality offices: Progress with the brakes on]. Oldenburg: Bibiliotheks-und Informations-system der Universität.

Gordon, L. (1979). The struggle for reproductive freedom. In Z. Eisenstein (Ed.), *Capitalist patriarchy and the case for socialist feminism* (pp. 107-132). New York: Monthly Review Press.

Gordon, L. (Ed.). (1990). *Women, the state, and welfare*. Madison: University of Wisconsin Press.

Guadagnini, M. (1993). A "partitocrazia" without women: The case of the Italian party system. In J. Lovenduski and P. Norris (Eds.), *Gender and party politics* (pp. 168-204). London: Sage.

Guadilla, N. G. (1981). *Libération des femmes: Le MLF* [Women's liberation: The MLF]. Paris: PUF.

Guy, M. E. (Ed.). (1992). *Women and men of the states: Public administrators at the state level*. Armonk NY: M. E. Sharpe.

Haavio-Mannila, E., Dahlerup, D., Eduards, M., Gudmundsdóttir, E., Halsaa, B., Hernes, H. M., Hänninen-Salmelin, E., Sigmundsdóttir, B., Sinkkonen, S., & Skard T. (1985). *The unfinished democracy—women in Nordic politics* (C. Badcock, Trans.). New York: Pergamon.

Hagman, N. (1992). Measures taken in Sweden to combat sexual harassment at work: Report to the International Labour Office (ILO). Stockholm: Stockholm University.

Hall, P. A. (1990). Pluralism and pressure politics. In P. A. Hall, J. Hayward, & H. Machin, (Eds.), *Developments in French politics* (pp. 77-94). New York City: St. Martin's.

Hall, S., & Hall, W. (Eds.). (1994). *Ego trip: Extra governmental organisations in the United Kingdom and their accountability*. London: The Charter 88 Trust.

Halsaa, B. (1989). *Policies and strategies on women in Norway*. Lillehamer: Oppland Regional College.

Halsaa, B. (1990). *The power of women in politics: So what?* Unpublished manuscript.

Hampele, A. (1993). "Arbeite mit, plane mit, regiere mit": Zur politischen Partizipation von Frauen in der DDR. [Work with us, plan with us, govern with us:

The political participation of women in the GDR]. In G. Helwig & H. M. Nickel (Eds.), *Frauen in Deutschland 1945-1992* (pp. 281-320). Bonn: Bundeszentral für politische Bildung.

Harlan, S. L., & Steinberg, R. J. (Eds.). (1989). *Job training for women: The promise and limits of public policies.* Philadelphia: Temple University Press.

Harrison, C. (1988). *On account of sex: The politics of women's issues, 1945-68.* Berkeley: University of California Press.

Hatem, M. F. (1992). Economic and political liberation in Egypt and the demise of state feminism. *International Journal of Middle East Studies, 24,* 231-251.

Hauser, E., Heyns, B., & Mansbridge, J. (1993). Feminism in the interstices of politics and culture: Poland in transition. In N. Funk & M. Mueller (Eds.), *Gender politics and post-communism* (p. 257-273). New York: Routledge.

Heclo, H., & Madsen, H. (1987). *Policy and politics in Sweden: Principled pragmatism.* Philadelphia: Temple University Press.

Hellevik, O., & Skard, T. (1985). *Norske kommunstyrer—Plass for kvinner?* [Norwegian local councils—A place for women?]. Oslo: Universitetsforlaget.

Hernes, H. M. (1987). *Welfare state and woman power: Essays in state feminism.* Oslo: Universitetsforlaget.

Hernes, H. (1988). The welfare state citizenship of Scandinavian women. In K. Jones & A. Jónasdóttir (Eds.), *The political interests of gender* (pp. 187-213). London: Sage.

Hernes, H. M., & Hanninen-Salmelin, E. (1985). Women in the corporate system. In E. Haavio-Mannila et al. (Eds.), *Unfinished democracy: Women in Nordic politics* (pp. 106-133). New York: Pergamon.

Hirdman, Y. (1994). *Women—From possibility to problem?: Gender conflict in the welfare state—the Swedish model* (Research Report No. 3). Stockholm: The Swedish Center for Working Life.

Hoffmann, S. (1987). Conclusion. In G. Ross, S. Hoffman, & S. Malzacher (Eds.), *The Mitterrand experiment* (pp. 341-353). New York: Oxford University Press.

Holter, H. (1970). *Sex roles and social structure.* Oslo: Universitetsforlaget.

Holter, H. (1981). Om kvinneundertrykkelse, mannsundertrykkelse og hesketeknikker [Concerning women's oppression, men's oppression, and techniques of domination]. In T. Andenaes et al. (Eds.), *Maktens ansikter* (pp. 218-229). Oslo: Gyldendal.

Honig, E., & Hershatter, G. (1988). *Personal voices.* Stanford: Stanford University Press.

Hood, C. (1982). Government bodies and government growth. In A. Barker (Ed.), *Quangos in Britain: Government and the networks of public policy making* (pp. 44-68). London: Macmillan.

Hopkins, A., & McGregor, H. (1991). *Working for change: The movement against domestic violence.* Sydney: Allen & Unwin.

Institut für Demoskopie Allensbach. (1993). *Frauen in Deutschland: Lebensverhältnisse Lebensstile und Zukunftserwartungen* [Women in Germany: Life situation, lifestyle, and expectations for the future]. Cologne: Bund Verlag.

Instituto de la Mujer. Metra seis (1985-1991). [Surveys on the opinions of the Spanish population about the Institute of the Woman]. Madrid: Author.

Instituto de la Mujer. (1990). *Primer plan para la igualdad de oportunidades de las mujeres 1988-1990. Evaluación* [First plan for equal opportunities for women, 1988-1990: Evaluation]. Madrid: Instituto de la Mujer.

Instituto de la Mujer. (1991). *Memoria* [Report]. Madrid: Author.
Instituto de la Mujer. (1992). *Memoria* [Report]. Madrid: Author.
Instituto de la Mujer. (1993). *Segundo plan para la iqualdad de oportunidades de las mujeres 1993-1995* [Second plan for equal opportunities for women, 1993-1995]. Madrid: Author.
Institute for Women's Policy Research. (1994, March). *Research-in-brief.* Washington, DC: Author.
JÄMO. (1992). *Report on equality between men and women, 1989-1991.* Stockholm: Author.
JÄMO. (1987, March). JÄMO-rapporten om sexuella-trakasserier mot kvinnor i arbetslivet [The ombudsman's report on sexual harassment against women at work]. *JÄMSIDES,* 3.
Jämställdhetsombudsmannen. (1987). *FRID-A projektet* [The Equality Ombudsman's investigation on sexual harassment in Sweden]. Stockholm: Author.
Jankowska, H. (1991). Abortion, church, and politics in Poland. *Feminist Review, 39*(Winter), 174-186.
Janowska, Z., Martini-Fiwek, J., & Goral, Z. (1991). *Female unemployment in Poland.* Warsaw: Friedrich-Ebert Foundation.
Jenson, J. (1989). Ce n'est pas un hasard: The varieties of French feminism. In J. Holyworth and G. Ross, (Eds.), *Contemporary France* (pp. 114-143). London: Frances Pinter.
Jobert, A. (1993). *Negociation collective et promotion de l'egalité en France* [Collective negotiation and the promotion of equality in France]. Rapport pour le Bureau International du Travail, Service du Droit et des relations du Travail. Paris: SEDF.
Jonung, C., & Thordarsson, B. (1980). Sweden. In A. Yohalem (Ed.), *Women returning to work: Policies and progress in five countries* (pp. 107-159). Montclaire, NJ: Landmark Studies.
Joppke, C. (1992, July). Models of statehood in the German nuclear energy debate. *Comparative Political Studies, 25*(2), 251-280.
Kahn, P. (1992). Introduction: Equal pay for work of equal value in Britain and the USA. In P. Kahn & E. Meehan (Eds.), *Equal value, comparable worth, in the UK and the USA* (pp. 1-25). London and Basingstoke: Macmillan.
Kaplan, G. (1992). *Contemporary Western feminism.* London: UCL Press & Allen & Unwin.
Kavanagh, D. (1980). Political culture in Great Britain: The decline of the civic culture. In G. Almond & S. Verba (Eds.), *The civic culture revisited* (pp. 124-176). Boston: Little, Brown.
Keane, J. (Ed.). (1988). *Civil society and the state.* London: Verso.
Keuzenkamp, S., & Teunissen, A. (1990). *Emancipatie ten halve geregeld. Continuiteit en inenging in het emancipatiebeleid* [Women's public policy half-done: Continuity and curtailment in policy]. The Hague: Ministerie van Sociale Zaken.
Kolarska-Bobinska, L. (1990). Civil society and social anomie in Poland. *Acta Sociologica, 33*(4), 277-288.
Kommissionen vedrørende kvindernes stilling i samfundet [The commission on the position of women in society]. (1974). *Betænkning nr. 715. Kvindernes stilling i samfundet* (Report no. 715, Women's position in society). Copenhagen: Author.

Koontz, E. D. (1971). Childbirth and child-rearing leave: Job-related benefits. *New York Law Forum, 17*, 480-502.

Koski, B. (1977). The situation of women in Poland. *Critique, 8*(Summer), 69-95.

Krautkrämer-Wagner, U. (1990). *Die Verstaatlichung der Frauenfrage: Gleichstellungs-institutionen der Bundesländer—Möglichkeiten und Grenzen Staatlicher frauen-politik* [Making the situation of women the business of the state: Institutions for equality in the federal states—opportunities and limits of state policy for women]. Bielefeld: Kleine Verlag.

Kurz-Scherf, I. (1992). *Nur noch Utopien sind realistisch: Feministische Perspektiven in Deutschland* [Only utopias are still realistic: Feminist perspectives in Germany]. Bonn: Pahl-Rugenstein.

Lange, P., & Regini, M. (Eds.) (1987). *Stato e regolazione sociale. Nuove prospettive sul caso italiano* [The state and social regulations: New perspectives on the Italian case]. Bologna: Il Mulino.

Lapidus, G. (1978). *Women in Soviet society.* Berkeley: University of California Press.

Leghorn, L., & Parker, K. (1981). *Woman's worth.* London: Routledge & Kegan Paul.

Leijon, A. (1968). *Swedish women—Swedish men.* Stockholm: Sweden Books.

Leira, A. (1993). The "woman-friendly" welfare state?—The case of Norway and Sweden. In J. Lewis (Ed.), *Women, work, and the family in Europe.* London: Edward Elgar.

Leven, B. (1991). The welfare effects on women of Poland's economic reforms. *Journal of Economic Issues, 25*(2), 581-588.

Levi, M., & Edwards, M. (1990). Dilemmas of femocratic reform. In M. F. Katzenstein & H. Skjeie (Eds.), *Going public: National histories of women's enfranchisement and women's participation within state institutions.* Oslo: Institute for Social Research.

Lévy, M. (1988). *Le féminisme d'etat en France 1965-1985: 20 ans de prise en charae institutionelle de l'égalité professionelle entre hommes et femmes* [State feminism in France, 1965-1985: Twenty years of institutional responsibility for equal employment between men and women]. Dissertation, Institut d'Etudes Politiques, Paris.

Lewis, J., & Astrom, G. (1992, Spring). Equality, difference, and state welfare: Labor market and family policies in Sweden. *Feminist Studies, 18*, 59-87.

Libreria delle donne di Milano. (1987). *Non credere di avere diritti* [Don't think you have any rights]. Turin: Rosenberg e Sellier.

Liga Kobiet Polskich. (1959). *Rocznik polityczny i gospodarczy 1958* [Political and economic yearbook]. Warsaw: Polskie Wydawnictwa Gospodarcze.

Liga Kobiet Polskich. (1961). *Rocznik polityczny i gospodarczy 1960* [Political and economic yearbook]. Warsaw: Polskie Wydawnictwa Gospodarcze.

Liga Kobiet Polskich. (1962). *Rocznik polityczny i gospodarczy 1961* [Political and economic yearbook]. Warsaw: Polskie Wydawnictwa Gospodarcze.

Liga Kobiet Polskich. (1964). *Rocznik polityczny i gospodarczy 1963* [Political and economic yearbook]. Warsaw: Polskie Wydawnictwa Gospodarcze.

Liga Kobiet Polskich. (1965). *Rocznik polityczny i gospodarczy 1964* [Political and economic yearbook]. Warsaw: Polskie Wydawnictwa Gospodarcze.

Liga Kobiet Polskich. (1966). *Rocznik polityczny i gospodarczy 1965* [Political and economic yearbook]. Warsaw: Polskie Wydawnictwa Gospodarcze.

Liga Kobiet Polskich. (1969). *Rocznik polityczny i gospodarczy 1968* [Political and economic yearbook]. Warsaw: Polskie Wydawnictwa Gospodarcze.

Liga Kobiet Polskich. (1979). *Rocznik polityczyny i gospodarczy 1978* [Political and economic yearbook]. Warsaw: Polskie Wydawnictwa Gospodarcze.

Liga Kobiet Polskich. (1987). *Rocznik polityczyny i gospodarczy 1986* [Political and economic yearbook]. Warsaw: Polskie Wydawnictwa Gospodarcze.

Ligestillingsrådet. (1993). *Vejen videre. Evaluering af Regeringens Handlingsplan for Ligestilling 1991-1993* [The road onwards: An evaluation of the government's plan of action on equality]. Copenhagen: Author.

Lijphart, A. (1971, September). Comparative politics and comparative method. *American Political Science Review, 65*(3), 682-693.

Lijphart, A. (1975, July). The comparable cases strategy in comparative research. *Comparative Political Studies, 8*(2), 481-496.

Lijphart, A. (1982). *Verzuiling, pacificatie en kentering in de Nederlandse politiek.* Amsterdam: De Bussy. (English Edition: *The politics of accommodation, pluralism and democracy in the Netherlands,* 1968, Berkeley: University of California Press.)

Lovenduski, J. (1986). *Women and European politics.* Amherst: University of Massachusetts Press.

Lovenduski, J., & Norris, P. (Eds.) (1993). *Gender and party politics.* London: Sage.

Lovenduski, J., & Randall, V. (1993). *Contemporary feminist politics: Women and power in Britain.* Oxford: Oxford University Press.

Lowi, T. (1964). American business, public policy, case studies, and political theory. *World Politics, 16,* 677-715.

Lowi, T. (1969). *The end of liberalism: Ideology, policy, and the crisis of public authority.* New York: Norton.

Lynch, L. (1984). Bureaucratic feminisms: Bossism and beige suits. *Refractory Girl, 27,* 38-44.

Macintyre, S. (1989). Neither capital nor labour. In S. Macintyre & R. Mitchell (Eds.), *Foundations of arbitration: The origins and effects of state compulsory arbitration 1890-1914* (pp.178-200). Melbourne: Melbourne University Press.

MacKinnon, C. (1989). *Toward a feminist theory of the state.* Cambridge, MA: Harvard University Press.

Mahon, E. (1987). Women's rights and Catholicism in Ireland. *New Left Review, 166,* 53-78.

Mahon, E. (1991). *Motherhood, work, and equal opportunities: A committee on women's rights.* Dublin: Stationery Office.

Maier, F. (1992). Frauenerwerbstätigkeit in der DDR und der BRD: Geminsamkeiten und Unterschiede [Women's employment in the FRG and GDR: commonalities and differences]. In G.-A. Knapp & U. Müller (Eds.), Ein Deutschland— Zwei Patriarchate? (pp. 23-35). Bielefeld: University of Bielefeld.

Maier, F. (1993). Zwischen Arbeitsmarkt und Familie: Frauenarbeit in den alten Bundesländer [Between the labor market and the family: Women's employment in the original federal states]. In G. Helwig & H. M. Nickel (Eds.), *Frauen in Deutschland 1945-1992* (pp. 257-280). Bonn: Bundeszentral für politische Bildung.

Marsden, L. R. (1980). The role of the National Action Committee on the Status of Women in facilitating equal pay policy in Canada. In R. S. Ratner (Ed.), *Equal employment policy for women* (pp. 242-60). Philadelphia: Temple University Press.

Mazur, A. (1992, October). Symbolic reform in France: Egalité professionnelle during the Mitterrand years. *West European Politics*, pp. 39-56.

Mazur, A. G. (1994, April). *Making and breaking symbolic reform: Equal employment policy for women in France, Great Britain, and the U.S.A.* Paper presented at the European Consortium for Political Research Joint Sessions of Workshops, Madrid, Spain.

Mazur, A. (in press). *Gender bias and the state: Symbolic reform at work in Fifth Republic France.* Pittsburgh, PA: University of Pittsburgh Press.

McConnell, G. (1966). *Private power and American democracy.* New York: Knopf.

McCulloch, D. (1988). Dear Deborah. *Femnews: A Feminist Newsletter, 13*, 19.

McIntosh, M. (1978). The state and the oppression of women. In A. Kuhn & A. Wolpe (Eds.), *Feminism and materialism: Women and the modes of production* (pp. 254-289). London: Routledge and Kegan Paul.

Mead, M., & Kaplan, F. B. (Eds.). (1965). *American women: The report of the President's Commission on the Status of Women and other publications of the commission.* New York: Scribner's.

Meehan, E. (1985). *Women's rights at work: Campaigns and policy in Britain and the United States.* New York: St. Martin's.

Ministère des Droits de la Femme. (1981). *Citoyennes à part entière* [Women citizens with full rights]. Paris: Author.

Ministère des Droits de la Femme. (1984). *L'égalité professionnelle, la loi du 13 juillet 1983: les rapports et les plans d'égalité* [Equal employment law of July 13, 1983: The reports and equality plans]. Paris: Author.

Ministerie van Sociale Zaken en Werkgelegenheid, Directie Coordinatie Emancipatiebeleid. (1992). *Met het oog op 1995* [With an eye to 1995]. The Hague: Author.

Ministry of Consumer Affairs and Government Administration. (1985). *The Norwegian plan of action and other measures related to the equality between the sexes.* Oslo: Norwegian Central Information Service.

Ministry of State for Women's Affairs. (1985). *Irish women: Agenda for practical action.* Dublin: Stationery Office.

Mink, G. (1990). The lady and the tramp: Gender, race, and the origins of the American welfare state. In L. Gordon (Ed.), *Women, the state, and welfare* (pp. 92-122). Madison: University of Wisconsin Press.

Mitchell, T. (1991). The limits of the state: Beyond statist approaches and their critics. *American Political Science Review, 85*, 77-96.

Moeller, R. (1993). *Protecting motherhood: Women and the family in the politics of postwar West Germany.* Berkeley: University of California Press.

Molyneux, M. (1985). Mobilization with emancipation? Women's interests, the state, and revolution in Nicaragua. *Feminist Studies, 11*(2), 227-255.

Morgan, R. (1984). *Sisterhood is global.* New York: Anchor Press.

Nave-Herz, R. (1994). *Die Geschichte der Frauenbewegung in Deutschland* [The history of the women's movement in Germany]. Opladen: Leske & Budrich.

Nesiah, V. (1993, Spring). Toward a feminist internationality: A critique of U.S. feminist legal scholarship. *Harvard Women's Law Journal, 16*, 189-210.

Nettl, J. P. (1968). The state as a conceptual variable. *World Politics, 20*, 559-592.

Noble, B. P. (1993a, October 17). At work: Reforming the talk on labor reform. *The New York Times*, p. 25.

Noble, B. P. (1993b, July 11). At work: Speaking for the working woman. *The New York Times*, p. 23.

Nolte, D. (1994, March 8). Verschlechtung in Grenzen halten [Keeping deterioration in bounds]. Non-traditional Education for Women Act, 29 U.S.C. 1501 (19xx). *Die Welt.*

Non-traditional Education for Women Act, 29 U.S. C. 1501 (1991).

Noonan, N. C. (1994). Does consciousness lead to action? Exploring the impact of Perestroika and post-Perestroika on women in Russia. *Journal of Gender Studies, 3*(1), 47-54.

Norton, P. (1994). *The British polity.* New York and London: Longman.

Norwegian Research Council for Applied Social Science. (1988). *Research to promote equal status and gender equality.* Oslo: Author.

Norwegian Research Council for Science and Humanities. (1987). *NAVF's Secretariat for Women and Research.* Oslo: Author.

O'Halpin, E. (1986). Oireachtas committees: Experience and prospects, *Seirbhis Phoibli, 7,* 3-9.

Outshoorn, J. (1986). The feminist movement and abortion policy in the Netherlands. In D. Dahlerup (Ed.), *The new women's movement: Feminism and political power in Europe and the USA* (pp. 64-84). London/Beverly Hills: Sage.

Outshoorn, J. (1991a). A distaste of dirty hands: Gender and politics in second-wave feminism. In T. Andreasen, A. Borchorst, D. Dahlerup, E. Lous, & H. Rimmen Nielsen (Eds.), *Moving on: New perspectives on the women's movement* (pp. 175-187). Aarhus: Aarhus University Press.

Outshoorn, J. (1991b). Is this what we wanted? Positive action as issue-perversion. In E. Meehan & S. Sevenhuijsen (Eds.), *Equality politics and gender* (pp. 104-122). London: Sage.

Outshoorn, J. (1992, April). *Femocrats in the Netherlands: Mission or career?* Paper presented at the European Consortium for Political Research Joint Sessions of Workshops, Limerick, Eire.

Outshoorn, J. (1994a, April). *The administrative accommodation of the "feminist question": State feminism in the Netherlands.* Paper presented at the European Consortium for Political Research Joint Sessions of Workshops, Madrid, Spain.

Outshoorn, J. (1994b). Between movement and government: "Femocrats" in the Netherlands. In H. Kriesi (Ed.), *Yearbook of Swiss political science* (pp. 141-165). Bern/Stuttgart/Wien: Paul Haupt Verlag.

Parti Socialiste. (1978). Manifeste du PS sur les droits des femmes [PS manifesto for women's rights]. *Le Poing et la Rose, 68*(Suppl.).

Pateman, C. (1988). *The sexual contract.* Stanford, CA: Stanford University Press.

Peterson, E. (1977). *Interest group incorporation in Sweden.* Paper presented to the Annual Meeting of the American Political Science Association.

Peterson, V. S., & Runyan, A. S. (1993). *Global gender issues.* Boulder, CO: Westview Press.

Phillips, A. (1993). *Democracy and difference.* University Park: Pennsylvania State University Press.

Picq, F. (1983, Fall). Droit de la femme or droits des femmes? [Woman's right or women's rights]. *La Revue d'en face, 14,* 5-22.

Picq, F. (1987). *Le Mouvement de Libération des Femmes et ces Effets Sociaux* [The women's liberation movement and its social effects]. In *ATP Recherches Féministes et Recherches sur les Femmes.* Paris: CNRS.

Pinl, C. (1993). *Vom kleinen zum großen Unterschied: "Geschlechterdifferenz" und konservative Wende im Feminismus* [From a small to a big difference: "Sex differences" and the conservative turn in feminism]. Hamburg: Konkret Literatur Verlag.

Praag, P. Van. (1985). Tien jaar emancipatiebeleid [Ten years of women's equality policy]. *Beleid en Maatschappij, 12*, 3-12.

Preddy, E. (Ed.). (1985). *Women's electoral lobbyAustralia/New Zealand 1972-1985.* Wellington: WEL Australia/WEL New Zealand.

Pringle, R. (1979). Feminists and bureaucrats—The last four years. *Refractory Girl, 18*(19).

Pringle, R., & Watson, S. (1992). Women's interests and the post-structuralist state. In M. Barrett & A. Phillips (Eds.), *Destabilizing theory: Contemporary feminist debates* (pp. 53-73). Cambridge, U.K.: Polity Press.

Prins, M. (1987). Emancipatie op maat gesneden. De totstandkoming van de Wet op de Emancipatieraad [Women's public policy cut to size: The establishment of the Emancipation Council]. In J. F. M. Koppenjan, A. B. Ringeling, & R. A. ter Velde (Eds.), *Beleidsvorming in Nederland: Een Vergeliijende studie naar de totstandkoming van wetten* (pp. 87-108). Den Haag: VUGA.

Prins, M. (1989). Emancipatie van vrouwen in beweging [Women's emancipation in motion]. Groningen: PP+Styx.

Przeworski, A., & Teune, H. (1970). *The logic of comparative social inquiry.* New York: John Wiley.

Radin, B. A. (1991). Occupational segration and its roots in education: A policy map. In L. R. Wolfe (Ed.), *Women, work, and school: Occupational segregation and the role of education,* (pp. 201-210). Boulder, CO: Westview.

Randall, V. (1982). *Women and politics.* London and Basingstoke: Macmillan.

Randall, V. (1987). *Women and politics: An international perspective* (2nd ed.). Chicago: University of Chicago Press.

Ratner, R. S. (1980). The policy and problem: Overview of seven countries. In R. S. Ratner (Ed.), *Equal employment policy for women* (pp. 1-52). Philadelphia: Temple University Press.

Reading, A. (1992). *Polish women, solidarity, and feminism.* London: Macmillan.

Reid, E. (1985). Interview. *Labor Forum, 7*(2), 10-15.

Reid, E. (1987). The child of our movement: A movement of women. In J. Scutt (Ed.), *Different lives* (pp. 9-20). Ringwood: Penguin.

Reinelt, C. (1994). Moving onto the terrain of the state: Battered women's projects in Texas. In M. M. Ferree & P. Y. Martin (Eds.), *Feminist organizations: Harvest of the new women's movement* (pp. 84-104). Philadelphia: Temple University Press.

Rhode, D. (1989). *Justice and gender: Sex discrimination and the law.* Cambridge, MA: Harvard University Press.

Rockman, B. A. (1990). Minding the state—or a state of mind? Issues in the comparative conceptualization of the state. *Comparative Political Studies, 23*, 22-55.

Rollén, B. (1980). Equality between men and women in the labor market: The Swedish National Labor Market Board. In R. S. Ratner (Ed.), *Equal employment policy for women: Strategies for implementation in the United States, Canada, and Western Europe* (pp. 179-198). Philadelphia: Temple University Press.

Rose, R. (1984). The political status of higher civil servants in Britain. In E. Suleiman (Ed.), *Bureaucrats and policy making* (pp. 136-173). New York: Holmes & Meier.

Ross, G., Hoffmann, S., & Malzacher, S. (Eds.). (1987). *The Mitterrand experiment.* New York: Oxford University Press.

Rossi Doria, A. (1994). Una rivoluzione non ancora compiuta [A revolution not yet accomplished]. In P. Ginsborg (Ed.), *Stato dell'Italia. Il bilancio politico, economico, sociale e culturale di un paese che cambia* (pp. 262-266). Milano: Il Saggiatore.

Royal Commission on Australian Government Administration. (1976). *Report*. Canberra: Australian Government Publishing Service.

Royal Commission on Equality in Employment. (1984, October). *Report*. Ottawa: Minister of Supply and Services Canada.

Royal Commission on the Status of Women. (1970, September). *Report*. Ottawa: Information Canada.

Royal Ministry of Foreign Affairs. (1989). *Women in Norwegian politics*. Oslo: Grayling A/S.

Ruggie, M. (1984). *The state & working women: A comparative study of Britain and Sweden*. Princeton, NJ: Princeton University Press.

Ryan, L. (1990). Feminism and the federal bureacracy, 1972-1983. In S. Watson (Ed.), *Playing the state: Australian feminist interventions*. Sydney: Allen and Unwin.

Sacks, V. (1986). The Equal Opportunities Commission—Ten years on. *The Modern Law Review, 49*, 560-592.

Sartori, G. (1970, December). Concept misformation in comparative politics. *American Political Science Review, 64*, 1033-1053.

Sarvasy, W. (1992). Beyond the difference versus equality debate: Post suffrage feminism, citizenship, and the quest for a feminist welfare state. *Signs, 17*(Winter), 329-362.

Sawer, M. (1990). *Sisters in suits: Women and public policy in Australia*. Sydney: Allen & Unwin.

Sawer, M. (1993, June). Reclaiming social liberalism: The women's movement and the state. *Journal of Australian Studies*, No. 37, 1-21.

Sawer, M. (1994). Reclaiming the state: Feminism, liberalism, and social liberalism [Special issue]. *Australian Journal of Politics and History, 40*.

Sawer, M., & Groves, A. (1994). *Working from inside: Twenty years of the Office of the Status of Women*. Canberra: Australian Government Publishing Service.

Scanlon, G. M. (1990). El movimiento feminista en España, 1900-1985: logros y dificultades [The feminist movement in Spain, 1900-1985: Successes and difficulties]. In J. Astelarra (Ed.), *Participación Política de las Mujeres* (pp. 83-100). Madrid: Centro de Investigaciones Sociológicas and Siglo XXI.

Schlapeit-Beck, D. (1988). Ermächtige Ohnmacht? Können Gleichstellungsstellen Einflußet auf die Kommunalpolitik gewinnen? [Empowering weakness? Can equality offices achieve influence in local politics?]. In M. Weg & O. Stein (Eds.), *Macht Frauen stark: Frauenpolitik für die 90er Jahre* (pp. 53-61). Hamburg: VSA-Verlag.

Scott, H. (1982). *Sweden's "Right to be Human."* New York: Sharpe.

Sealander, J. (1983). *As minority becomes majority: Federal reaction to the phenomenon of women in the work force, 1920-1963*. Westport, CT: Greenwood Press.

Side by side: A report on equality between men & women in Sweden 1985. (1985). Stockholm: Liber.

Siemienska, R. (1990). *Plec, Zawod, Polityka: Kobiety w zyciu publiczynym w Polsce* [Gender, occupation, politics: Women in public life in Poland]. Warsaw: Uniwersytet Warszawski, Instytut Socjologii.

Siemienska, R. (1991). Polish women and Polish politics since World War II. *Journal of Women's History, 3*(1), 108-125.

Siemienska, R. (1994). Polish women as the object and subject of politics during and after the Communist period. In B. J. Nelson & N. Chowdhury (Eds.), *Women and politics worldwide* (pp. 610-624). New Haven, CT: Yale University Press.

Siim, B. (1991). Welfare state, gender politics, and equality policies: Women's citizenship in the Scandinavian welfare states. In E. Meehan & S. Sevenhuijsen (Eds.), *Equality, politics, and gender* (pp. 175-193). London: Sage.

Siim, B. (1993). The gendered Scandinavian welfare states: The interplay between women's roles as mothers, workers, and citizens in Denmark. In J. Lewis (Ed.), *Women and social policies in Europe* (pp. 175-193). London: Edward Elgar.

Sjerps, I. (1987). Indirect discrimination in social security in the Netherlands: Demands of the Dutch women's movement. In M. Buckley & M. Anderson, (Eds.), *Women, equality, and Europe* (pp. 95-107). Basingstoke/London: Macmillan.

Skard, T., & Haavio-Mannila, E. (1986). Equality between the sexes—Myth or reality in Norden? In S. Graubard (Ed.), *Norden: The passion for equality* (pp. 176-199). Oslo: The Norwegian University Press.

Skjeie, H. (1991, May/June). From movements to governments: Two decades of Norwegian feminist influences. *New Left Review, 187*, 15-26.

Skjeie, H. (1992). *Den Politiske Betydningen Av Kjonn* [The political meaning of gender]. Oslo: Institute for Social Research.

Skjeie, H. (1993). Ending the male political hegemony: The Norwegian experience. In J. Lovenduski & P. Norris (Eds.), *Gender and party politics* (pp. 231-262). London: Sage.

Skocpol, T., & Somers, M. (1980). The uses of comparative history in macrosocial inquiry. *Comparative Studies in Society and History, 22*, 174-197.

Skocpol, T. (1985). Bringing the state back in: Strategies of analysis in current research. In P. B. Evans, D. Ruechemeyer, & T. Skocpol (Eds.), *Bringing the state back in* (pp. 3-37). Cambridge, MA: Cambridge University Press.

Skocpol, T. (1988, August 31). *Comparing national systems of social provision: A polity-centered approach.* Paper presented at the IPSA meeting, Washington DC.

Skocpol, T. (1992). *Protecting soldiers and the mothers: The political origins of social policy in the United States.* Cambridge, MA: Belknap Press.

Smart, C. (1990). Law's power, the sexed body, and feminist discourse. *Journal of Law and Society, 17*(2), 194-210.

Soper, K. (1991). Postmodernism and its discontents. *Feminist Review, 39*, 97-108.

SOU. (1990). 41, Tio år med jämställdhetslagen—utvärdering och förslag [Ten years with the equality act—evaluation and suggestions]. Stockholm: Liber.

Status of Women Canada. (1993, May). *Canada's national machinery for the advancement of women.* Ottawa: Author.

Staudt, K. (Ed.). (1990). *Women, international development, and politics: The bureaucratic mire.* Philadelphia: Temple University Press.

Steinberg, R. (1988). Women, the state, and equal employment. In J. Jenson, E. Hagen, & C. Ruddy (Eds.), *Feminization of the labor force: Paradoxes and promises* (pp. 189-213). New York: Oxford University Press.

Stephan, A. (1978). *The state and society: Peru in comparative perspective.* Princeton, NJ: Princeton University Press.

Stetson, D. M. (1987). *Women's rights in France*. Westport, CT: Greenwood Press.
Stetson, D. M. (1991). The political history of parental leave policy. In J. S. Hyde & M. J. Essex (Eds.), *Parental leave and child care: Setting a research and policy agenda* (pp. 406-423). Philadelphia: Temple University Press.
Stromberg, E. (1980). *The role of women's organizations in Norway*. Oslo: Equal Status Council.
Suleiman, E. (1974). *Politics, power, and bureaucracy in France: The administrative elite*. Princeton, NJ: Princeton University Press.
Suleiman, E. (1979). *Elites in French society: The politics of survival*. Princeton, NJ: Princeton University Press.
Suleiman, E. (1987). *Private power and centralization in France: The notaries and the state*. Princeton, NJ: Princeton University Press.
Sullivan, B. (1994). Contemporary Australian feminism: A critical review. In G. Stokes (Ed.), *Australian political ideas* (pp. 152-167). Sydney: University of N&W Press.
Summers, A. (1986). Mandarins or missionaries: Women in the Australian federal bureaucracy. In N. Grieves & A. Burns (Eds.), *Australian women: New feminist perspectives* (pp. 59-67). Melbourne: Oxford University Press.
Sundin, E. (1992). Equality through regional policy: Report from a Swedish project. In M. Eduards, E. Lundgren, & U. Wikander (Eds.), *Rethinking change: Current Swedish feminist research* (pp. 105-129). Uppsala: Swedish Science Press.
Swedish Institute. (1993). Equality between men and women in Sweden [*Fact Sheets on Sweden*]. Stockholm: Author.
Swiebel, J. (1988). The gender of bureaucracy: Reflections on policy-making for women. *Politics, 8*, 14-19.
Swiebel, J., & Outshoorn, J. (1990, September). *Feminism and the state: The case of the Netherlands*. Paper presented at the International Conference, Lima, Peru.
Tatafiore, R. (1992). Femminismo [Feminism]. In *Enciclopedia Italiana di scienze, lettere ed arti, 1979-1992*. Roma: Istituto della Enciclopedia Italiana-Treccani.
Threlfall, M. (1985). The women's movement in Spain. *New Left Review, 151*, 44-73.
Titkow, A. (1984). Let's pull down the bastilles before they are built. In R. Morgan (Ed.), *Sisterhood is global* (pp. 560-566). New York: Doubleday.
Titkow, A. (1993). Political change in Poland: Cause, modifier or barrier to gender equality. In N. Funk & M. Mueller (Eds.), *Gender politics and post-Communism* (pp. 253-256). New York: Routledge.
United Nations. (1987). *The development of national machinery for the advancement of women and their characteristics in 1985*. Vienna: Seminar on National Machinery for the Advancement of Women.
United Nations. (1991). *The world's women 1970-1990: Trends and statistics*. New York: United Nations.
United Nations. (1993a). *Directory of national machinery for the advancement of women*. Vienna: Division for the Advancement of Women.
United Nations. (1993b). The Nairobi forward-looking strategies for the advancement of women adopted by World Conference. New York: Author. (Original work published 1985)
U.S. Department of Labor, Women's Bureau. (1975). *Women's bureaus and commissions on the status of women, a guide to functions and services*. Washington, DC: GPO.

U.S. Department of Labor, Women's Bureau. (1978). *Women's bureaus and commissions on the status of women—avoiding an obstacle course.* Washington DC: GPO.

U.S. House of Representatives. (1984, July 26). *The women's bureau: Is it meeting the needs of women workers?* [Hearing]. Washington, DC: GPO.

U.S. Department of Labor, Women's Bureau. (1994). *Working women count: A report to the nation.* Washington, DC: GPO.

U.S. House of Representatives. (1993). *Departments of Labor, Health and Human Services, Education and related agencies, appropriations for 1994* [Hearing]. Washington, DC: GPO.

Valiente, C. (1994). *Políticas públicas para la mujer trabajadora en Italia y España (1900-1991)* [Public policies for the woman worker in Italy and Spain]. Madrid: Instituto Juan March.

Van der Ros, J. (1994, April). *The organization of equality policies at the local level: The case of Norway.* Paper presented at the 22nd ECPR Joint Workshop Sessions, Madrid.

Vickers, J., Rankin, P., & Appelle, C. (1993). *Politics as if women mattered.* Toronto: University of Toronto Press.

Vollmer, C. (1988). Das Netzwerk der kommunalen Frauenbüros [The network of local women's offices]. In M. Weg & O. Stein (Eds.), *MACHT macht Frauen stark: Frauenpolitik für die 90er Jahre* (pp. 46-52). Hamburg: VSA-Verlag.

Vries, P. de. (1981). Feminism in the Netherlands. *International Women's Studies Quarterly, 4*(4), 389-409.

Wadstein, M. (1989). Så trubbig är inte jämställdhetslagen [The equality law is not so blunt]. *Lag & Avtal, 3,* 29-30.

Walker, G. (1990, Fall). The conceptual politics of struggle: Wife battering, the women's movement, and the state. *Studies in Political Economy, 33,* 63-90.

Wandersee, W. D. (1988). *On the move: American women in the 1970s.* Boston: Twayne.

Watson, P. (1993). Eastern Europe's silent revolution: Gender. *Sociology, 27*(3), 471-487.

Watson, S. (Ed.). (1990). *Playing the state: Australian feminist interventions.* London: Verso.

Weber, M. (1981). *From Max Weber: Essays in sociology* (H. H. Gerth & C. W. Mills, Eds.). New York: Oxford University Press.

Weg, M., & Stein, O. (Eds.) (1988). *MACHT macht Frauen stark: Frauenpolitik für die 90er Jahre.* Hamburg: VSA-Verlag.

Wilken, L. (1992). *Einmischung erlaubt? Kommunale Frauenbüros in der Bundesrepublik* [Is getting involved permitted? Local women's offices in the Federal Republic]. Hamburg: VSA-Verlag.

Wilsford, D. (1989). Tactical versus administrative heterogeneity: The strengths and the weaknesses of the French state. In J. A. Caporaso, (Ed.), *The elusive state* (pp. 128-172). Newbury Park, CA: Sage.

Wilsford, D. (1991). *Doctors and the state: The politics of health care in France and the United States.* Durham, NC: Duke University Press.

Wilson, E. (1977). *Women & the welfare state.* London: Tavistock.

Wilson, F. L. (1987). *Interest group politics in France.* New York: Cambridge University Press.

Wistrand, B. (1981). *Swedish women on the move.* Stockholm: The Swedish Institute.

Yeatman, A. (1990). *Bureaucrats, technocrats, femocrats: Essays on the contemporary Australian state.* Sydney: Allen & Unwin.

Yuval-Davis, N. (1991). The citizenship debate. *Feminist Review, 39,* 58-68.

Zelman, P. G. (1980). *Women, work, and national policy, the Kennedy-Johnson years.* Ann Arbor, MI: University Microfilms Research Press.

Zimmerman, J. (1988). An innovation: Backbench committees. *Administration, 36*(3), 265-289.

Zincone, G. (1978). Costruzione e costrizione della donna in Italia [Construction and constraints of the Italian woman]. In G. Zincone (Ed.), *Un mondo di donne* (pp. 69-70). Turin: Quaderni di Biblioteca della Libertà.

Zincone, G. (Ed.). (1983). *Decision-making arenas affecting women at work in four European countries* (Final report to the Directorate, General Employment, Social Affairs and Education of the Commission of the European Community)

APPENDIX

Women's Policy Machinery
in Fourteen Countries

This appendix provides a summary of the various structures that make up women's policy machineries discussed in each chapter. For each agency the table shows type of structures, as follows

M = Ministry
EEA = Equal Employment Agency
A = Agency within a department
I = Independent Agency
C = Commission

It also gives the party or coalition of parties in control of the chief executive when the office was created and the years during which the office has been active. For agencies that were still active in the summer of 1994, the text places a dash after the first date.

	Type of Structure	Party (ies) in Power	Dates
Australia			
Women's Affairs Branch	A	Conservative	1975-1977
Intergovernmental Working Group on Women's Affairs	C	Conservative	1970s-1977
Minister Assisting the Prime Minister on Women's Affairs	M	Conservative	1976—
Office of Women's Affairs	A	Conservative	1977-1982
Office of the Status of Women	M/A	Conservative	1982—
Canada			
Women's Bureau	A	Liberal	1954—
Interdepartmental Committee	C	Liberal	1971
Minister Responsible for the Status of Women	M	Liberal	1971—
Canadian Advisory Council on the Status of Women	I	Liberal	1973—

	Type of Structure	Party (ies) in Power	Dates
Women's Program	A	Liberal	1973—
Status of Women Canada	A	Liberal	1976
Denmark			
Women's Commission	C	Social Democrat	1967-1974
Danish Equal Status Council	C	Social Democrat	1975—
France			
Comité d'Etudes et de Liaison des Problèmes du Travail Féminin	A	Gaullist	1965-1971
Comité du Travail Féminin	A	Gaullist	1971-1983
Secrétariat d'Etat à la Condition Féminine	M	Centrist	1974-1976
Délégation Nationale à la Condition Féminine	I	Centrist	1976-1978
Secrétariat d'Etat à l'Emploi Féminin	M	Centrist	1978-1981
Ministère Déléguée auprès du Premier Ministre à la Condition Féminine et à la Famille	M/A	Centrist	1978-1981
Ministère des Droits de la Femme	M/A	Socialist	1981-1986
Conseil Supérieur de l'Egalité Professionnelle	EEA	Socialist	1983—
Mission pour l'Egalité Professionelle	EEA	Socialist	1983—
Délégation Nationale à la Condition Féminine	A	Gaullist	1986-1988
Secrétaire d'Etat des Droits des Femme	M/A	Socialist	1988-1991
Secrétaire d'Etat aux Droits des Femmes et à la Vie Quotidienne	M/A	Socialist	1991-1993
Service des Droits aux Femmes	A	Gaullist	1993
Germany			
Arbeitsstab Frauenpolitik	A	Social Democrats	1974-1982
Frauenbeauftragte	A	all parties	1982—
Frauenbeauftragte (in certain states)	M	Social Democrats/ Greens	1985—
Ministry for Health, Family, Youth, and Women	M	CDU/CDU/FDP	1986-1991

	Type of Structure	Party (ies) in Power	Dates
Great Britain			
Equal Opportunities Commission	EEA	Labour	1975—
Ireland			
Employment Equality Agency	EEA	Fine Fail	1977—
Ministry of State for Women's Affairs	M	Fine Gael/Labour	1982-1987
Joint Oireachtas Committee on Women's Rights	M	Fine Gael/Labour	1992
Ministry of Equality and Law Reform	M	Fine Fail	1992—
Italy			
Equal Status Committee	C	PSI/DC coalition	1983—
Equal Status and Equal Opportunity National Commission	A/M	PSI/DC coalition	1984—
The Netherlands			
Emancipatiekommissie	C	Labor	1974-1979
Directie Coordinatie Emancipatiebeleid	A	Labor	1978—
Emancipatieraad	C	Labor	1981—
Stimuleringsgroep Emancipatieonderzoek	C	Labor/CD coalition	1985-1991
Cabinet Committee for Women's Policy	C	Labor/CD	1986
Norway			
Equal Pay Council	C	Labor	1959-1972
Norwegian Equal Status Council	C/A	Labor	1972—
Equal Status Ombud	I	Labor	1978—
Equal Status Appeals Board	I	Labor	1978—
Department of Family Affairs and Equal Status	A	Labor	1977
Secretariat for Equal Opportunities in Education	A	Labor	1981
Secretariat for Women in Research	A	Labor	1981
Poland			
Liga Kobiet	I	PUWP	1945-1989
Office of Women's Affairs	A	PUWP	1986-1989

	Type of *Structure*	*Party (ies)* *in Power*	*Dates*
Undersecretary of State for Women and Family	M		1989—
Spain			
Instituto de la Mujer	A	Socialists	1983—
Consejo Rector	C	Socialists	1985—
Comisión consultiva para el seguimiento del Primer Plan	C	Socialists	1988
Sweden			
Jämställdhetsombudsmannen	EEA	Center/Right	1980—
Equal Affairs Division	A	Labor	1982—
Advisory Council to the Prime Minister on Equality Between Men and Women	C	Labor	1972-1976
United States			
Women's Bureau	A	Democrat	1920—
President's Commission on the Status of Women	C	Democrat	1960-1963
Citizens' Advisory Council on the Status of Women	C	Democrat	1963-1975

Index

About the Authors

Anette Borchorst is Associate Professor at the Institute of Political Science at Aarhus University, Denmark. Since November 1988 she has been a member of the Danish Equal Status Council, representing Women's Studies. Her research interests relate to women, care, and welfare states in a cross-national context; child care policies; motherhood and fatherhood; the interface between family and work; and the effects of the European Union on gender differences. She has published in the *International Journal of Contemporary Sociology* and in a book, *Gendering Welfare States* (1994). From 1986 to 1987 she was one of two coordinators of Women's Studies in Denmark. From August 1993 to August 1994 she was visiting scholar at the Center for Research on Women, Wellesley College, Massachusetts.

Jill M. Bystydzienski is Associate Professor of Sociology at Franklin College in Indiana, where she also teaches courses in Women's Studies and Canadian Studies. She has B.A. and M.A. degrees in Sociology from McGill University and a Ph.D. from State University of New York at Albany. She is the author of numerous articles on women in politics and cross-cultural comparisons of women. Her edited book,

Women Transforming Politics: Worldwide Strategies for Empowerment, was published in 1992, and she coedited *Women in Cross-Cultural Transitions* with Estelle Resnik. Her most recent book is *Women in Electoral Politics: Lessons From Norway.*

R. Amy Elman is Assistant Professor in the Department of Political Science at Kalamazoo College, where she teaches an array of courses concerning contemporary European politics. From 1989-1990 she was a Fulbright fellow in Sweden. She has since published on that state's responsiveness to women in *Women's Studies International Forum* and elsewhere. Her book, *Sexual Subordination and State Intervention: Comparing Sweden and the United States* (forthcoming) examines development and implementation of programs and policies for battered women. Her edited book, *Sexual Politics and the European Union: The New Feminist Challenges,* is forthcoming. Her research interest include a feminist analysis of the Holocaust.

Myra Marx Ferree is Professor of Sociology and Women's Studies at the University of Connecticut. She is coauthor with Beth Hess of *Controversy and Coalition: the New Feminist Movement Through Three Decades of Change* (1994), a revised and expanded version of their earlier book, and she is coeditor with Patricia Yancey Martin of *Feminist Organizations: Harvest of the New Women's Movement* (1994). She has also published numerous journal articles on West and East German feminism. Her current research includes a collaborative project analyzing German and American media discourse on abortion from the 1960s to the 1990s.

Linda Geller-Schwartz teaches in the Women's Studies program at Florida Atlantic University and is also a consultant on issues concerning women in the workforce. She is a former head of the Women's Bureau of Canada and has had extensive experience in government and academia. She obtained her M.Sc. in Comparative Politics from the London School of Economics and her Ph.D. from University of Toronto. She has taught in the fields of political science and women's studies in both Canada and the United States and is the author of a number of publications in these fields.

Marila Guadagnini teaches the Italian political system at the University of Turin. She has written articles on parties and the party system, including "Partiti" in *Il Mondo Contemporaneo* (1981), and an introduction to the volume *Sistemi di partito* (1986). Her major field of research on women has focused on women's presence in Italian decision-making arenas at the national and local level since 1948. She has published articles in such journals as the *Rivista Italiana di Scienza Politica* and the *Quaderni di Sociologia*. Her latest publications are "A partitocrazia without women: The case of the Italian party system," in J. Lovenduski and P. Norris (eds.), *Gender and Party Politics* (1993) and *Il sistema politico italiano, Temi e prospettive di analisi* (1995).

Joni Lovenduski is Professor of Politics at Southampton University, UK. She is author of *Women and European Politics* (1986), coauthor of *Parliamentary Representation* (1994), *Contemporary Feminist Politics* (1993), and *Politics and Society in Eastern Europe* (1987). She coedited *Gender and Party Politics* (1993), *The New Politics of Abortion* (1986), *The Politics of the Second Electorate* (1981), and numerous papers, articles, and chapters on gender and politics. She was codirector of the British Candidate Study from 1988 to 1992 and a founding convener of the Standing Group on Women and Politics of the European Consortium for Political Research and of the Women and Politics Group of the Political Studies Association of the United Kingdom.

Evelyn Mahon is Lecturer in Sociology at Trinity College, Dublin. She has also taught at the University of Limerick and University College, Galway. A founding member and former secretary of the Women's Studies Association of Ireland, she has presented many papers at international conferences on the role of women in Irish society and politics. Her publications include "Gender Equity in the Irish Civil Service," in *Equality Politics and Gender* (1991) and *Motherhood, Work and Equal Opportunity: A Case Study of Irish civil Servants* for the Third Joint Oireachtas Committee on Women's Rights.

Amy G. Mazur is Assistant Professor of Political Science at Washington State University. She received a joint Ph.D. in Political Science and French Studies from New York University. She studies feminist policy formation in comparative perspective and has focused her empirical work on France. She is the author of *Gender Bias and the State: Symbolic Reform at Work in Fifth Republic France* (1995) and chapters in two recent books, *Sexual Politics and the European Unions: The New Feminist Challenge* (1995) and *Gender and Party Politics* (1993). She is currently working on a continuation of the *State Feminism Project* with Dorothy McBride Stetson and Joyce Outshoorn and is co-organizing a curriculum development workshop on *Gender and Politics in European Society*.

Joyce Outshoorn is Professor of Women's Studies and Chair of the department at Leiden University, where she is also director of the research program on Gender and Power. She studied political science and contemporary history at the University of Amsterdam, where she was Associate Professor in Political Science. Her most recent publications include articles on the women's movement (in *Moving on: New Directions in Social Movement Research, See* 1991), and feminist theory (*Een irriterend onderwerp. Verschuivende conceptualiseringen van het sekseverschil*, 1989). Currently she is working on state feminism and femocrats and has published an article, *Between Movement and the Government Femocrats in the Netherlands* (1994). Another project (for the Council of Europe) involves work on equal representation and democracy.

Jean Robinson is Associate Professor of Political Science and Women's Studies at Indiana University, where she has also served as Director of the Women's Studies Program. She earned her B.A. at Oberlin College and M.A. and Ph.D. degrees from Cornell University. A specialist on contemporary Chinese politics, her chapter in this volume builds on teaching interests in gender, socialism, and postsocialist societies. She was a Visiting Professor at Warsaw University in 1989-1990. She is author of "Women Under the Collective: the Exigencies of Family Policies in China" in *The Reconstruction of Family Policy* (1991) and "China's Special Economic Zones, Labor and Women," in *Communist Dialectic: the Political Implications of Economic Reform in Communist Countries* (1990).

Marian Sawer is Senior Lecturer in Politics, Faculty of Management, at the University of Canberra. She earned B.A., M.A., and Ph.D. degrees at Australian National University. A pioneer in the study of women's policy machinery, she has published *Sisters in Suits: Women* *and Public Policy in Australia* (1990), *A Woman's Place: Women and Politics in Australia* (1984, 1993), and many other books, articles, and chapters. She is an expert on public administration and has served as a consultant to the Australian government. She recently coauthored, on request of the prime minister, a history of the Office of the Status of Women for the Australian government.

Dorothy McBride Stetson is Professor of Political Science at Florida Atlantic University, where she is an active participant in the Women's Studies program. She earned a B.A. at the University of Montana and an M.A. and Ph.D. at Vanderbilt University. A specialist in the comparative study of women and public policy, she is the author of three books: *A Woman's Issue: The Politics of Family Reform in England* (1982); *Women's Rights in France* (1987); and *Women's Rights in the U.S.A.* (1991; 2nd ed., 1996) and numerous articles and conference papers. She is presently working with Amy Mazur on an expanded study of comparative state feminism. She is a founding member of the Women and Politics Section of the American Political Science Association.

Celia Valiente is Associate Professor of Sociology at the Autonomous University of Madrid. Her current research deals with women and the Spanish welfare state. She received an undergraduate degree in history and a Ph.D. in Sociology from the Autonomous University of Madrid, Spain, and an M.A. in Social Sciences at the *Instituto Juan March de Estudios e Investigaciones*, Madrid. She wrote a docctoral dissertation titled *Public Policies for Women Workers in Italy and Spain, 1900-1991* (in Spanish), under the supervision of Juan J. Linz.